Going Global
Connecting cultures,
forging futures

IOE Press

Going Global

Connecting cultures, forging futures

Edited by

Mary Stiasny OBE
University of London, UK

Tim Gore OBE
University of London, UK

UCL Institute of Education Press

First published in 2016 by the UCL Institute of Education Press,
20 Bedford Way, London WC1H 0AL

www.ucl-ioe-press.com

Copyright © 2016 British Council
British Library Cataloguing in Publication Data:
A catalogue record for this publication is available from the British Library

ISBNs
978-0-86355-784-2 (paperback)
978-0-86355-783-5 (ePub eBook)

Typeset by Quadrant Infotech (India) Pvt Ltd
Printed by CPI Group (UK) Ltd, Croydon, CR0 4YY

Contents

List of contributors

Joyce Achampong	*Director of Engagement, Association of Commonwealth Universities, UK*
Paul Kwadwo Addo	*Assistant Registrar, Kwame Nkrumah University of Science and Technology, Kumasi, Ghana*
S. Kojo Mbra Assan	*Assistant Registrar, Kwame Nkrumah University of Science and Technology, Kumasi, Ghana*
Pavel G. Arefiev	*Principal Researcher, National Training Foundation, Russian Federation*
Irina V. Arzhanova	*Executive Director, National Training Foundation, Russian Federation*
Graeme Atherton	*Director, AccessHE and the National Education Opportunities Network, UK*
Marina Y. Baryshnikova	*Deputy Executive Director, National Training Foundation, Russian Federation*
Jo Beall	*Director Education and Society, British Council, UK*
Nilton N. Cometti	*Professor, Federal Institute of Espirito Santo, Brazil*
Catriona Cunningham	*Academic Development Partner, University of Stirling, UK*
Dmitriy O. Derman	*Head, Department of Higher Education, National Training Foundation, Russian Federation*
Sir Ciarán Devane	*Chief Executive, British Council*
Hans de Wit	*Director, Center for International Higher Education, Boston College, USA*
Philip Esterhuizen	*Lecturer, Adult Nursing, University of Leeds, UK*
Dawn Freshwater	*Senior Deputy Vice Chancellor, University of Western Australia*

List of contributors

Anne Marie Graham — *Head of Programme, Outward Student Mobility, UK Higher Education International Unit*

Elizabeth Halford — *Head of Research and Intelligence, QAA, UK*

Catriona Hanks — *Outward Mobility Policy Researcher, UK Higher Education International Unit*

John Hearn — *Chief Executive, Worldwide Universities Network*

Laura Howard — *President, European Association for International Education*

Fiona Hunter — *Associate Director, Centre for Higher Education Internationalisation, Università Cattolica del Sacro Cuore, Italy*

Wendy Jordan — *Director, British Universities Iraq Consortium*

Susanne Kammüller — *Senior desk officer, Transnational Education and Co-operation Programmes division, German Academic Exchange Service*

Tom Kennie — *Founding director, Ranmore education consultancy, UK*

Takehiko Kitamori — *Professor, Department of Applied Chemistry, University of Tokyo, Japan*

Alexandr V. Klyagin — *Deputy Head, Department of Higher Education, National Training Foundation, Russian Federation*

Jane Knight — *Adjunct Professor, Ontario Institute for Studies in Education, University of Toronto, Canada*

Annamarie Lawrence — *Programme Manager, Management, Bahrain Polytechnic*

Jonathan Ledger — *Chief Executive Officer, Proskills UK Group*

Paul Manners — *Associate Professor in Public Engagement, University of the West of England, UK*

John McNamara — *Director of Research, McNamara Economic Research, Ireland*

Robin Middlehurst — *Professor of Higher Education, Kingston University, UK*

Cameron Mirza	*Director for Programmes and Strategy, Bahrain Higher Education Council, Kingdom of*
Rajani Naidoo	*Professor of Higher Education and Director of the International Centre for Higher Education Management, University of Bath, UK*
Ruth Najda	*Writer and editor; adviser to the British Council's intercultural fluency initiative*
Patricia G. Owusu-Darko	*Director, Graduate School, Kumasi Polytechnic, Ghana*
Sibilla Robutti	*Study Abroad Coordinator, St Mary's University Twickenham, London, UK*
Dorothea Rüland	*Secretary General, German Academic Exchange Service*
Elizabeth J. Sandell	*Professor, College of Education, Minnesota State University, Mankato, USA*
Melissa Schuessler	*Faculty International Director, Leeds University Business School, UK*
Neil Shaw	*Global Employability Portfolio Manager, British Council, UK*
Christina Slade	*Vice-Chancellor, Bath Spa University, UK*
Alfred Tan	*Head of Knowledge Transfer Office, Hong Kong Baptist University*
Mark Thorley	*Head of Music and Creative Technologies, Coventry University, UK*
Hilligje Van't Land	*Director of Membership and Programme Development, International Association of Universities, France*

Foreword

I am very pleased to introduce this fifth volume of the Going Global education papers. These were presented and discussed at the British Council's Going Global Conference 2015, held in London, and taken together they highlight latest developments in international education and the benefit of global collaboration.

Engagement in international education is vital in our connected world. It helps countries achieve their economic and development goals and supports their citizens' aspirations and life chances. For students who take the opportunity to study overseas, the benefits can be life-changing.

The UK has a long history of reaching out globally in education. Our university exams were taken by students all over the world long before the new digital world. And for centuries we have been a magnet for brilliant minds to study at our institutions. Like other countries, we have also gone abroad to seek education and understanding. I am very pleased that more UK students are now going abroad than ever before, both within Europe and further afield. This experience fosters new knowledge and understanding, which is vital in our modern and increasingly connected knowledge economy.

We warmly welcome international students to the UK. Last year the Prime Minster said that 'we will roll out the red carpet to the brightest and best, to the talented workers and brilliant students that help Britain's success'. We value the considerable contribution international students bring to the UK, to university campus life, to our research base and wider economy. Because of this there is no cap on the number of overseas students that can come to study in the UK.

Conferences such as Going Global provide the opportunity to promote the value of international partnership and explore innovation in education. International collaboration is now an important enabler to economic growth and development, not just in education, but also in science and innovation. Perhaps even more important for the long term, collaboration also broadens our understanding and our horizons.

Jo Johnson MP
Minister of State for Universities and Science
Department for Business, Innovation and Skills
United Kingdom

Introduction

We live in an age of disconnection and fracture, just as much as we live in an age of connection and networks. That struggle between connection and disconnection is one that will define our times.

The veteran observer of Eastern European politics Timothy Garton Ash, who spent the early 1990s chronicling the collapse of the Soviet empire, has recently written of walls going up again around the world. They are walls and fences separating different pieces of territory on the ground. But they also represent divisions in people's minds – barriers to understanding and fellow feeling.

Our job, as educators and promoters of culture, is to oppose that trend for all we're worth. Because education is about connection – connection with the ideas of the past, connection between learners and teachers, connection between problems and their solution.

The British Council's Going Global programme brings together government ministers, heads of institutions, and policy advisers each year for two days of lively exchange, debate and conversation, focused on the most significant topics in the higher education sector. In 2015 more than a thousand leaders of international further and higher education, representing some eighty nations, came to London to explore the broad theme of *'Connecting cultures, forging futures'*. This collection of papers from contributors is a record of the conference, and a means of continuing the Going Global conversation – a conversation that will never be completed, and which changes from year to year and place to place, but within which certain themes, and certain questions, recur.

As a newcomer to Going Global, my initial impression was of an almost ungraspable variety of people and ideas. I had already done some thinking about the purpose and practice of international higher education, of course, both as incoming British Council chief executive, and prior to that as an overseas master's student myself, at George Washington University. But those few days in London brought home to me the fact that international education is a heady mix of the political (nations' ambitions on the world stage, their hopes for their young people, horizon scanning to figure out their place in a changing world); the personal (individual ambitions for betterment and discovery); and the philosophical (What kind of education is 'good'? Is technology a game-changer, or simply an improved enabler of conventional approaches?).

All of these perspectives, and more, were on display in the workshops and seminars of Going Global 2015. I left the conference with a real feeling of optimism and energy – the sense that we are moving forward, and that by moving forward together we will go further, and faster.

One unspoken theme that has been constant since the first Going Global in 2004, and essential if cultures are truly to be connected, and futures forged, is that of *openness*. There was much debate in the United Kingdom in 2015 about 'open doors' of all kinds – doors to migration, to influence, to ideas. These are discussions that will continue for years to come, and the conclusions we arrive at will shape the societies we live in for much longer than that. Recent terrorist actions in Tunisia and Paris, and all over the Middle East and Africa, can be seen as a symptom of doors closing in people's minds, of closed thinking – rigid, disconnected, unable to see beyond its own narrow certainties. The provision of alternative pathways for a generation of poorly served young people in some of the most unstable parts of the world is a priority for the British Council – and for the UK government. Education is central to that agenda. Because what is education, if not a way of providing young people with the skills and qualifications that will help to connect them to their own futures and with the world? People who are connected – who feel they are part of the fabric of life, with an ability to contribute – are by and large not those who join the forces of *dis*-connection. Those with a stake in the world *as it is* do not seek to live in dangerous utopias.

The wider agenda of the British Council's work in education – beyond the search for knowledge and the provision of skills and qualifications – might be seen as a means of undoing this kind of dangerous disconnection. That is why we work – for instance – to ensure continuity of education for Syrian refugee children in Jordan; and help to facilitate transnational education in Burma. It's why we offer scholarships to young Africans in technical and engineering subjects. In each case, it's with the underlying motive of connecting young people with their potential.

With a global network of over a hundred countries, we have a habit of taking the 'helicopter view' (or perhaps the 'satellite view') of which methods and approaches are most effective. My own tendency, as a person with a scientific background, is to ask of any project: Does it work? What does the data say? Is this the best way of making an impact? Openness can be a challenge, of course: to individuals, to institutions, to cultures. It involves exposing yourself to the possibility that you are wrong, that you have something to learn. But that is why, as educators, we must be explicit about the fact that openness is the lifeblood of learning. It's also the *sine qua non* of collaborative working.

As Rajani Naidoo of the University of Bath's School of Management says, 'Many of the major issues facing humankind, such as the destruction of the environment, rising inequality and violence across borders, can only be solved by countries and universities working together'.

We should remember that there is nothing new in this. For the whole of their history, universities have engaged in this kind of cross border connection and collaboration: the creation of a republic of ideas, regardless of distance. Universities' ancient responsibility to reach beyond national boundaries is even more critical in a time of instant global communication, when an almost limitless number of individuals can be in connection with innumerable others. Modern communications technology gives universities an historic opportunity to move beyond national competition and embrace a new concept of collaboration. To 'go global' in ways that previous generations of vice-chancellors, professors, and students could only dream of.

The British Council's understanding of 'intercultural fluency' (or Sybilla Robutti's 'intercultural competence') is vital here. Ruth Najda and Neil Shaw's paper ('Intercultural fluency: A practice-led approach') explores the importance of students', and organizations', ability to understand and operate with, and within, different cultural environments – which implies far more than a simple familiarity with foreign language. It's that 'ease of being' in different cultural settings that will make this generation of students truly global in their outlook.

There are roughly half a million international students currently at British universities and colleges, and a further 600,000 undertaking UK higher education courses abroad. That's over a million people from other countries coming into intimate contact with a UK education – not just with the content of their courses, whether it's philosophy or engineering or app design; but with the particular approach to the world that comes from a UK education. That includes the concept of openness to new ideas, to sharing results and research, and to genuine intellectual exchange. The kind of approach, in other words, that leads to new ideas and better solutions. It means that when those million-plus people go on with their lives at the end of their studies, they carry within them, as well as skills and qualifications that will help them to build their careers, a special strand of international DNA.

Yet this is not – as far as the UK is concerned – a two-way process. As Catriona Hanks and Anne Marie Graham point out in their paper ('Why do students make the decisions they make on mobility programmes?'), the great communicating device of the English language may actually be serving young *British* people poorly. Our own outward mobility is a small fraction of that of many of our neighbours, who speak our language, and understand our culture, in addition to their own.

In my first year as Chief Executive of the British Council, I have 'gone global' myself, visiting more than twenty countries to see that connection-making in action. What I have seen, from Uganda to South Korea to Pakistan, is work that connects people to their potential – and that means, more often than not, connecting them to other people in other parts of the world who are facing similar challenges. Predicting the future is always a risky activity, and perhaps especially so today. But there are some trends we can be fairly certain will continue, and which will affect the way most of us live in coming decades. In particular, these are the various forms of globalization: of economies, of climate change, of technology, of epidemic disease.

And to set against the concerns raised by some of this global connectivity, there is the *globalization of aspiration* – the free movement of skills and knowledge around the world – with which many of us are directly concerned. Many of the contributions to Going Global 2015, and to this volume, explicitly relate to this kind of connection.

Graeme Atherton's contribution, 'Access and equality in higher education: Building the global dialogue' references Amitia Etzioni's concept of the 'megalogue' – a conversation involving millions of individuals, and taking place in homes and workplaces (and, today, via numerous digital channels). Perhaps this is a helpful way of envisioning the transmission of education in the coming decades.

At the same time, higher education professionals are not blind to the fact that conditions for both learners and teachers vary hugely from place to place – even on a 'globalized' planet.

The paper from Wendy Jordan (British Universities Iraq Consortium) – 'Higher education in emergency environments' – argues the importance of protecting universities in developing countries and fragile states when disaster strikes. Aid agencies and friendly governments understandably seek to mitigate the immediate effects of warfare or natural disaster, perhaps forgetting that the impact of such events can last for generations. Higher education, in this context, is just as vital for the long-term health of a nation as a functioning health service or legal system. Like many of the authors, Jordan argues that higher education is one of the most significant engines of progress in society. Not only a generator of research and innovation to the benefit of the economy, but one of the principal creators of a nation's intellectual capital.

Another metaphor (and I don't think these are mutually exclusive by any means – rather they serve to reinforce and inform each other) is the vision of education's role as 'international bridge'. Cameron Mirza of the Kingdom of Bahrain's Higher Education Council and Annamarie Lawrence of Bahrain Polytechnic propose internationalization as a key part of closing the kingdom's skills gap; as well as building the country's credentials as a genuine knowledge economy. Such 'bridges', Mirza and Lawrence write, can help bring about the creation of a national innovation and skills 'ecosystem'. This is a well-chosen word. For if one model for the developing higher education landscape is the computer matrix of multiply-connected nodes, then the other is nature itself, with its web of exchanges and mutual influence.

And of course our global education network, like nature, must adapt itself to local conditions. One size certainly does not fit all when it comes to national and regional educational needs. What works in Brasilia may not work so well in Beirut – which is not to say that Brasilia and Beirut have nothing to teach one another. Getting educational adaptation right, while at the same time aspiring to global standards of quality and accessibility, will keep all of us occupied for a considerable time to come.

Education, in the broadest sense, is the engine at the heart of all the great advances in society. Without a profound commitment to education, we are all lost. As that big-picture thinker and visionary H.G. Wells once said, 'Civilisation is a race between education and catastrophe'.

That's why education is one of the key pillars of the British Council. It's not our only area of activity, but it's central to our mission to create 'a friendly knowledge and understanding' between the people of the UK and the wider world.

I have no crystal ball in which to divine the future of higher education, despite the many prognostications on offer at Going Global ('forging futures' was one half of the 2015 equation, after all) and in many other places. But it seems clear that we should be looking at the teaching institution as both connector and fixed point.

In other words, we should think of the connecting qualities of education as having both a global and a local aspect – reaching out to exchange ideas beyond national boundaries – while at the same time being anchored in a community of place and thought. A bridge is necessarily fixed at both ends, after all: one end is not more important than the other. Indeed it is the failure to recognize that education systems and individual learning establishments sit within (and are vitally connected to) wider society, that provokes the 'ivory tower' jibes that have been levelled at out-of-touch institutions since time immemorial.

Over the last decade, Going Global has established itself as the international education event for those who wish to make intellectual connections – to engage with peers in the kind of discussions that are education's life-blood – but who also want to reach out in practical ways, to industry, to policymakers, to communities. But 'event' is probably the wrong word. Going Global was not conceived as a one-off event, but a series: each iteration building on the last and looking forward to the next. This book offers a flavour of the conversations of 2015 – as an appetizer for the discussions of 2016.

There is nothing resembling an 'ivory tower' in any of the papers that follow.

Sir Ciarán Devane
Chief Executive, British Council

Section 1

Structures and mechanisms of internationalization

1

Editors' introduction to Section 1

Structures and mechanisms of internationalization

Internationalization has, in the last 10 years, become the norm in tertiary education. While originally we used to focus on the recruitment of international students to our home campuses, now, with the growing complexity of TNE and international strategies within our institutions, we see a set of emerging patterns forming across the range of our HE institutions and vocational education provision. The structures and mechanisms of the different forms of internationalization are explored in this section of the book. As awareness of the existence of TNE in different shapes and forms becomes accepted, and as its very existence becomes established, we develop increased understanding of, and clarity about, those same structures and mechanisms. The papers in this section approach this issue from a variety of different perspectives.

Hunter, Howard and de Wit explore the key trends in internationalization as identified in a study of the internationalization of higher education. In the course of establishing a list of ten trends, the authors not only explore the common characteristics, but also indicate the direction in which internationalization of higher education can be said to be heading. **Knight and McNamara** explore the rationale, enablers and challenges for collecting the data relating to TNE, in order to develop a framework for TNE data collection systems across nations. **Rüland and Kamüller** examine the issue of data collection further, and highlight its difficulties in the absence of internationally agreed standards – and in the context where there is a lack of standardized terminology.

Turning to the students themselves, **Robutti's** paper looks at student mobility and the importance of intercultural competence within the internationalization agenda. This becomes really important when we are concerned about how to support students. **Hanks and Graham's** study analyses two reports on what students perceive as the drivers and barriers to outward mobility. While students are motivated by personal and cultural factors, they are, simultaneously, deterred by a range of barriers, of which financial concerns are the most significant.

Halford then moves us into a consideration of the significance of the structures and frameworks of quality assurance organizations in a range of countries – and the role these play in measuring quality in higher education. Continuing the theme of quality assurance, the paper by **Addo, Assan and Owusu-Darko** discusses its importance as a global imperative, and its role more specifically as a driver in the African context.

Inspired within the context of our Going Global conferences, this collection of papers enables us to examine more forensically the bones of what internationalization means to the sector, and what the key and critical elements are for us as internationalizers.

Key trends in the internationalization of higher education: Are we heading in the right direction?[1]

Fiona Hunter, Hans de Wit and Laura Howard

While the concept of internationalization of higher education (IoHE) is a relatively new one, it has rapidly become both broad and varied. It is driven by a dynamic and constantly evolving combination of political, economic, socio-cultural and academic rationales and has recently been strongly influenced by the globalization of our economies and societies and the increased importance of knowledge as a driver of development. While IoHE itself is becoming globalized and is increasingly considered a high-level priority in all world regions, it nevertheless takes on different forms and dimensions in different regions, countries and institutions as each seeks to use IoHE as a means to position itself beyond its own borders. There is quite clearly no one model that fits all.

This contribution presents the ten key trends identified in a recent study on IoHE, interspersed with reflections and recommendations that led the authors to revise the most commonly accepted working definition for IoHE in an attempt to give it a clearer focus and recalibrate its principal purpose. While the main focus of the European Parliament study 'Internationalisation of higher education' (de Wit *et al.*, 2015, on which this contribution is based) was Europe, it also examined the phenomenon in a number of countries in other world regions to get a sense of what was emerging globally.

Despite the many distinctive features and diversified approaches that can be observed in the 17 country reports of the study – ten from Europe and seven from other continents –a number of global trends can be identified, which give an indication of the direction in which IoHE is heading. This raises the questions of whether or not it is always the most appropriate one and if it is possible to change course.

Becoming more strategic

Overall, there is a clear trend towards more and broader internationalization of higher education, one that is also more strategic in its approach. Its importance is growing everywhere as a response to the challenges faced by universities and countries. All reports call for greater effort towards internationalization in the belief that it can make a difference and bring about necessary change.

National strategies for internationalization emerge as governments begin to see it as part of a bigger undertaking to position their country, improve economic standing or reinvigorate the higher education system. When linked to national ambitions, it is generally better supported and funded, with a clear trend away from an ad hoc to a more systematic approach, in order to promote the national higher education system globally. In countries where there is no national strategy, or where national support of IoHE is happening to a lesser degree or at a reduced speed, lack of strategy is generally perceived as a weakness.

In Europe, it is apparent that this process began with Erasmus, which created common understandings and drivers for internationalization in most countries, although the UK, like other English-speaking countries around the world, focused more on recruitment of international students than on student exchange and cooperation.

This European approach was then further reinforced by the Bologna Process, but, while the rhetoric speaks of more comprehensive and strategic policies for internationalization, in reality there is often still a long way to go. Accomplishment across the different countries is uneven, with parts of Southern and, in particular, Central and Eastern Europe lagging behind.

Impact on institutional strategies

There is a clear trend of policy cascade from the European and national to the institutional level. While national strategies may be supportive of institutional strategies, the use of standardized targets and performance-based indicators across the system can lead to a homogenization of institutional strategies, as HEIs tend to adhere closely to national guidelines (linked to funding) rather than develop their own agendas.

Moreover, when indicators are being used, they tend to focus on quantitative rather than qualitative results, which puts pressure on the institutions to focus on increasing numbers rather than looking at the outcomes of internationalization in terms of enhancement of education, research and service, according to their own specific missions and contexts.

In many countries, governments and HEIs are still struggling to find a balance between autonomy and accountability, and this is reflected in the capacity for institutions to develop their own internationalization agenda. This challenge is particularly evident in Central and Eastern Europe, as well as in emerging and developing economies. Regional- and national-level policies are key external drivers and influencers of institutional policies for IoHE, but it is key that they operate in a way that is supportive, seeking to overcome obstacles and offer opportunities. This can also mean turning to areas that still need attention, such as aligning IoHE with internationalization at other levels of education (primary, secondary, vocational and adult), or stimulating bilingual and multilingual learning at earlier education levels as a basis for a language policy based on diversity.

Insufficient funding

Funding remains a challenge, although a number of countries and institutions are in the fortunate position of being well supported in their internationalization efforts by their national governments, or in the case of Europe, by the European Union. However, some Central and Eastern European countries and institutions can become over-reliant on European funding when there is no substantial investment in internationalization from their national and institutional resources, and this can create problems of sustainability.

The level of importance attached to internationalization impacts on the range of funding mechanisms available and the stakeholders involved. These can include a variety of public bodies that provide funding, such as government agencies, regions and cities, but investment can also come from private stakeholders, for instance, businesses and foundations. In the emerging and developing economies, there is still a tendency to depend on external international development funds for internationalization in the absence of regional, national or institutional investments.

Generally, higher education funding models, tuition fee policies and scholarship schemes follow diverse strategies, but can also impact on internationalization, not only in terms of international student recruitment but also by facilitating or hindering mobility and cooperation between countries.

Increasing privatization

The trend towards privatization of higher education is visible in internationalization, increasingly seen as a means to replace shrinking public funds through revenue generation from international students. However, even in well-supported systems, universities are being encouraged to become more entrepreneurial in their approaches and to develop new income streams through commercial activities. While this is more apparent in some regions than in others, there are increasing trends towards privatization in continental Europe, and in Central and Eastern Europe, in particular.

Higher education as a public good, and in the public interest, is not necessarily in conflict with increased entrepreneurship and private ownership. However, it is important to ensure that the internationalization process acts in line with the values and principles as described in the IAU declaration 'Affirming academic values in internationalisation of higher education: A call for action' (IAU, 2012) and the 'International Student Mobility Charter' (EAIE, 2012).

Effects of globalization

All higher education systems are dealing with the competitive pressures of globalization, the pace of (unexpected) change it is generating and the expectations that are being placed on its institutions to make a key contribution to national development in terms of employable graduates and transferable knowledge. The need to attract talented international students and scholars, in particular in the STEM fields, to meet the needs of academia and industry, is generated not only by increased demand for innovation in the knowledge economy but also by declining demographic trends and insufficient local student participation in these fields in many European countries.

Beyond Europe, this competitive trend is even more manifest, although in the race for talent, rankings and positioning there are substantive risks, such as brain drain and dependency in developing countries. The successes and failures of internationalization are linked to the strengths and weaknesses of the national higher education system, which is, in turn, embedded in the economic, political and social development of each country. Although the same trends are apparent everywhere, all countries have had different starting points. There may be increasing global convergence in aspirations, if not yet in actions.

From (only) cooperation to (also) competition

There is an evident shift from an almost exclusive focus on cooperation and exchange to a broader and more competitive understanding of internationalization, such as the race for talent, international student recruitment, income generation, rankings and institutional positioning. Strategic partnerships are developed not only between HEIs but with HEIs and other stakeholders in industry, business and other sectors, although there is still much to be done in this area.

In Europe, where there is often both demographic decline and shrinking national funding, many HEIs are developing a more competitive approach to internationalization. Three models can be identified: internationalization as soft power with long-term economic goals, evident in Scandinavian countries and in Germany; those with a stronger focus on shorter-term economic goals, such as the United Kingdom; and others such as the Netherlands and France that have developed a mixed approach.

In Europe, Erasmus and the Bologna Process have also opened up opportunities for closer collaboration, although countries in Central and Eastern Europe had to struggle with the upheaval of the post-communist period and many of the challenges are still there. This requires attention from the national governments in these countries but also at the European level, to avert an increased divide in higher education in the region.

In other world regions, emerging countries are still consolidating their national higher education systems, and South Africa has had to deal with the consequences of the former apartheid system. This creates significant challenges in terms of how to cooperate and compete on an equal footing at a global level, although those countries that are successfully developing their economies begin to emerge as new competitors and collaborators.

Growing regionalization

There is an evident trend towards regionalization, often taking inspiration from the European model. European influence in other regions is also apparent, but to varying degrees. This often depends on the EU programmes and level of funding made available, but there has also been careful attention paid to how European models (mobility programmes under Erasmus+, Tempus, ECTS, Tuning, Diploma Supplement and so on) might be adapted to enhance internationalization in other countries and regions.

Asia emerges increasingly as a region of focus, both within the region itself and for other countries and institutions, including Europe. Asian, African and Latin American countries are increasingly looking to develop special relations with their neighbours and facilitate interaction through the development of shared systems and procedures. In identifying target regions, countries and institutions focus not only on emerging clusters, such as BRICS, but also begin to explore less well-known clusters such as CIVETS (Colombia, Indonesia, Vietnam, Egypt, Turkey and South Africa) and CLMV (Cambodia, Laos, Myanmar and Vietnam).

However, Europe emerges as the region most often prioritized in institutional internationalization activities in other parts of the world. The importance of the role of the European Union and the Bologna Process in the development of IoHE, in Europe but also around the globe, is undeniable, and has to be built on even further. In this process, however, it is essential to focus on partnerships and collaboration that recognize and respect the differences in contexts, needs, goals, partner interests and prevailing economic and cultural conditions. Europe can be an example only if it is willing to acknowledge that it can also learn from elsewhere. It offers an important model, but not the only one for the internationalization of higher education.

Rising numbers

The numbers are still rising everywhere. The increase may be fast or slow, large or small, but the numbers for all international activities and, in particular, student mobility whether credit- or degree-seeking, show a clear upward trend, and more countries are becoming involved. Moreover, major sending countries of degree-seeking students are increasingly becoming receiving countries as well.

However, in developing countries there is an imbalance between outgoing and incoming students and scholars, resulting in brain drain and decreasing quality and reputation. There is also concern in Central and Eastern Europe about the imbalance in both credit and degree mobility, with more outgoing than incoming students, and this is further exacerbated by the challenges of demographic decline and a shrinking student population.

Increasing numbers have led to a debate on quantity versus quality in a number of countries. Internationalization exposes and magnifies institutional weaknesses, and as international student numbers rise, along with the subsequent impact on funding and/or reputation, some countries and institutions are turning their attention and efforts to improving the quality of the student experience. Development of strong quality assurance mechanisms for internationalization is increasingly perceived as key to providing a high level of education and service to students and in creating transparent institutional standards for all aspects of internationalization.

Insufficient data

Despite the increasing requirements to produce evidence of impact, the perception often exists that there are still insufficient data about internationalization to carry out accurate analysis and comparison and inform decision making. In Europe, data on European programmes and

European mobility trends are collected regularly, and studies on their impact and outcomes are made freely available. While some countries have sophisticated tools for data collection, others produce only limited information on international activities. Beyond data collection, there is a need for more impact studies that can demonstrate outcomes of internationalization. The level and usefulness of data on internationalization is clearly linked to the importance attached to IoHE as a component in broader national policies.

New areas of development

Three emerging areas are identified for the years ahead: internationalization of the curriculum (IoC), transnational education (TNE) and digital learning.

Internationalization of the curriculum

There is much discussion about internationalization of the curriculum (and of learning outcomes) and the need to pay greater attention to developing an international dimension for all students, not just the mobile minority. However, in many countries the question has not yet been addressed as a strategic priority, while in others it is understood as teaching in another language, predominantly English, or offering joint and/or double programmes. Such programmes are clearly growing in number and importance in many countries as a key tool for internationalization, despite the many legal, financial and quality assurance constraints that still prevail, but do not, by themselves, constitute an internationalized curriculum.

It is crucial to perceive the key benefits and reasons for pursuing internationalization as the improvement of the quality of teaching and learning and preparing students to live and work in a globalized world. Most national strategies are still predominantly focused on mobility, short-term and/or long-term economic gains, recruitment and/or training of talented students and scholars, and international reputation and visibility.

This implies that far greater efforts are still needed to incorporate these approaches into more comprehensive strategies, in which internationalization of the curriculum and learning outcomes, as a means of enhancing the quality of education and research, receive more attention. The inclusion of 'internationalization at home' as a third pillar in the internationalization strategy of the European Commission (2013), 'European higher education in the world', as well as in several national strategies, is a good starting point, but it will require more concrete actions at the European, national and, in particular, the institutional level for it to become reality.

Transnational education

While less widely discussed, there is also a clear growth of transnational education, with a range of different models developing out of the opportunities offered to different national systems from their historical ties, languages offered or the presence of diaspora. While this has traditionally been a sector for English-speaking countries, a number of European and non-English-speaking countries elsewhere are now entering the field. Host countries are often interested in opening up their system to foreign providers as a means of coping with higher education demand and/or to accelerate the pace of reform.

Digital learning

On the other hand, digital learning and in particular MOOCs have been at the centre of many higher education debates, and yet the question can be asked whether HEIs seek to develop digital learning as part of their internationalization strategy. Despite its high profile, there is very little sign of any significant activity in the development of digital learning in the countries surveyed, even those with high levels of technological development. Europe is still playing catch-up in the digital revolution, but it is well placed to be in the vanguard of new thinking on how the digital revolution can improve both quality and access to higher education as well as develop innovative models of virtual exchange and collaborative, online, international learning as an instrument to complement IoHE.

Recalibrating the focus of IoHE

The analysis of these trends in the internationalization of higher education emerging from the 17 country reports and the literature in the study led to the question of whether IoHE is heading in the right direction and whether rethinking the most commonly accepted working definition for internationalization by Jane Knight might help provide greater focus. While the new version may not be one that is easily committed to memory, it is meant to serve as a basis for reflection for those who engage in the internationalization endeavour. The words highlighted in bold show how the definition has been expanded to:

> … the **intentional** process of integrating an international, intercultural or global dimension into the purpose, functions and delivery of post-secondary education, **in order to enhance the quality of education and research for all students and staff, and to make a meaningful contribution to society**.

This definition highlights that IoHE is a planned process that implies consideration, decision and action. It reflects growing awareness that internationalization has to become more inclusive and less elitist by not focusing predominantly on mobility but more on the curriculum and learning outcomes. The 'abroad' component (mobility) needs to become an integral part of the internationalized curriculum to ensure internationalization for all, not only the mobile minority.

It re-emphasizes that internationalization is not a goal in itself, but is a means to enhance quality, and that it should not focus solely on economic rationales. We cannot ignore the fact that we live in a world challenged by increasingly profound social, economic, ethnic and religious tensions. If internationalization of higher education is to make a meaningful contribution to overcoming these challenges, it must be more than a solution to financial shortfall.

Note
[1] This contribution is based on: de Wit *et al.* (eds) (2015) 'Internationalisation of higher education'. Brussels: European Parliament, Directorate-General for Internal Policies.

References
De Wit, H., Hunter, F., Howard, L. and Egron Polak, E. (eds) (2015) 'Internationalisation of higher education'. Brussels: European Parliament, Directorate-General for Internal Policies.

European Association for International Education & International Education Association of Australia (2012) 'International Student Mobility Charter'. Online. www.eaie.org/home/in-the-field/policy-advocacy/international-student-mobility-charter (accessed 16 November 2015).

European Commission (2013) 'European higher education in the world'. Communication from the Commission to the European Parliament, the Council, the European Economic and Social Committee and the Committee of the Regions. Brussels, 11.7.2013 COM(2013) 499 final. Online. http://eur-lex.europa.eu/LexUriServ/LexUriServ.do?uri=COM:2013:0499:FIN:en:PDF (accessed 10 June 2014).

International Association of Universities (2012) 'Affirming academic values in internationalisation of higher education: A call for action'. Paris: International Association of Universities.

Importance and dynamics of TNE data collection systems
Jane Knight and John McNamara

Introduction: The changing landscape of TNE and the need for TNE data collection

Transnational education (TNE) – briefly described as *programme and provider mobility* for the purposes of this article – is a dynamic, vibrant sector of higher education internationalization. Not only has there been an exponential increase in the number of new TNE programmes being offered, there are new forms of TNE partnerships and delivery modes emerging onto the TNE landscape. The past decade has seen a steady increase in the number of branch campuses and the development of internationally cofounded institutions, such as binational universities. Franchised universities are new to the TNE landscape and involve a foreign or local entity establishing a private independent university in a host country, which offers franchised academic programmes from different foreign providers. The number of twinning and franchise programmes is now being surpassed by the staggering increase in double and multiple degree programmes, and distance education is being revolutionized by the development of new technologies and massive open online courses (MOOCs).

However, the research and monitoring of these new developments is simply not keeping pace with the accelerated pace of change. While opinion and anecdotal evidence reveal the benefits and risks attached to this burgeoning field, there continues to be a significant lack of research, robust data and information regarding TNE programmes and enrolments. This is especially true in terms of host country TNE activity. Institutions and national agencies in major sending countries, such as the UK, Australia, Germany and the USA, seem to be more active in tracking their TNE activities and producing data for use in their home context. Host countries, in contrast, especially those with developing higher education systems, are lagging behind in obtaining solid information on standalone TNE institutions, such as branch campuses, franchises and virtual universities, as well as partnership programmes between local and foreign institutions, including twinning and joint/double/multiple degree programmes.

Thus, in spite of the fact that TNE is increasing in scope and scale, there is a significant lack of reliable information regarding the characteristics of the TNE programmes such as numbers, mode, level, discipline, duration and partners. Furthermore, student enrolment data is scarce. Of course, there are highly active TNE countries such as Malaysia, Hong Kong and Mauritius, which have developed TNE regulatory processes and databases on all TNE activity under their jurisdiction. However, it is fair to say that the majority of TNE host countries, especially those who have only recently become more TNE active, do not have appropriate registration of foreign programmes or TNE data collection systems in place and, therefore, are not able to monitor TNE activity. This means that there is insufficient information to effectively include TNE provision in their higher education planning processes, policies and regulatory functions.

This article builds on the research completed for the British Council and the German Academic Exchange Service (DAAD) on the importance and development of TNE data collection systems at all levels – institutional, country and international (McNamara and Knight, 2015). It is worth noting that a long-term need and goal regarding TNE data collection systems is the development of an international mechanism or framework to promote transparent, consistent and comparable TNE data across all TNE active countries, similar to the way that UNESCO and OECD have an international protocol in place to collect, monitor and analyse the international trends of student mobility. The first part of the article reviews the reasons why countries need to collect TNE data and the major enablers and challenges inherent in doing so. The second part addresses the critical issue of developing a common framework or classification system so that there is a common interpretation of different modes of TNE. A work-in-progress framework is provided. In the third and final part of the article, the impact and use of developing this kind of common TNE framework or classification system is discussed.

TNE data collections systems: Rationales, enablers and challenges

Rationales for collecting TNE data

A major driver for collecting TNE data relates to the regulatory functions associated with registration, accreditation and, to a lesser extent, quality assurance, of TNE providers and programmes. Even countries at an early stage of collecting TNE data appear to be motivated to collect TNE data by the need for developing and implementing regulatory processes. This highlights the important role that regulatory bodies, as opposed to statistical agencies, play in gathering TNE data.

The motivations for collecting TNE data can also be framed within a policy development and decision-making context. Examples of national policy areas influenced by the existence of TNE data include: accreditation and quality assurance, recognition of foreign qualifications, visa and immigration, promoting access to higher education, and knowledge and innovation. The scale of TNE activity relative to domestic programmes appears to be an important factor in establishing data collection systems. Furthermore, and not surprisingly, the most active data collection systems are generally in the countries with most experience of hosting TNE programmes.

In some cases, the reason for collecting TNE data is simply explained as being a natural extension of the data collection on higher education. This then leads to the question of whether TNE data is integrated into an overall higher education database and therefore is sometimes difficult to extract or whether it is collected as standalone disaggregated data, thereby being much easier to access and analyse.

Enablers and challenges for collecting TNE data

The key challenge identified in collecting TNE data is the categorization and definitions used to label different types of TNE modes and partnerships. There is much confusion within and across countries about what different types or modes of TNE actually involve. For example, a twinning programme or a branch campus in one country can be understood as something completely different in another country. This definitely affects how data is collected, interpreted and used and makes cross-country comparisons impossible. While most countries recognize this problem, to date there has not been any kind of solution provided. This has led to the proposed common TNE framework in the following section.

Challenges originate both from the HEIs providing the data and the agencies collecting the TNE data, such as the higher education, quality assurance and statistical bodies. Concerns raised by data collection agencies include: non-response to information requests, late provision of data and inconsistent quality and gaps in the data, all of which are compounded by a lack of HEI capacity to assist with queries. On the other hand, HEIs identify issues about the procedures used by data collection agencies, such as poor coordination between different government agencies resulting in duplication of data requested, inappropriate and impractical deadlines; poor lines of communication with HEIs; lack of detailed guidelines to assist with completing the data templates; and lack of expertise in government agencies. The use of outdated or poorly structured data templates is considered a major reason for lack of TNE data in a few countries, and lack of clear guidelines can result in HEIs developing their own templates, resulting in inconsistent data returns.

In terms of major enablers for collecting TNE data, a coherent strategic approach at the national policy level is considered an important enabler for the collection of TNE data. This includes having a well-developed regulatory system in place to oversee the establishment and recognition of TNE providers and programmes. For HEIs, clear and efficient lines of communication between the data collection agencies and the HEIs is the main issue. The optimal approach involves education and training for HEIs on the importance of providing the requested information, including briefings and meetings between HEIs and data collection agencies. Development of online data collection portals is generally enthusiastically supported, but often the technical capacity is missing. Linking HEI and government data collection systems is considered a good way to drive data consistency and comparability across the HE sector. Finally, the importance of having a clear and enforced legal requirement for private HEIs to provide data to government is considered an essential enabler.

Towards a common TNE categorization framework

Without question, there is much confusion within and among countries about what different types or modes of TNE actually mean and involve. While it is important for each country to use terms that fit into the domestic higher education landscape, it is equally important that there is a shared understanding and use of TNE terms across countries. The lack of a common understanding of the terms raises serious issues related to appropriate quality assurance processes, qualification recognition procedures, registration of new providers or programmes, completion rates and the collection of programme-level information and enrolment data.

A step forward in addressing the confusion and misunderstandings is the development of a common framework of TNE terms. The framework needs to be robust enough to ensure that the characteristics of each mode of TNE are clearly defined, but flexible enough to reflect the realities faced by more than 120 countries involved in TNE. Furthermore, the differences between terms need to be explicit, so as to avoid two different terms being used to describe the same activity, or one term describing very different TNE activities. A framework also needs to take into consideration the perspectives of both host and sending countries, as research shows most TNE activities are collaborative in nature, making communication between partners essential. Finally, terms will need to be translated into different languages. This emphasizes again the need for clarity, conciseness and consistency.

Collaborative or independent activity

A key issue is the necessity to delineate:

1. whether the TNE activity is a joint effort between host and sending HEIs
2. whether the TNE activity could be described as a standalone or independent activity without direct academic involvement with a local partner HEI. This distinction has important implications for both host country and sending country regulations and policies related to registration, quality insurance, degree recognition, availability of scholarships and, of course, data collection.

Table 1 categorizes the different TNE modes into two groups – collaborative or independent – and provides a concise description of the mode through identifying who is responsible for providing the curriculum and qualification/s with some explanation notes relating to QAA.

Table 1: Common TNE framework

TNE mode	Description	Notes
Collaborative TNE provision		
Twinning programme	A foreign sending HEI offers academic programme(s) through a host country HEI. Foreign sending HEI provides curriculum and awards the qualification while the host country provides academic administrative support.	Joint/double degrees from host country HEI and from foreign sending HEI are increasingly being offered. QAA dependent on national regulations of host and sending country. Twinning is often labelled *franchise* in some countries.

TNE mode	Description	Notes
Collaborative TNE provision		
Joint/double/ multiple degree programme	Curriculum is jointly designed, delivered and monitored by all local and foreign partners. Different combinations of qualification provided, depending on host country regulations.	The different types of qualification include: • A joint degree programme offers one qualification with badges of both sending and host HEI on the certificate. • A double degree programme offers two qualifications – one certificate/qualification from each partner. • A multiple degree programme offers three or more certificates/ qualifications, depending on the number of partners. QAA normally the responsibility of each partner HEI.
Cofounded/ developed universities	An HEI is established in the host country in collaboration with foreign sending HEIs. The academic programmes are offered through twinning or joint/ double/multiple degree arrangements. Local host HEI also develops academic programmes independent of foreign partners.	Different kinds of qualifications are awarded and can include: • host country HEI qualification • joint qualification with foreign sending HEI • double or multiple qualifications depending on number of foreign sending HEIs. QAA dependent on host and foreign country regulations.

TNE mode	Description	Notes
Collaborative TNE provision		
Locally supported distance education programmes	A foreign distance education HEI/provider offers programmes with academic support for students, available from local entity. Qualification and curriculum offered by foreign distance education provider.	QAA normally undertaken by sending HEI and host country.
Independent (foreign) TNE provision		
Branch campus	A foreign sending HEI offers academic programmes through its own satellite campus, located in the host country. Qualification and curriculum offered by foreign sending HEI.	QAA dependent on national regulations of both host and sending countries.
Franchise university	A private independent host country HEI/provider offers a series of franchised academic programmes from different foreign sending HEI/providers. Qualification and curriculum offered by foreign sending HEIs.	QAA dependent on national regulations of host and sending country. Joint/double degrees between foreign sending HEIs and local private franchise university are increasingly being offered.
Distance education	Foreign sending distance education provider offers academic programmes directly to host country students. No local academic support available. Qualification, curriculum and QAA offered by foreign sending HEI.	QAA from foreign sending country.

Source: J. Knight (2015) 'Transnational education remodeled: Toward a common TNE framework and definitions'. *Journal of Studies in International Education*. Online: doi: 10.1177/1028315315602927.

Much meaning can be lost when a framework becomes too complex and the definitions too nuanced or, conversely, too generic. *Too nuanced* means that some TNE activity can get excluded; too generic creates overlap and lack of clarity about the various modes of TNE. The same challenges of clarity, conciseness, rigour and flexibility faced the development of terms to describe the many different forms of student mobility. However, without a common definition of international student or student mobility, information on source country, destination country, discipline, level of programme, type of mobility, etc. cannot be collected or analysed. The same situation now faces TNE. A common framework or classification system of TNE activities is critical.

Impact and use of a common TNE framework

For such a framework to be useful, it must be robust enough to differentiate between the two categories of TNE provision (collaborative and independent) and each mode of TNE, but flexible enough so that countries with different approaches and levels of involvement can use it to meet their particular needs and circumstances.

Consequently, the use of the common TNE framework for data collection will vary from country to country. It is important to emphasize that it is the use of the TNE framework that will vary, not the actual content. Countries are at different stages in terms of establishing TNE data collection systems and may have to develop their capacity over several phases. To allow for an incremental approach to data collection, the framework must be flexible and have different entry points, but still have robust definitions.

How a country uses the common TNE framework and definitions will depend on a number of factors, such as:

1. the most prevalent TNE category – collaborative or independent
2. the most popular mode – twinning, joint/double/multiple degree programmes, branch campus, franchise university or distance education
3. the use that will be made of the information collected from such as analysis of enrolments, TNE programme trends, QAA conditions and the need for new policies or regulations.

The use of the common TNE framework will also determine the kind of data that is to be collected. The following list demonstrates very clearly that there is a wide variety of information that can be collected to assist a host or sending country in analysing TNE provision trends and develop appropriate policies and regulations.

Examples of types of information that could be collected by host countries using the Common TNE Framework include:

- The degree to which TNE provision is collaborative between local and foreign providers and how much is provided exclusively by foreign sending country HEIs and providers. This is valuable information for host country higher education long-term planning and development of appropriate policies and regulations.

- Within the collaborative category of TNE provision, how much of the TNE curriculum is imported/exported and how much is jointly developed? This is useful in terms of capacity building of local host HEIs and for determining how relevant programmes and curriculum are to the local environment.

- For each TNE mode, programme information on discipline, level (undergraduate, master's, PhD), qualification(s) offered, tuition fees, duration, internships and study abroad opportunities etc. This is instrumental in determining the overlap of TNE programmes with those provided by local HEIs and current trends.

- For each TNE mode, information on enrolment data by programme, gender, level of programme and country of origin of student. This is helpful in assessing whether TNE does increase access to education and for which categories of student.

- For each independent TNE programme: source country of provider, type of provider, QAA procedures and tuition fees. This information is useful for determining the priority of foreign TNE countries and for developing QAA procedures.

- For each collaborative TNE programme: local HEIs involved, source country of partner, number of qualifications being offered (joint, double, multiple), etc. This helps establish what kind of local HEIs are active in TNE collaborative activities and which are the prevalent foreign TNE countries and HEI partners involved. This will help to evaluate TNE provision and, if appropriate, develop a more strategic approach to choice of countries, counterpart HEIs, registration processes, monitoring policies, etc.

The type of information that can be collected is extensive. These examples show the breadth of information and how it can be used. Similarly, the information that can be collected by sending countries is extensive and can be utilized for different purposes, both at institutional and national levels.

Next steps

It is important to note that this framework provides a starting point only, and will require considerable political leadership within and across countries to produce an international framework robust enough to ensure that the characteristics of each mode of TNE are clearly defined, yet flexible enough to reflect the realities faced by the more than 120 countries involved in TNE. To find an example of how to collect comparable international higher education in a consistent and transparent way it is useful to look at the process used by UNESCO and OECD in terms of collecting information on international student mobility from across many countries in all regions of the world. Collecting TNE data will be different but equally complex and challenging and is probably a multiyear initiative. It is not a question of whether TNE data collection systems can be created, but one of when and how they can be developed and used.

References

British Council and German Academic Exchange Service (DAAD) (2014) 'Impacts of transnational education on host countries: Academic, cultural, economic and skills impacts and implications of programme and provider mobility'. Online. www.britishcouncil.org/education/ihe/knowledge-centre/transnational-education/impacts-transnational (accessed 16 November 2015).

Knight, J. (2015) 'Transnational education remodeled: Toward a common TNE framework and definitions'. *Journal of Studies in International Education.* Online. doi:10.1177/1028315315602927 (accessed 16 November 2015).

McNamara, J. and Knight, J. (2015) 'Transnational higher education data collection systems: Awareness, analysis, action'. British Council and German Academic Exchange Service. Online. www.britishcouncil.org/education/ihe/knowledge-centre/transnational-education/tne-education-data-collection-systems (accessed 16 November 2015).

Terminology counts: Towards a mutual basis for transnational education statistics

Dorothea Rüland and Susanne Kammüller

Introduction

Transnational education (TNE) has developed rapidly since the beginning of the millennium and the sector continues to be one of the most dynamic in international higher education. The growth of TNE and its increasing importance for national higher education systems and international HE entails new needs for monitoring, analysing and comparing the scope, extent and impact of TNE activities for institutional and national planning and decision making. Higher education statistics, however, have not kept up with the pace of TNE development, and a lack of sound and internationally comparable data has been a long-felt hindrance in analysis. Recent research has identified an absence of shared terms and definitions as a major stumbling block for the development of a common database on TNE.

The following paragraphs explore some of the issues arising from the lack of a generally accepted terminology, illustrating the challenges of national TNE data collection in the absence of internationally agreed standards through the example of Germany, and argue for a joint effort to create a basis for shared data on global TNE activity.

TNE development amid expectations and doubts

TNE raises hopes and expectations in host countries with regard to its potential for improving the quality of national higher education. This is through the importation of alternative teaching models, scientific knowledge and know-how from abroad, widening overall access to higher education as well as to international higher education without the risk of losing a sizeable portion of national young talent to other countries, or attracting larger numbers of international students into the host country. On the other hand, there are concerns about the impact of TNE related to the quality of study programmes offered by foreign providers, or to a commercialization of HE provision that might fail to meet the education needs of local societies and economies and instead withdraw urgently needed financial and human resources from host countries without creating an appropriate benefit for them.

In TNE providing countries, HEIs see their engagement abroad as a means of accessing additional target groups among students for their study programmes, increasing their international visibility and enhancing their international networks for teaching and research. Nonetheless the inevitable adaptation of study programmes offered across borders to the needs and regulations of the target region raises concerns that this might result in a dilution of academic standards at the foreign 'outposts'. This may in turn threaten the reputation not only of individual higher education institutions that offer their programmes abroad, but may also cast a shadow on the reputation of the TNE providers' national higher education systems as a whole.

This was the backdrop to initial research dedicated specifically to analysing the impact of TNE study offers in host countries. The study, jointly commissioned by the British Council and the German Academic Exchange Service (DAAD) and presented at the Going Global conference 2014, revealed that the overall effects of the presence of TNE study offers are clearly perceived as positive by all host country stakeholders. It also showed that the scope and size of TNE activity is expected to rise even further.[1] The results of the study and all other indicators strongly support the assumption that the growth of TNE actors, programmes and enrolments seen in the past decade will continue, and that the range and diversity of TNE activities will grow even more in the years to come. With this prospect, the issue of monitoring and evaluating the development, scope and impact of TNE gains ever more importance.

Lack of global TNE data

Over the past years, several studies into different aspects of TNE activity have yielded important insights into, for example, the possible effects of TNE on international student mobility, the specific characteristics of students who choose transnational qualifications over domestic study opportunities or studying abroad, and the effects of the presence of TNE on the higher education environment in host countries.[2] Notwithstanding the value of the results gained so far, what all these studies have in common is that they rely on very limited statistical information.

Sound, comprehensive and internationally comparable data on TNE have been a desideratum in higher education research for a long time. Existing data sources, especially on the numbers of enrolled and graduating students in TNE programmes, on the levels of qualification they pursue and the types of study offers they choose, are scarce and vary in depth and coverage. Only very few countries collect and publish TNE enrolment data at all. The existing national data collections often treat TNE from the perspective of providers, counting, for instance, the number of students in China enrolled in programmes offered by German universities, but not the overall number or portion of the total number of students in China enrolled in study courses offered by HEIs from other countries. In addition, the existing sources differ as to the definitions and terms they use to describe various forms of higher education activities offered across borders and also as to the range of activities to be counted under the collective term 'transnational education'. In other words, when we talk of TNE at an international level, it is not only the quantities of the phenomenon of which we cannot be sure – we cannot even safely assume that we are talking about the same things. Some results of this 'chaos and confusion' in TNE terminology, as the authors of a study on TNE data collection systems jointly commissioned by the British Council and DAAD described it, will be illustrated below in the example of Germany.[3]

The challenges of TNE data collection: Example of Germany

With regard to TNE, the situation in Germany is largely determined by two factors: the German system of higher education is almost entirely publicly funded, and German HEIs, based on a broad political consensus, do not demand tuitions fees for the vast majority of the study options they offer to German and international students in Germany. For their study courses offered outside Germany, German HEIs charge tuition fees to sustain the continuation of the programme at the host location.[4] Unlike universities in the UK and Australia, which initially turned to TNE primarily as a means of countering a rapid decline in public funding, German HEIs therefore are not challenged to find alternative sources of revenue outside their national borders, neither can they expect to create additional income by attracting international students to Germany. Their motivation to engage in TNE, which they began on a larger scale from 2003 onwards, originally sprang from the need to internationalize the German system of higher education and establish an international presence and standing that would deepen their integration into an increasingly globalizing higher education landscape, expand their course portfolios and better enable them to compete in the global 'race for talent'. In these endeavours, they were – and are – financially supported by the German Government via DAAD. In addition to motivations of higher education policy, the German Government also sponsors TNE activities of German universities in the context of foreign cultural policy and development cooperation.[5]

These basic parameters are reflected in the development of specific forms of engagement and a distinct profile of Germany as a TNE providing country on the one hand. On the other hand, they also fostered the evolution of a specific understanding of TNE, as distinct from other aspects of internationalization.[6] This in turn influences the treatment of TNE in German higher education statistics.

German national HE statistics, which are mainly collected by the Federal Statistical Office and the statistical offices of the German federal states, in general do not cover enrolments in study courses offered abroad by German HEIs. In registering enrolments of international students in Germany, they do not distinguish between students who stay for an entire study course in Germany and students who spend part of their studies in Germany as part of a double/joint degree programme. In spite of a highly developed system of data collection on higher education, transnational activities of German universities therefore elude government statistics.

Nonetheless, *Wissenschaft Weltoffen*, the key source for data and figures on all aspects of internationalization in German higher education, publishes data on enrolment numbers, geographical distribution, fields of study and degrees sought by students in German TNE study offers.[7] These TNE data are provided by DAAD, which collects them from the reports of German universities whose TNE projects receive support from some of the organization's funding schemes. As the majority of Germany's TNE activity is part-funded by DAAD at one stage, the data cover a very large part of German TNE activity. Nevertheless, they cannot be considered complete since TNE activity outside DAAD funding cannot be included.

The data in *Wissenschaft Weltoffen* also differ from other national collections, for instance, the Higher Education Statistics Agency (HESA) data on TNE enrolment in study courses offered by UK universities, with respect to the underlying understanding of TNE. DAAD's definition of TNE, as explained in a position paper in 2012, stresses as the main features of TNE:

- the provider's academic responsibility for educational content
- a main target group of students from the country or region in which the study programme is offered.[8]

As a logical consequence, the definition excludes cross-border activities that target German students to the same degree as students abroad. Referring to TNE statistics, this means that a major portion of students studying for a German degree outside Germany in double or joint degree courses are not included in the published data. As of October 2015, German universities maintain more than 500 double and joint degree programmes on bachelor's and master's level and 111 *cotutelle* PhD programmes with university partners abroad according to the online database of the German Rectors' Conference.[9] The majority of these double/joint degree courses are with partners in Europe or North America and include a strong element of reciprocal exchange: the double degree option is offered to students of both institutions, who are required to spend a substantial part of their study programme at the partner institution, where they are exempted from local tuition fees. From the perspective of German HEIs, these joint programmes are a way to attract international students, but an even more important function is that of providing mobility windows for German students in which they can gain relevant study experience abroad without loss of time and without additional cost for tuition fees, which they would not have to pay in Germany. The German government provides funding for this type of collaborative delivery via DAAD or the Deutsch-Französische Hochschule,[10] mainly within the context of its strategic goal to increase the portion of higher education graduates from German universities with substantial international study experience to 50 per cent. Corresponding with this view on the function of joint programmes within the national strategy for the internationalization of higher education, the interest in Germany in enrolment numbers of these study courses tends to focus on German students.

As a second consequence, the above definition, in contrast to the understanding of TNE prevalent in English-speaking countries, does not necessarily require the award of a German degree as a criterion for inclusion. This point is of particular importance with regard to the type of institutions known as 'binational universities', which has evolved as a specifically German mode of collaborative TNE engagement. The term covers a group of HEIs established and run in close cooperation with German universities in countries as diverse as Egypt, Jordan, Oman, Kazakhstan, Russia, Turkey and Vietnam. They are independent, private or state-run institutions, governed by the national law of the seat country; in some cases they operate on a special legal status.[11] The involvement of German HEIs takes different forms, including responsibility for curricular development, quality assurance, capacity building, delegation of teaching staff and representation on the institutional boards and committees, among other things. In most cases, several German universities team up to support the binational institution abroad. Corresponding to their differing surrounding conditions and development histories, there is no general rule concerning degree-awarding powers at the binational universities. At the Vietnamese-German University in Ho Chi Minh City, for example, students receive a degree from a German university, while the oldest and biggest of these institutions with more than 10,000 students, the German University in Cairo, awards its own degrees, which are accredited in Germany according to the standards set by the German Accreditation Council.

Compared with British TNE data, German data therefore do not comprise a considerable number of students in double and joint degree programmes with a focus on reciprocal exchange, which would be counted as TNE students in HESA statistics. On the other hand, the German data do comprise a substantial portion of enrolments that would not appear in British statistics, namely the enrolment numbers of collaborative provision without award of a German degree, as is the case at some of the binational universities.

These are just two examples to illustrate how TNE statistics are influenced by specific national concepts and strategic perspectives. Other possible examples include the use of terms such as 'franchise', whose underlying concept of higher education as a tradeable commodity conflicts with the understanding of education as a common good and public task in predominantly public-funded higher education systems, or the inclusion of online distance learning, which raises new questions concerning the 'nationality' of study programmes that are no longer tied to fixed learning or teaching locations. Generally accepted terms and definitions of what constitutes TNE and which aspects we describe by the names we give to its different types and forms would need to accommodate such different concepts and strategic approaches concerning the form and function of study opportunities offered across national borders. Without them, our statistics on TNE will necessarily remain incomparable.

Based on previous research, the study 'Transnational education data collection systems: Awareness, analysis, action' proposed a common terminological framework for TNE data collections that should be 'robust enough to ensure that the characteristics of each mode of TNE are clearly defined, but flexible enough to reflect the realities faced by more than 120 countries involved in TNE'.[12] The framework now put up for discussion by the international community is a valuable advancement. The next step will be the formation of an international working group to discuss, test and refine the proposed framework, and DAAD, together with the British Council, is happy to further support this effort.

Use and benefit of TNE data for hosts and providers

In view of the rising global demand for higher education worldwide, the growth of TNE provision and the continuing disputes in academia and politics on the benefits and risks of this segment of internationalization, solid statistical data on TNE enrolment are increasingly needed as a basis for informed decisions in order to shape higher education landscapes in a way that suits the needs and interests of all parties involved. The continuing lack of reliable quantitative information hinders a full verification of our assumptions and theses on the effects, benefits, potentials and threats of TNE.

For governments and HEIs in TNE hosting countries, information gained from systematic data collection could be a tool to:

- monitor the range of activities of foreign higher education providers in their country and compare these with other countries
- evaluate the contribution of existing TNE provision to fill gaps or cater to specific educational demands of their society and economy
- identify points that require political reaction, for example, to steer the strategic development of TNE in certain fields or geographical regions or support TNE in specific segments of the HE system
- assess needs to adapt the regulatory framework for foreign HEI providers or transnational inter-university cooperations
- support effective quality assurance of TNE study offers.

For governments and HEIs in providing countries, systematic TNE data collections would help them to:

- better assess the conditions and demands for TNE engagement overall or in specific regions or countries
- evaluate their own activity and potential as TNE providers in comparison with others
- appraise the effect of their TNE engagement on their economies and higher education systems, for instance, with regard to international student mobility.

Thus, a systematic approach to TNE data collection in host and providing countries could effectively influence the framework conditions for TNE activity and ultimately impact the scope, form and direction of transnational HE provision by informing strategic decisions of institutions and governments for the further development of the global higher education landscape.

Conclusion

As the preceding examples have shown, the lack of reliable and comparable information on the overall scope and extent of TNE engagement is an issue that affects a growing number of countries and stakeholders. The development of a common database to systematically monitor student numbers and types of activities in TNE on the basis of national data collections should therefore be regarded as a joint challenge requiring international combined efforts in order to achieve mutual benefit from this special field of international higher education. A fundamental prerequisite for the creation of a comprehensive stock of information would be an agreement on a common terminology.

In recognition of the challenges presented by the lack of available data and the complexity of TNE terminology, the British Council and DAAD together commissioned research and supported the development of a first proposal towards a terminological framework for TNE data collections. In a joint declaration published on the occasion of the Going Global conference in London in May 2015,[13] the two organizations called on the international higher education community, national governments and international stakeholders concerned with collecting data on higher education to work together for the development of a better global understanding of TNE. A joint effort is needed, and the international HE community is invited to participate in it as a further contribution towards the development of an international data collection protocol that might enable the inclusion of TNE data in national and international data collections on higher education such as the statistics of UNESCO or the OECD.

Notes

[1] British Council/DAAD (ed.) (2014) *Impacts of Transnational Education on Host Countries: Academic, cultural, economic and skills impacts and implications of programme and provider mobility*, p.61 ff.

[2] See British Council/DAAD (2014); British Council (ed.) (2013) *The Shape of Things to Come. The evolution of transnational education: Data, definitions, opportunities and impacts analysis*. V. Tsiligiris (2014) *Transnational Education vs International Student Mobility: Substitutes or distinct markets?*. Observatory on Borderless Higher Education (ed.), to name just a few examples.

[3] British Council/DAAD (ed.) (2015) *Transnational Education Data Collection Systems: Awareness, analysis, action*. Authors: John McNamara and Jane Knight, p.9.

[4] In the 'Code of Conduct for German Higher Education Projects Abroad', approved in 2013, the members of the German Rectors' Conference have recorded a conscious policy of voluntary self-restraint with regard to tuition fees in their TNE activities.

See hrk.de/resolutions-publications/resolutions/resolution/convention/code-of-conduct-for-german-higher-education-projects-abroad/.

[5] For an outline of the different motivations underlying government support for TNE in Germany, see Dorothea Rüland, 'Transnational education: The German approach' in Mary Stiasny and Tim Gore (eds) (2014) *Going Global: Global Education – Knowledge based economies for 21st century nations*. Bingley, UK: Emerald Books.

[6] See DAAD (2012) 'Transnational education in Germany – DAAD position paper' (English translation 2014), p.3f.

[7] See DAAD/DZHW (2015) *Wissenschaft weltoffen 2015: Daten und Fakten zur Internationalität von Studium und Forschung in Deutschland* [Facts and Figures on the International Nature of Studies and Research in Germany], p. 96ff. Online. www.wissenschaftweltoffen.de/publikation/wiwe_2015_verlinkt.pdf.

[8] See DAAD (2012), p.3.

[9] See www.hochschulkompass.de/en/partnerships/search-for-partnerships.html.

[10] The Deutsch-Französische Hochschule or Université Franco-Allemande is a bilateral French-German umbrella organization that currently supports and coordinates more than 180 double and joint degree courses offered in collaboration by universities from both countries (see dfh-ufa.org/de).

[11] See Stephan Geifes and Susanne Kammüller (2014) 'Transnational, bi-national, international? The German approach'. *EAIE Forum*, summer edition, p.17f.

[12] British Council/DAAD (eds) (2015), p.43.

[13] 'Joint declaration British Council and the German Academic Exchange Service (DAAD): The critical need to support collection of TNE data', britishcouncil.org/sites/default/files/1.1_tne_joint_declaration.pdf.

1.5

Encouraging and supporting student mobility: The role of a pedagogy of intercultural competence

Sibilla Robutti

Our contribution to the *Broadening Horizons* session at the Going Global conference 2015 sought to investigate the rationale for including mobility within the HE curriculum. Why should UK students be encouraged to engage in a period of study abroad, when the rest of the world looks at the UK as one of the topmost providers of HE?

Among the wide range of skills impacted by mobility, as evidenced by previous research conducted at St Mary's University Twickenham, London (Coombs and Robutti, 2014) and by key literature within the sector (for example, Brandenburg and team, 2014), this paper focuses specifically on intercultural competence. The positive impact of mobility on intercultural competence is identified as key for positioning mobility firmly within the HE curriculum, and for counteracting the treatment of mobility activities as secondary to subject knowledge.

The paper sets out to identify the key ingredients of a pedagogy of intercultural competence to accompany mobility programmes. Analysing the potential offered by a range of educational tools to act on barriers and drivers of mobility identified by the British Council's *Broadening Horizons* research (2015), it argues that a pedagogy of intercultural competence has a significant role to play in encouraging and supporting mobility.

Why should we include mobility in the curriculum? A key tool for developing intercultural competence

Equipping students to face the challenges of globalization: The internationalization agenda

Our starting point is an approach to curriculum design in which the wider context plays a significant part, and that aims to address the challenges of a changing world. The curriculum should equip students with personal qualities for lifelong independent learning, and 'a continual capacity for remaking the self' to face such challenges (Barnett and Coate, 2005: 43).

In the current scenario of globalization, the internationalization agenda has earned widespread consensus in the HE sector. While this has most commonly been realized by increasing international student numbers, it has been argued that the scope of internationalization is more fully embraced when it also includes an ethos of internationalism (Sweeney, 2013). Internationalization aims to prepare '... 21st century graduates to live in and contribute responsibly to a globally interconnected society' (Higher Education Academy, 2014: 1). Student mobility is but one among the several tools in the internationalization kit. We however argue for its importance, because of its potential for equipping students with intercultural competence.

Developing intercultural competence through mobility: A key tool for internationalizing the curriculum

The literature on student mobility widely evidences its positive impact on the development of key abilities related to intercultural competence (see, for example, Doyle, 2009). This has been identified by the British Council as the core skill set for the twenty-first century, without which we are simply not equipped to function in a globalized world (Ferrier, 2015).

The abilities within the intercultural competence skill set can be grouped into three dimensions: a *cognitive* dimension, relating to awareness and knowledge of a range of cultural perspectives; an *interpersonal* dimension, relating to the ability to translate these into effective performance in diverse contexts; and an *intrapersonal* dimension, relating to an inclusive identity and ethos (see Braskamp *et al.*, 2007, cited in Doyle, 2009). These three dimensions can be directly related to the three key dimensions targeted by curriculum design, namely *knowing*, *acting* and *being* (Barnett and Coate, 2005).

We wish to highlight here the relevance of the relationship between intercultural competence and the *acting* and *being* dimensions of the curriculum. The *knowing* dimension can also be internationalized to a certain extent by adding international perspectives to content. International perspectives, however, do not necessarily act on students' sense of self, equipping them with personal qualities to face shifting global challenges (Coate, 2009); nor do they engender the translation of analytical knowledge into effective performance. The *acting* dimension of intercultural competence relates to employability skills that are key for thriving in a globalized job market (see CBI/Pearson, 2014). While other employability skills impacted by mobility can also be developed through different curricular activities, such as work placements, intercultural competence seems to be more exclusively linked to mobility.

We therefore argue that curriculum design should actively target the development of intercultural competence through mobility. This would realize the internationalization agenda on all of the three key dimensions of the curriculum, and link it to employability.

We now wish to take a closer look at how intercultural competence is developed during mobility, to better understand how HEIs can support this process.

The learning process engendered by mobility

Living in a different context constitutes the experience that is central to experiential learning in mobility, and which differentiates mobility from study at home. It is however necessary to demystify the belief that mere exposure to difference is transformative in itself (Pedersen, 2010). Rather, it is 'focused and reflective interaction with the host culture' that has been identified as the key enabler of learning in mobility (Engle and Engle, 2003, cited in Vande Berg *et al.*, 2009: 6).

Context in itself is not a stable construct, but derives from students' capacity to engage in this focused and reflective interaction, their ability to set learning goals for themselves and act accordingly, and the negotiation between these and the intentions of the other actors present in the context (Allen, 2010). The *self* of the student therefore comes prominently into play. The experience of otherness is core to this process (Talburt and Stewart, 1999). The desire to be *personally* accepted in the host community, where the pressure for learning the rules of behaviour and feedback are constant, motivates students to learn how to *act* appropriately. This mechanism, engendered by sustained immersion in the host context, is key to the special learning potential of mobility for equipping students with intercultural competence. During mobility, all informal living experiences are framed by the host culture, and become learning opportunities (Kawamura, 2007). Students' strong motivation to learn, in order to be able to 'fit in' and function as part of the community, influences the learning strategies they enact. Constant feedback allows them to monitor their progress and readjust their strategies, accelerating the development of intercultural competence.

The skills required in this process are also key for a career of lifelong independent learning (ibid.). These echo the capacity to continuously update knowledge, skills and attitudes in interaction with shifting global contexts, which is targeted in our approach to curriculum design (Coate, 2009). Not surprisingly, literature on the impact of student mobility has highlighted that the learning benefits expected from the experience are not achieved consistently, but are more prominent in individuals with an established capacity for independent learning and reflection (Allen, 2010; Vande Berg *et al.*, 2009).

The key ingredients of a pedagogy of intercultural competence

If intercultural competence is to be treated as a key curricular goal, it is crucial that governmental policies to encourage mobility are complemented by HEIs' pedagogical intervention to support all students in making meaning out of their experiences abroad.

Informed by the experience of St Mary's University in designing mobility learning resources (Coombs and Robutti, 2014) and by best practice within the sector, we propose an intercultural competence pedagogical toolkit. Guided reflection and structured opportunities for interaction with the host culture are identified as its core ingredients, to support reflection and participation.

The intervention should be implemented 'just in time' (Pedersen, 2010: 78), from promotion throughout the mobility experience. HEIs have a variety of media at their disposal – coaching by on-site cultural mentors or via email, group discussions, e-portfolios, photo or audio diaries, blogging, applications, learning resources in a virtual learning environment, etc. Blended learning and a range of written/audio/video resources should be utilized, to suit a variety of learning styles.

Independent methods of critical reflection and peer discussion should be complemented by the intervention of a 'well-trained cultural mentor' (Vande Berg *et al.*, 2009: 25). The mentor should possess an intimate understanding of the host and home socio-cultural contexts, and of the goals of the learners (Kawamura, 2007). He or she would act as an intermediary between the student and the host country (Talburt and Stewart, 1999) to suggest meaningful directions for participation and reflection, and to enable the widening of personal interpretations through discussion. Rather than delivering lectures, the mentor can offer prompts for reflection in the form of open-ended questions, guide further reflection through feedback, and integrate into the curriculum increased opportunities for contact with the host culture through cultural immersion assignments.

The following criteria for intervention design provide avenues to enhance learning, and to act on key barriers to and drivers of mobility perceived by students.

An intentional approach to learning aims

Goal-setting is a particularly valuable tool to support reflective learning. HEIs' intervention can encourage students to be aware of the learning aims of mobility even prior to departure and throughout the experience (Williams, 2009), using questions, group discussions and multimedia material as prompts for reflection. Having a clear idea of what they wish to achieve has a powerful influence on what strategies students enact and how they engage in learning. Input from the mentor throughout the experience can then guide students in reflecting on and monitoring their progress, and adjusting their goals and strategies accordingly, so that they themselves can regulate and take charge of their learning process (Allen, 2010).

A multi-method assessment plan, when used in a formative capacity, is a valuable tool to aid goal-setting and progress-tracking. Assessment should be underpinned by frameworks articulating progressively more sophisticated degrees of intercultural competence (Deardorff, 2006; see also the Intercultural Competence and Knowledge Value Rubric in Rhodes, 2010). Methods such as the evaluation of students' reflective work, observation by others and student interviews should be incorporated throughout the experience.

By asking students to articulate their learning progress, and providing examples of instances in which they had to make use of skills related to intercultural competence, HEIs can support students in learning how to communicate their achievements to others in meaningful ways (Williams, 2009). This is a skill that can be used in job interviews and applications, positively impacting students' employability (Coombs and Robutti, 2014).

Assessment should be accompanied by initiatives to recognize achievements, in order to incentivize learning. Different options for this were discussed by the conference audience: credit-bearing reflective work; a cumulative system whereby accreditation occurs after a set threshold of mobility experiences has been completed; and where accreditation is not feasible, certificates or degrees with international or intercultural experience recognized on the transcript.

Guided reflection on the goals of mobility is also a valuable tool at the promotional stage, for acting on key drivers and barriers. This can be combined with celebrative events of returned students' achievements, engaging faculty and the returned students – inspirational lectures from teachers about the benefits of the experience, and information sessions from mobility alumni, indeed figure among the top five incentives to mobility (British Council, 2015).

The *Broadening Horizons* research has specifically identified wanting to have fun travelling and experiencing other cultures as the most frequent motivation for mobility (ibid.). Guided reflection during promotion can build on students' desire for a cultural experience, by raising their awareness of the impact of this experience on intercultural competence. Crucially, it can help students recognize the significance of the intercultural competence skill set as a facilitator of academic and employability outcomes (see Bridger, 2015). A shift in perception of mobility, from a fun experience to one with crucial implications for academic and professional development, can be used to alter perceptions of the cost/benefit ratio of mobility. This would complement funding-related initiatives to mitigate the top non-academic deterrent represented by cost. It is furthermore crucial at the organizational level, for embedding a culture-making space for mobility in curriculum design.

Framing reflection through the concept of culture

Students require support in developing the skills to identify the host culture's underlying values, and to frame their reflections through the concept of culture (Vande Berg *et al.*, 2009). This type of support can be used to further stimulate students' desire for a cultural experience. Moreover, the *Broadening Horizons* research has identified fear of not being able to fit into another culture as the fifth top non-academic deterrent to mobility (British Council, 2015). Support can thus empower students with the tools to react positively to disorientation, and use it to trigger reflection and learning. This would contribute to mitigating such fears during promotion, and possible phases of culture shock while abroad.

An important step to be taken right from the pre-departure phase is to guide students in recognizing that culture is not something that concerns their host community alone, but themselves too, and in de-universalizing their own cultural constructs (Kawamura, 2007). In order then to structure cultural comparison, it is useful to familiarize students with certain core dimensions of cultural analysis – for example, the values attributed to the individual and to community, communication styles, the use of body language, attitudes to time, rule application, age, gender, sexuality, religion, family structure, social stratification, etc. The comparison between target and base culture can be articulated through each of these dimensions (see Peace Corps, 1997). Examples of practical behaviours should be sought to support reflection. Students should then be guided to formulate hypotheses on the cultural values and logics that underpin the prevailing attitude of a culture towards each of the dimensions being analysed.

Discussion is also fed by the personal experiences students bring to the table. These are shaped by students' socio-cultural positioning, and by the extent to which they are visibly marked as outsiders within a particular context. Peer discussion, explicitly approaching a range of socio-cultural variables, should be used to encourage students to learn from others' experiences, so that their learning can develop from a multiplicity of vantage points (Talburt and Stewart, 1999).

For capacity building at home, HEIs can make use of the great resource represented by international students, engaging them in these discussions through promotional and academic group activities, buddy systems and an International Society.

Additionally to guided reflection, the role of language support in offering students insights into their host culture's prevailing tendencies should not be overlooked. Language support is also obviously crucial to overcome the lack of language skills, the first academic and second non-academic deterrent to mobility (British Council, 2015).

Using cultural immersion assignments and mentoring to achieve the right balance of challenge

Considering cultural meaning as emerging from social interaction (Kawamura, 2007), HEIs can also support students' meaning-making process by modulating the interactions to which they are exposed during mobility. Their intervention should create an environment with enough challenge to exert on students the amount of pressure required to prompt their learning, in their desire to be accepted by the host community.

HEIs can 'facilitate student exploration out of their comfort zone', by designing specific cultural assignments for students to actively engage with the host community (Pedersen, 2010: 73). Examples include participating in events to which they would not necessarily be exposed, interviewing locals to understand their views on a certain topic, researching specific information/products, opportunities for service learning, and housing arrangements involving staying with a family or with local students (ibid.; Kawamura, 2007).

Cultural assignments can target interaction with a more varied range of actors than those with whom students would normally come into contact. This would help students to avoid developing a highly skewed vision of their host culture, more closely aligned with that of the age group with which they mostly interact (Meredith, 2010).

While challenge has been identified as an important enabler of learning, it has also been noted that an optimum level can be reached, after which the learning curve reverses and students tend to retreat from difference (Martinsen, 2011). HEIs' intervention needs therefore to carefully balance challenge with support (Sanford, 1966), and create a sort of buffer zone using guided reflection and group discussion (Talburt and Stewart, 1999). This would function as a safe space of mediation between students and the host country, in which students are gently encouraged to take on challenges and to build their confidence in their ability to tackle them, and are provided with opportunities to debrief the feelings they experience.

Concerns around access to quality health care and feeling unsafe in another country figure as the third and fourth top non-academic deterrents to mobility respectively (British Council, 2015). These concerns about personal well-being, which might be underpinned by a more general fear of the unknown represented by the host context as opposed to the familiar territory of home, can be mitigated by the support mechanisms established by HEI's pedagogical intervention. This would familiarize students with the host context right from the promotional stage, integrating first-hand knowledge from returned and international students, and emphasizing the support available throughout the experience.

Challenge can also be modulated according to the varying ranges of students' comfort zones and personal circumstances, by offering a wide range of mobility options including domestic, virtual and shorter-term choices. These can be used in a staged approach to build students' levels of intercultural competence, mitigating their fears and progressively creating an appetite for more challenging opportunities.

Conclusions

The place awarded to mobility within the HE curriculum is more fully justified if mobility programmes are supported by a pedagogy of intercultural competence, incorporating the key ingredients outlined in this paper. Such intervention would enable HEIs to support the entire student population engaged in mobility to develop intercultural competence – the key skill set for the twenty-first century – including students with a less established capacity for independent learning.

The pedagogical intervention outlined provides educators with a tool for stimulating students' desire for a cultural experience, as a driver of mobility. It also opens avenues for mitigating concerns related to personal well-being. Supplementing funding-related initiatives, it could furthermore contribute to shifting perceptions of the cost/benefit ratio of the experience. In this sense, the proposed pedagogy of intercultural competence harbours significant potential for increasing mobility numbers, complementing continued governmental effort through the UK's Strategy for Outward Mobility, but crucially also for enhancing the mobility experience.

References

Allen, H.W. (2010) 'What shapes short-term study abroad experiences? A comparative case study of students' motives and goals'. *Journal of Studies in International Education*, 14 (5), 452–70.

Barnett, R. and Coate, C. (2005) *Engaging the Curriculum in Higher Education*. Buckingham: Open University Press.

Brandenburg, U. and team (2014) 'The Erasmus Impact Study – Effects of mobility on the skills and the internationalisation of higher education institutions'. European Commission. Online. http://ec.europa.eu/education/library/study/2014/erasmus-impact_en.pdf (accessed 27 September 2015).

Bridger, K. (2015) 'Academic perspectives on the outcomes of outward student mobility'. Online. www.heacademy.ac.uk/sites/default/files/resources/academic_perspectives_on_the_outcomes_of_outward_student_mobility_-_final_report.pdf (accessed 24 May 2015).

British Council (2015) 'Broadening Horizons: The value of overseas experience'. British Council. Online. www.britishcouncil.org/sites/britishcouncil.uk2/files/6.3_broadening-horizons-2015.pdf (accessed 12 September 2015).

CBI/Pearson (2014) 'Gateway to Growth: CBI/Pearson education and skills survey 2014'. CBI/Pearson. Online. www.cbi.org.uk/media/2807987/gateway-to-growth.pdf (accessed 14 January 2015).

Coate, K. (2009) 'Curriculum'. In Tight, M., Mok, K.H., Huisman, J. and Morphew, C.C. (eds), *The Routledge International Handbook of Higher Education*. London: Routledge. 77–90.

Coombs, L. and Robutti, S. (2014) 'Developing Employability through the Study Abroad Experience: A structured and supported activity to enhance international experience'. London: the Higher Education Academy. Online. www.heacademy.ac.uk/sites/default/files/tdg_liz_coombs_1.pdf (accessed 2 March 2016).

Deardorff, D.K. (2006) 'Identification and assessment of intercultural competence as a student outcome of internationalization'. *Journal of Studies in International Education*, 10 (3), 241–66.

Doyle, D. (2009) 'Holistic assessment and the study abroad experience'. *Frontiers: The Interdisciplinary Journal of Study Abroad*, XVIII, 143–55.

Ferrier, T. (2015) 'What does it take to develop intercultural competence?'. Paper presented at British Council's Conference *Going Global 2015: Connecting cultures, forging futures*, London, 1–2 June.

Higher Education Academy (2014) 'Internationalising higher education framework: Preparing 21st century graduates to live in and contribute responsibly to a globally interconnected society'. Online. www.heacademy.ac.uk/sites/default/files/resources/internationalisingheframeworkfinal.pdf (accessed 27 September 2014).

Kawamura, H. (2007) 'Participant observation for language learners: A performance-based approach to language learning during study'. *Japanese Language and Literature* 'Study Abroad for Advanced Skills', 41 (2), 333–49.

Martinsen, R. (2011) 'Predicting changes in cultural sensitivity among students of Spanish during short-term study abroad'. *Hispania*, 94 (1), 121–41.

Meredith, A. (2010) 'Acquiring cultural perceptions during study abroad: The influence of youthful associates'. *Hispania*, 93 (4), 686–702.

Peace Corps (1997) *Culture Matters – The Peace Corps Cross-Cultural Workbook*. Washington D.C.: Peace Corps Information Collection & Exchange.

Pedersen, P. J. (2010) 'Assessing intercultural effectiveness outcomes in a year-long study abroad program'. *International Journal of Intercultural Relations*, 34, 70–80.

Rhodes, T.L. (ed.) (2010) *Assessing Outcomes and Improving Achievement: Tips and tools for Using Rubrics*. Association of American Colleges and Universities.

Sanford, N. (1966) *Self and Society: Social change and development*. New York: Atherton Press.

Sweeney, S. (2013) 'Encouraging outward student mobility'. In Westminster Higher Education Forum Keynote Seminar: Internationalisation of Higher Education – UK Competitiveness, Student Mobility and the Development of Overseas Campuses, London: Westminster Higher Education Forum, 21 March.

Talburt, S. and Stewart, M. (1999) 'What's the subject of study abroad?: Race, gender, and "living culture"'. *The Modern Language Journal*, 83 (2), 163–75.

Vande Berg, M., Connor-Linton, J. and Paige, R.M. (2009) 'The Georgetown Consortium Project: Interventions for student learning abroad'. *Frontiers: The Interdisciplinary Journal of Study Abroad*, XVIII, 1–75.

Williams, T.R. (2009) 'The reflective model of intercultural competency: A multidimensional, qualitative approach to study abroad assessment'. *Frontiers: The Interdisciplinary Journal of Study Abroad*, XVIII, 289–306.

Why do students make the decisions they make on mobility programmes?

Catriona Hanks and Anne Marie Graham

Introduction

The United Kingdom excels in many areas of higher education: through world-class institutions, through excellence in teaching and research, and through its appeal for international students. However, there is one area in which it lags behind: its own students' outward mobility. Figures released this year by the Higher Education Statistical Agency (HESA) place the overall proportion of UK-domiciled students who were mobile in 2013/14 at 1.2 per cent (or just 22,100 students), meaning that 98.8 per cent of students did not choose to study, work or volunteer overseas, and therefore did not profit from the unique personal, academic and career opportunities that time spent abroad can offer.

Although this percentage is low, the profile of student mobility has increased in the past few years. With greater awareness of the benefits of mobility, and the evidence base growing, UK universities are already playing their part in encouraging students to go mobile, through the increased provision and promotion of mobility programmes. The UK government has also launched its own Strategy for Outward Mobility aimed at increasing the proportion of UK-domiciled students who access an international experience as part of their UK higher education.[1] This strategy and its associated campaign, 'Go International', are being implemented by the UK Higher Education International Unit, which works with the sector to provide a hub for research, advice, best practice and opportunities on outward mobility.[2] With new research in place, and with political momentum behind it, outward mobility may yet become higher education's new cause célèbre, offering a more international higher education package and benefitting students, institutions and international cooperation.

The new research available on graduate outcomes and student perspectives is of particular interest to those institutions developing or implementing outward mobility strategies.[3] This paper will look at two such reports into student perspectives, from the UK Higher Education International Unit and the British Council, the findings of which were presented at the Going Global Conference 2015. Both reports explore what motivates students towards, or deters them from, mobility, while surveying different student populations: those considering mobility as well as those who have decided for or against it.

The reports

In September 2015 the UK Higher Education International Unit and the British Council released *Student Perspectives on Going International*, a report that examines the perspectives of 1,588 UK-domiciled students regarding the benefits of, and barriers to, spending up to one year abroad as part of a UK undergraduate degree.[4] Just a few months earlier, the British Council published its third annual *Broadening Horizons* report, which examines how 7,481 UK and US students, aged mainly between 16 and 30 years, perceive study abroad and what they see to be the main drivers of and barriers to overseas study.[5] Both reports give us a wealth of insight into students' current thinking on mobility, and why they take the decisions they do. Their main findings will be outlined in the 'Key findings' section below.

The reports compare different student populations – an important factor in considering the similarities and differences in their findings. On the one hand, *Student Perspectives* included students considering different types of mobility, including study abroad, work abroad and volunteering, and mobility lengths of up to a year. It looked primarily at undergraduate students who were either openly considering such mobility, who had made a 'positive decision' and were waiting to go abroad, or who were post-mobile. Only 2 per cent of students in this report had decided against mobility. On the other hand, *Broadening Horizons* surveyed a broader range of students, from high school students to postgraduates, and incorporated students who were considering mobility lengths of longer than a year, including full degree mobility. Of this group, 47 per cent had already taken a 'negative' decision, deciding against going abroad. Unlike *Student Perspectives*, this report considered only one type of mobility: study abroad.

Both reports offer valuable findings for institutions looking to identify strategies to increase their number of mobile students. *Broadening Horizons* fills out the background to the detailed picture in *Student Perspectives*, offering a broader view of study abroad across the UK-domiciled student body (its main aim is to look at how UK and US students' perceptions differ). *Student Perspectives* focuses on undergraduate short-term mobility and presents a breakdown of findings by mobility length and type.

Key findings from *Student Perspectives* and *Broadening Horizons*

This section will explore what *Student Perspectives* and *Broadening Horizons* can tell us about why students decide to go, or not to go, abroad. Following the structure of the reports themselves, this paper will look at key motivations, impacts, barriers and information sources, as perceived by students, to gain a better understanding of why students make the decisions they do.

Motivations

Key to any institution's marketing and recruitment strategy on outward mobility is an understanding of what really motivates students to go abroad. Both *Student Perspectives* and *Broadening Horizons* explore these motivations in some detail, and both arrive at similar findings. *Student Perspectives* finds that the key motivation for students, across mobility types and durations, is first and foremost a personal and cultural one: to have an interesting and enjoyable experience, broaden horizons, improve intercultural skills and learn about a new country and culture. Likewise, *Broadening Horizons* finds 'having fun travelling and exploring different cultures' outweighs more calculated external motivations such as increased employability prospects or improved academic outcomes (although employment and academic motivations were still very much in the mix). While *Student Perspectives* does make the point that many of the personal skills developed through mobility are also valuable to employers, it is still the case that students chose to report these as motivations over those that directly refer to employment. Students also tended to select more general 'enhanced employability' outcomes over more specific employment aspirations, such as securing a particular job in the UK.

While these responses were largely consistent across different student groups, it is worth mentioning some small differences in the mix. Two of these differences are intuitive: *Student Perspectives* found that language students saw language improvement as a very important motivation, and that volunteers were more motivated than others by the charitable and humanitarian dimension. The other differences between groups are less intuitive. *Student Perspectives* found that women tended to be more driven by employment and academic factors than men, and that those from disadvantaged backgrounds tended to place more emphasis on employment factors. *Broadening Horizons* found that UK students were more likely to be motivated by employability concerns than their US counterparts. That women are more motivated by external considerations is of particular interest given that, at least in 2013–14, there are more women as a proportion of UK-domiciled students, Erasmus participators and mobile students more generally.[6]

Impacts

The perceived value of time spent abroad as part of their degree can in itself be a strong motivator for students. But are students already aware of the benefits that this activity can offer and, critically, is it informing their decisions? *Student Perspectives* and *Broadening Horizons* both find that it is. The development of personal skills and increased employability both featured highly as motivating factors for students in the two reports, and very few students in *Student Perspectives* reported a lack of evidence of personal impact as a barrier to mobility. Equally, across students who had already decided for or against mobility, or who were still making their decision, *Broadening Horizons* found that the majority of students were very aware that their degree alone was not enough in an increasingly competitive job market, and that study abroad could give them the edge they needed. In general, though, the report found that students were more likely to view study abroad as having cultural value rather than as having employment and academic value – by introducing them to new cultures, giving them a cosmopolitan identity and allowing them to travel. This tallies with the main motivation we found for students considering mobility: the personal and cultural impetus.

Meanwhile, *Student Perspectives* found an equally strong grasp of the value of an overseas experience by students who had already been mobile, with a particularly strong emphasis on its impact on personal development. Independence, intercultural understanding, new social networks and self-confidence were reported by over 90 per cent of respondents to be outcomes of their time spent abroad. Strong academic and career impacts were also reported, if to a lesser extent. The perceptions of these post-mobile students is important not only because they are a key source of information for students still making their decisions, but because they may decide on further mobility themselves: indeed, the most commonly reported 'academic and career' impact by mobile students in *Student Perspectives* was interest in more study abroad. This accords with findings from *Broadening Horizons* that 31 per cent of students reporting an interest in study abroad had already completed one mobility placement. As focus groups confirmed, once students experienced what mobility could offer, they often wanted more, and 'serial' mobility was not unusual among mobile respondents.

Another important finding from *Student Perspectives* was that mobile students perceived strong personal development impacts regardless of different types and durations of mobility. Currently the *Broadening Horizons* report finds that UK students are most likely to be interested in studying abroad for a one-year period at the undergraduate level; however, with this new evidence, institutions have a strong argument to make for shorter-term mobility programmes.

Decision-making factors and barriers

With so many motivations for, and positive impacts of, mobility, the question arises, why aren't all of our students going abroad? The answer, of course, is that it is not that easy. As both *Student Perspectives* and *Broadening Horizons* report, a multitude of factors feed into student decisions on mobility, and as many factors draw students towards mobility as deter them. At least two-thirds of the overall *Student Perspectives* survey population reported nine out of eleven given factors as very important or important in their decision, ranging from social or practical to academic and institutional. The factors they identified as most important were the attractiveness of the location and the availability of funding. The report also separates out those considering mobility from the rest of the survey population, which otherwise has a somewhat 'positive' bias, given that 91 per cent of students had already decided to go, or had indeed gone, abroad. Making this distinction changes slightly what students perceive to be the most important considerations, with funding availability and total cost now considered (by over 90 per cent) to be the most important factors, followed by personal safety concerns.

Both *Broadening Horizons* and *Student Perspectives* look in detail at what students perceive to be the main barriers to mobility, and agree that funding availability was the number one 'perceived barrier' for students considering mobility, or in the *Broadening Horizons* case, students both considering and decided against mobility.[7] Both reports also found language to be a significant barrier: in *Broadening Horizons* this was found to be the number one 'academic' deterrent by a significant margin, outweighing factors such as inflexible degree structures or problems with credit recognition, and the number two 'non-academic' deterrent. However, when broken down by mobility types, and students' socio-economic status, *Student Perspectives* found that language as a barrier varied widely between groups. For example, it was found to be more of a concern for students still considering whether to go abroad (and in particular, students considering work experience), and among students from more disadvantaged backgrounds.

Student Perspectives found that the most important perceived barriers to mobility varied more by student type (those who had been abroad or were waiting to go, as opposed to those still considering it) and relatively little across different types or durations of mobility. Those waiting to go abroad were less concerned about the lack of opportunities, greater debt or loss of earning potential, and more worried about social implications, such as interruption to friendships and fear of isolation.

However, it did find that funding and knowledge of opportunities, the top two concerns overall, were greater concerns for very short mobility periods than for longer durations. As the report points out, this may be due to the better-known and more established semester and year abroad programmes such as Erasmus, which carry with them their own funding schemes.

Building on the reports' findings regarding financial barriers, focus groups in *Student Perspectives* and undecided or uninterested students from *Broadening Perspectives* all emphasized that help with funding could be an important motivating factor in deciding whether to go abroad. For those students surveyed by *Student Perspectives*, this was based on real experience of the full costs of studying abroad. Second to funding, *Broadening Horizons* also found that help with foreign language skills could be a motivating factor.

Information and support

The decisions that students make on mobility are necessarily informed and influenced by the information they have to work with, and the support they are given by family, peers, academics and institutions. We have already seen that information plays a key role in forming both drivers (evidence of impact of mobility) and barriers (knowledge of opportunities) to mobility. *Broadening Horizons* delves more deeply into this relationship, finding a positive correlation between information and openness to study abroad – only 14 per cent of students still considering and 32 per cent of students not interested in study abroad said that they had enough information, compared with 56 per cent of students who were waiting to go abroad.

Student Perspectives asked students what they considered to be the most important information sources and influences during their decision-making process. Those considered most helpful were reported to be previous student experiences and information about funding opportunities, the latter being particularly valued by students considering short mobility periods. Support from the study abroad office and institution, including help in choosing a destination and support with the application, were also highly rated, in particular by students from disadvantaged backgrounds, as was support from parents and academics.[8] Students in focus groups also emphasized the importance of the timing of information: there was a consensus that learning about opportunities earlier on in their degrees was preferable, giving them more time for consideration, as well as allowing more time for multiple mobility opportunities.

Conclusion

What can institutions take away from these detailed reports on why students make the decisions they do on mobility programmes? Both *Student Perspectives* and *Broadening Horizons* provide a broad evidence base for UK-domiciled student perspectives of outward mobility, and help institutions to create a picture of why students do, or do not, choose to be mobile. They identify key perceived drivers of mobility that are consistent across different types of mobility, such as having an interesting and enjoyable experience, or enhancing employability, which institutions can tap into in their promotion strategies. Equally, they identify a number of perceived barriers to mobility for institutions to consider in terms of how they engage students, such as lack of knowledge of opportunities, total cost and funding availability and personal safety concerns.

Lessons can also be learned from *Student Perspectives*' focus on students considering short-term mobility. Although *Broadening Horizons* finds that few students are interested in mobilities shorter than a quarter, these short-term programmes have been found to be an effective way of engaging 'widening participation' students, as a shorter and less costly commitment than semester or year-long programmes. Engaging more of these students in outward mobility, and moving beyond the traditional, middle-class participation, will be critical in increasing our overall outwardly mobile numbers. Importantly, *Student Perspectives* finds that these short-term mobility placements have just as big an impact on students as do longer durations, a finding that should both encourage more students to take them up and justify more institutions in offering them. However, institutions should note that in making their decisions, students considering short-term mobility are found to need just as much support from institutions in terms of information, advice and guidance (particularly on financial considerations) as those considering embarking on longer-term mobilities. Faculty support was also found to be more important for short-term mobility than other durations, while for all less-established study or work abroad schemes, academic support, and engagement in mobility programmes, would be welcomed.

On a final note, these two reports offer a cautiously optimistic view of student perceptions and decisions on outward mobility in the future. Coming out at around the same time that HESA released its 1.2 per cent figure for mobility in 2013/14, *Broadening Horizons* found that, in fact, 34 per cent of the broad range of students they surveyed were interested in study abroad. Even those students who expressed no interest in mobility or who were undecided widely reported an interest in travel. Added to this, *Student Perspectives* found that students who had already been abroad were almost all interested in further mobility.

Many students are clearly keen to go abroad, even if currently the uptake is low. But with a better understanding of what influences their decisions, institutions can continue to tailor their student mobility strategies, and enable even more students to access this life-changing opportunity.

Notes

[1] Read the UK Strategy for Outward Mobility at: www.international.ac.uk/media/2468186/uk-he-international-unit-uk-strategy-for-outward-mobility.pdf.

[2] See the Go International website for further details on the campaign: www.go.international.ac.uk.

[3] The UK Higher Education International Unit's report 'Gone International: Mobile students and their outcomes' explores mobile graduate outcomes for a specific cohort.

[4] Referred to subsequently as *Student Perspectives*.

[5] *Broadening Horizons 2015: The value of the overseas experience*, henceforth referred to as *Broadening Horizons*.

[6] British Council Erasmus statistics: student and staff numbers by gender 07–14: www.erasmusplus.org.uk/erasmus-projects

[7] *Broadening Horizons* separates perceived barriers into 'academic' and 'non-academic' – funding availability was top of the 'non-academic' category.

[8] This contrasted with *Broadening Horizons'* finding that study abroad officers were consulted by only 22 per cent of students as an information source.

References

British Council (2015) *Broadening Horizons 2015: The value of the overseas experience*. Retrieved from https://ei.britishcouncil.org/educationintelligence/broadening-horizons-2015-value-overseas-experience

Careers Research & Advisor Centre (CRAC) (2015) *Student perspectives on outward mobility*. Powerpoint slides presented at Going Global 2015 conference.

European Commission (2014) *The Erasmus Impact Study. Effects of mobility on the skills and employability of students and the internationalisation of higher education institutions*. Retrieved from http://ec.europa.eu/education/library/study/2014/erasmus-impact_en.pdf

Higher Education Statistics Agency (HESA) (2015) Data on student mobility in 2013/14 from the HESA Student Record. Retrieved from http://go.international.ac.uk/who-went-abroad-201314-updated-summary-recent-hesa-data

UK HE International Unit, Go International Programme (2015) *Gone International: mobile students and their outcomes* (Report on the 2012/13 graduating cohort).

UK HE International Unit, Go International Programme, and British Council (2015) *Student Perspectives on going international.* Produced by the Careers Research & Advisory Centre (CRAC).

UK HE International Unit, Go International Programme, and the Higher Education Academy (2015) *Academic perspectives on the outcomes of outward student mobility.* Produced by BSV Associates Ltd.

Encouraging cultures of quality in higher education: An international perspective

Elizabeth Halford

Introduction

This paper presents Phase 1 of a collaborative research project with the British Council, considering how the structures and frameworks of quality assurance organizations in nine countries (**the UK, USA, Australia, India, China, Brazil, Mexico, Colombia** and **Chile**) encourage cultures of quality in higher education systems. Specifically:

1. The extent to which quality assurance cultures affect quality development cultures.
2. The opportunities to build international partnerships between the UK and other countries to address collective concerns.

These countries have been selected as the basis for comparative case studies because they: represent the three largest TNE higher education systems (USA, UK, Australia); are expanding economies (India and China), with their concomitant expansion of higher education and world-class universities; are the developing economies of four Latin American countries (Brazil, Mexico, Colombia and Chile), each with its own particular agenda for higher education.

This project relates to the following conference perspective of Going Global 2015:

> National, regional and local cultures and the extent to which connecting people and ideas across these cultures generates a creative force leading to innovation.

Methodology

The research is being undertaken in conjunction with the British Council in the Americas and is being conducted in three stages, exploring what constitutes higher education in different national contexts, in terms of purpose, level, delivery mode and setting.

It will investigate how and why higher education is regulated in the nine different countries and what impact this has on teaching and learning – does it improve the student experience and outcomes?

Phase 1 of the research has provided nine comparative case studies, identifying the relative size and nature of the higher education systems in each country. This used a desk-based analysis of secondary sources to provide a quantitative and qualitative scoping of the higher education systems in each country. In each case, the following aspects are outlined:

- history and context of the higher education system
- GDP indicators
- size of the higher education system
- shape of the higher education system
- definitions of higher education.

Phase 2 will focus on detailed studies of teaching, learning and quality in the four Latin American countries, and Phase 3 will reflect upon the possible lessons to be learned between systems, connecting systems, institutions and individuals in communities of practice, to encourage an international perspective of how higher education supports the needs of students and national economies.

Findings

The findings indicate that all nine HE systems are expanding rapidly and becoming more differentiated, with quality assurance systems reflecting this differentiation in their complexity and authority. These case studies enable collective reflection upon the changing role of HE in developed and developing economies.

GDP, student population, the number of HE providers and the system growth of the past decade are compared in each of the nine countries and any apparent relationship between these factors is considered. The nine countries in question now all have mass or universal systems of higher education, where demand-led growth has resulted in expanding private provision. This creates mixed economies of higher education, with impacts on the prevailing cultures of quality and the need for regulatory coherence in an international HE market. Some particular dimensions of quality cultures are now explored.

What the case studies tell us about higher education and its quality assurance systems

In all nine countries, two major trends were observed. First, there has been a major expansion of higher education systems, whether as measured by the number of higher education institutions or by the number of students enrolled in them. Second, there was an increasing differentiation of institutions, as new providers joined established systems. Typically, this was a case of an expanding private element in an existing public system, creating a mixed economy of higher education provision. For example, in China the number of private providers increased from 173 in 2003 to 717 in 2013. In several systems, especially in Latin America, there are far more private providers than public ones. In Brazil, 87 per cent of institutions are private, in Chile it is 85 per cent, in Colombia 72 per cent. In Mexico, however, private provision constitutes only 34 per cent of institutions. Private providers in most countries consist of relatively small specialized institutions, whereas public institutions may represent a small proportion of the total number of providers, but enrol the majority of students. In Brazil, for example, public universities represent only 8 per cent of institutional provision but they enrol 53 per cent of students.

Another prevalent form of differentiation is of institutional type, including universities, colleges, polytechnics, technical institutes and teacher training colleges, plus a range of private provision and partnership arrangements. However, in considering questions of diversity and differentiation, it is necessary to be aware of differences in how higher education is defined in different countries, to encompass post-compulsory, tertiary and higher provision, with the terms being used interchangeably in some instances. In the established systems of the UK and Australia, however, there are national qualification frameworks to enable a demarcation of higher education and specific criteria for the title of university. Boundaries and linkages between higher and further education are becoming increasingly blurred, along with definitions of what constitutes professional or vocational education.

In relation to the role of new private providers, it might be assumed that market forces would be replacing the state as a major controlling force; however, in several higher education systems, it was clear that new private providers were granted less autonomy than established state institutions. In some cases, these were dependent on public universities for the award of degrees and the accreditation formalities that preceded them. This was partly a deliberate exercise of state control, in order to ensure the 'public good', protect the consumer and benefit the broader society, but it was also partly a deliberate attempt by small private universities to enhance their reputation and public acceptability. Thus, in a number of places where higher education accreditation arrangements were optional, it was the smaller private universities that applied for accreditation because it was something that could enhance their reputation and acceptability. For well-established state institutions, accreditation offers less and indeed could be regarded as a distraction from the core university activities of research and teaching.

The distinction between public and private providers is sometimes unclear. In cases where students receive grants or loans from the state, irrespective of where they study, public money can flow into private providers via the state-subsidized consumer. And similarly, some state institutions receive substantial amounts of funding from non-public sources, via research and consultancy contracts, recruitment of overseas students and numerous other means.

Bearing in mind these complexities of differentiated higher education systems, some features of the quality assurance arrangements within the nine case studies are examined. Differentiated higher education systems appear to require differentiated quality assurance arrangements. Different kinds of institutions have different needs and require different forms of control and support. In general, the national profiles reveal quite complex and multilevel quality assurance arrangements, sometimes allowing institutions some degree of choice. At the same time, national authorities are able to exercise differential degrees of control, according to the reputation, experience and track record of the individual institution. The Australian Higher Education Standards Framework allows, at least in principle, the delivery of risk-based quality assurance arrangements proportionate to institutional characteristics and history.

At the system level, quality assurance is an important part of the 'licensing' process for individual institutions. It thus has a fundamental significance for new providers. In many countries, it may provide limitations to the practice of an institution, in terms of qualification levels and subjects of study, for example. The 'licence' might be time limited. However, for established providers, quality assurance may become a process of 'routine compliance', a necessary undertaking to avoid potential embarrassment and reputational damage, although it can also enhance and develop reputation. Quality assurance systems and processes can also provide linkages and networking across institutional boundaries, especially when processes of peer review are involved. At the same time, they can be part of a growing competitiveness in relationships between institutions, especially in systems marked by strong vertical forms of differentiation. More generally, quality assurance processes can play an important role in reinforcing differentiation within higher education systems.

What the national reports are not telling us about higher education and its quality assurance systems

In the nine case study countries, higher education systems have moved from elite to mass or universal, as defined by Trow (2010). An important point about Trow's typology is that the smaller system types are not removed by the arrival of the larger systems, but continue alongside them. Thus the universal systems can exist alongside the elite and the mass. This can be helpful in understanding the expanded and differentiated systems that have been reviewed for this project. What is not clear from the national profiles is whether differentiated quality assurance arrangements mainly reflect or can be an important cause of perceived quality differences between institutions.

More generally, very limited evidence is available from which to conclude that differences in reputation, funding or size are related to differences in educational content and processes, the student experience and learning outcomes, or the social and economic impact of different types of institution.

This is part of a more general observation: it is not clear how comparable the quality assurance processes are between different systems and agencies. This has implications for the comparability of standards and qualifications gained from different higher education systems. With the increasing international mobility of students, many of whom are acquiring a bachelor's degree from one national system then moving to a different system for a master's degree, questions about comparability of qualifications across national system boundaries become increasingly important. In large differentiated systems, there can also be questions of comparability *within* the system.

Two further issues are raised: first, the sheer increase in the volume of institutions, students and curricula range poses major resource issues for quality assurance and related agencies. One approach to dealing with the significantly increased requirements in order to continue to adequately assure taxpayers, students and governments that quality and standards are rigorously scrutinized is to adopt risk-based classifications of institutions. Broadly, those deemed most at risk receive greatest external regulatory attention from agencies, while those regarded as mature and relatively riskless are the focus of a more light-touch regime.

A second approach is for external quality assurance, accreditation and professional and statutory bodies to share information and for quality assurance bodies to utilize data and verdicts found in the reviews by other regulatory bodies.

A second issue raised by the case studies is the extent to which the student experience is becoming a touchstone for quality judgements (as in the UK, USA and Australia). This poses the question: 'Are consumerist notions of quality and standards, reinforced by the growth of university rankings, found in the approaches in the different countries?'

Some unanswered questions about quality assurance arrangements in higher education systems

The nine national profiles of higher education systems revealed much in common – expansion of student numbers and institutional providers, increasing differentiation of provision and providers, changing and complex regulatory frameworks. However, questions remain concerning the processes involved and the impacts and outcomes of those processes.

1. THE AIMS OF QUALITY ASSURANCE

Essentially, there is need for greater clarity in particular systems and contexts about the questions that quality assurance is asking of higher education. These are likely to include some combination of the following:

- Is this higher education good enough?
- How does it differ from some other higher education?
- Is it better than that other higher education? (How and why?)
- How can it be made even better?

These questions are relevant at all levels within quality assurance systems, from the system level itself down to quality processes at programme levels.

2. QUALITY ASSURANCE PROCESSES

These questions are particularly important if we want to improve the understanding of different higher education systems and the similarities and differences that exist between them. They include:

- Who is responsible?
- What is the unit of analysis? (Course? Qualification? Institution?)
- What is the method? (Peer review? Performance indicators? Risk analysis?)
- What is assessed? (Input? Process? Output?)
- How does it differ according to institutional (or programme) type?

3. Audiences and impacts

Bearing in mind the different levels of authority and decision making in higher education (and the variations that exist at both system and institutional levels), questions need to be asked in order to identify:

- internal and external audiences
- uses of information obtained through quality assurance processes by these different audiences
- evidence of impacts on practices and priorities within higher education systems and institutions, and on the users of those systems and institutions
- evidence of the development of quality cultures – what are they and where are they?

4. Wider system questions

Finally, there are questions concerning the rapid changes occurring in the size and shape of higher education systems, which provide both changing contexts for quality assurance as well as potentially changing needs and changing outcomes. Wider system questions concern:

- The place of private (for-profit and not-for-profit) providers and their relationship to public providers, the types of education they provide and the kinds of students who receive it.
- The relationship between higher education system differentiation and student diversity.
- Are there national or regional systems? Or is a 'global' system emerging?
- Is there clarity about the differentiation and boundaries between 'higher' education and 'tertiary' education? What are the relationships between the two and is demarcation helpful?

In relation to all of the above questions, we may find that answers differ between national systems and between sectors and institutions within national systems. There may also be evidence of both convergence and divergence (internationally) in terms of how higher education is developing globally and in how its quality assurance arrangements are adapting to this development.

Acknowledgements

With thanks to Leon Cremonini, with John Brennan, Richard Lewis and Roger King for their contributions to the country case studies.

Reference

Trow, M. (2010) 'Reflection on the transition from elite to mass to universal higher education'. In M. Burrage (ed.), *Martin Trow: Twentieth century higher education, elite to mass to universal*. Baltimore: John Hopkins University Press.

Data sources for case studies

British Council (2014) 'Understanding India: The future of higher education and opportunities for international cooperation'. Online. www.britishcouncil. org/sites/britishcouncil.uk2/files/understanding_india_report.pdf (accessed 13 November 2015).

Department of Higher Education (2013) 'All India Survey on Higher Education 2011–12'. Government of India, Ministry of Human Resource Development.

De Wit, H., Gacel-Ávila, J., Jaramillo, I.C. and Knight, J. (eds) (2005) 'Higher Education in Latin America: The international dimension'. The World Bank. Online. http://siteresources.worldbank.org/EXTLACREGTOPEDUCATION/ Resources/Higher_Ed_in_LAC_Intnal_Dimension.pdf (accessed 13 November 2015).

Eaton, J.S. (2012) 'An Overview of US Accreditation'. Online. www.chea.org/ pdf/Overview%20of%20US%20Accreditation%202012.pdf (accessed 13 November 2015).

Halford, E., Jackson, S., McClaran, A. (2015) 'Diversity and its discontents: An examination of how UK higher education is responding to diversity and the implications for quality assurance'. In *Higher Education and Development*, Vol. 9, No. 1. Higher Education Evaluation and Accreditation Council of Taiwan.

Jacob, W.J. and Hawkins, J.N. (2013) 'Trends in Chinese higher education: Opportunities and challenges'. Paper presented at the 10th International Workshop on Higher Education Reform, Ljubljana, Slovenia, October 2013. Online. www.pef.uni-lj.si/fileadmin/Datoteke/Mednarodna/conference/wher/ after/JacobHawkins-proceedings.pdf (accessed 13 November 2015).

Ministry of Education, Brazil (2012a) 'Análise sobre a expansão das Universidades Federais (2003–12)'.

— (2012b) 'Principais ações e programas de responsabilidade do Ministério da Educação no PPA 2012–15'. Online. http://portal.mec.gov.br/ (accessed 13 November 2015).

OECD (2010) 'Higher education management and policy'. *Journal of the Programme on Institutional Management in Higher Education*, 22 (1). Online. www.oecd.org/edu/imhe/50310012.pdf (accessed 13 November 2015).

— (2012) 'Quality assurance in higher education in Chile: Reviews of national policies for education'. Online. www.oecd.org/chile/Quality%20Assurance%20 in%20Higher%20Education%20in%20Chile%20-%20Reviews%20of%20 National%20Policies%20for%20Education.pdf (accessed 13 November 2015).

— (2014) 'Country note: Chile. Education at a glance 2014: OECD Indicators'. Online. www.oecd.org/education/Chile-EAG2014-Country-Note.pdf (accessed 13 November 2015).

OECD/International Bank for Reconstruction and Development/The World Bank (2012) 'Reviews of national policies for education: Tertiary education in Colombia'. Online. www.oecd.org/education/skills-beyond-school/Reviews%20 of%20National%20Policies%20for%20Education%20Tertiary%20 Education%20in%20Colombia%202012.pdf (accessed 13 November 2015).

QAA (2015) 'The UK Quality Code for Higher Education'. Online. www. qaa.ac.uk/assuring-standards-and-quality/the-quality-code (accessed 13 November 2015).

State Higher Education Executive Officers (SHEEO) (2013) 'State Higher Education Finance (SHEF) Study'. Online. www.sheeo.org/sites/default/files/ publications/SHEF_FY13_04292014.pdf (accessed 13 November 2015).

TEQSA (2012) 'Information sheet: TEQSA's approach to quality assessments'. Online. http://teqsa.gov.au/sites/default/files/TEQSAs_Approach_to_Quality_ Assessments_web_121112.pdf (accessed 13 November 2015).

— (2014) 'TEQSA's Risk Assessment Framework'. Online. www.teqsa.gov.au/ sites/default/files/publication-documents/TEQSARiskAssessFramework_2.pdf (accessed 13 November 2015).

UNESCO (2012) 'Desafios e perspectivas da educação superior Brasileira para a próxima década 2011'. Online. http://unesdoc.unesco.org/ images/0021/002189/218964POR.pdf (accessed 13 November 2015).

Universities Australia (2013) 'Universities Australia submission to the Review of Higher Education Regulation'. Online. www.universitiesaustralia.edu.au/ (accessed 13 November 2015).

University Grants Commission (2013) 'Annual Report 2011–12'. Secretary, University Grants Commission.

The role of quality assurance in building and maintaining a culture of excellence in higher education: The African perspective

Paul Kwadwo Addo, S. Kojo Mbra Assan and Patricia G. Owusu-Darko

Introduction

The need for quality assurance (QA) for organizational effectiveness and excellence beyond prior standards has become a global imperative. Higher education institutions (HEIs) are responding to this demand by strategically initiating the incorporation of quality measures into systems and structures in their institutions. QA is now featured in the strategic plans of higher institutions in their quest for improvement, quality control and higher performance aimed at building and maintaining a strong culture of excellence. This is needed for fitness for purpose (Mizikaci, 2006), stakeholder satisfaction, continuous improvement and brand identity. This paper explores the historical backgrounds, philosophical underpinning and current approaches in QA measures to create and maintain a strong institutional culture of excellence. The paper provides a perspective of the attempts by Kwame Nkrumah University of Science and Technology (KNUST), Kumasi, Ghana, to build a culture of excellence using the Total Quality Management (TQM) approach. The paper further shares the continental efforts in Africa to assist in the development of capacity in institutions in Africa and to strengthen their quality control measures. The paper concludes with recommendations for building a culture of excellence.

The concept of higher education

In order to appreciate the organizational type in focus, it is imperative to appreciate the concept of higher education institutions. Though the term may be broadly used to include professional organizations, agencies and foundations focused on research, policies and other operations of colleges and universities, the literature varies when it comes to defining what really constitutes higher education institutions (HEIs).

Generally, HEIs may refer to formalized educational institutions with a strong academic post-high school orientation or similar. Several professional institutions require at least high school-equivalent credentials, but their orientations are less academic. Again, HEIs are distinct from adult/continuing education, which often tends to be concerned with basic life skills and civic education among other things.

The concept would also have a different meaning in different places and at different times. An institution considered to be an HEI in one country may not be labelled as such in another country. Over time an institution that was previously not regarded as an HEI could assume a new status. For instance, in Ghana, colleges of education previously known as training colleges, which require high school credentials for admission, are now classified as HEIs. For the purposes of this paper, HEI refers to colleges and universities as earlier specified.

The concept of quality assurance in higher education

Perhaps the difficulty in satisfactorily defining quality control in higher education is due to the fact that the concept originated from the manufacturing industry. According to Harvey and Green (1993), different meanings are assigned to quality as a result of the complex nature of the stakeholders in higher education. Quality assurance has different interpretations from the user's perspective (students, teaching, administrative and various other professional staff members, quality control agencies, etc.), so creating a culture of quality in higher education institutions means agreeing on a common definition of the quality concept. The issue of academic freedom in higher education has also affected the acceptance of quality assurance measures. Kinser (2011) indicates that QA is a relatively new concept in higher education, even though systems of quality assurance can be traced back more than a century in the United States and the United Kingdom. He further states that few other countries developed their own systems before the mid-1980s. Historically, HEIs have tended to regulate themselves and such a great degree of autonomy has sometimes prevented them from embracing change through quality assurance mechanisms. The above notwithstanding, several institutions are incorporating QA systems and policies in their system of operations.

Vught and Westerheijden (1994) observed that quality assessment in higher education dates back to the medieval era. The authors identified two major models of quality assessment that had been in use prior to the introduction of modern systems. The first was the French model of vesting control in external authority, the second was the English model of self-governing a community of fellows. The French model, they observed, was characterized by the struggle for self-autonomy by the University of Paris in the early thirteenth century. The English model of self-governance took inspiration from the masters at the medieval universities of Oxford and Cambridge, who were independent of external control. These major models are still in use but in modified forms. They are termed external and internal quality assurance according to the source of control. External measures are all the requirements demanded by the accreditation/governmental agency from an institution, often backed by law. According to Harvey (2005), external quality assurance is not necessarily government controlled – though it tends to be established in response to a public policy demand – but it ensures the need for greater accountability. Internal quality assurance will include all of the measures an institution puts in place to ensure quality.

Institutional approach to QA

National bodies are set up to regulate higher education in most countries. They set up rules and benchmarks/standards to which each institution should adhere. According to Oyewole (2012), the enforcement of QA standards are in response to the demand for:

- efficiency and competitiveness
- increased mobility, globalization and cross-border recognition of qualifications
- the involvement of private interest in higher education
- the challenge of mode of delivery
- an expansion in enrolment
- market demands for quality and relevance of education
- the challenge of brain drain.

Based on these and other factors, institutions set up quality assurance/control units/departments to coordinate all quality matters.

The Kwame Nkrumah University of Science and Technology, for example, has established the Quality Assurance and Planning Unit (QAPU). QAPU is responsible for strategic planning and overseeing quality assurance, as well as the management of the university's information systems. The unit uses a three-stage approach, made up of inputs, process and output, to ensure quality. The inputs stage involves all of the activities conducted to admit/recruit students and staff. Measures are in place to ensure that only qualified students are admitted and qualified staffs are recruited. The next stage involves all of the internal and external processes to ensure that there is customer satisfaction, value for money and continuous professional improvement. These are applied to the following areas: teaching and learning, students' affairs, quality research, community outreach, governance structures, resource utilization, internationalization, regulations/accreditations and academic freedom. The output stage involves evaluation to see if the desired outcomes are obtained. These include: examination audit, graduation rate, satisfaction survey, tracer studies for curriculum improvement and exit interviews, among others.

Policies and guidelines have been developed as well as regular periodic training. This is offered through a summer school arrangement, with all members of staff being instructed on the planned agenda before the beginning of the academic year. Continuous training programmes use the TQM principle, ensuring that KNUST remains committed to constant improvement in order to fulfil a new philosophy of zero errors/defects. The culture of quality is emphasized, which has led to the establishment of a quality assurance subunit in every operational area of the university.

QA initiatives in HEIs in Africa

The focus of quality assurance measures in Africa has mainly been on accreditation and academic evaluation. Accreditation is concerned with institutions meeting standards set by governments, national agencies or professional bodies. In Ghana, for example, there is institutional accreditation whereby the institution is accredited to function as such by the National Accreditation Board (NAB). There is also programme accreditation, where each programme of an institution goes through periodic accreditation/ reaccreditation. Academic evaluation/assessment/audit, on the other hand, is undertaken by governments or national agencies to assess the HEIs' academic processes to ensure quality of teaching and learning. The audit involves preparing an institutional self-assessment report, which is reviewed by a panel of external assessors who undertake a site visit and submit their report. The objective of the academic evaluation is for development and enhancement, but in some countries it is linked to accountability and public funding. The evaluation process is now widely used internationally. Both accreditation and evaluation processes are important for improving quality in African HEIs.

Most HEIs in African countries have had collaborations with European institutions, which implies that the Bologna Process was adopted by those African institutions with regards to QA. However, by the end of the 1990s and early 2000s, several HEIs in Africa, such as the University of Mauritius, St Mary's University College, Ethiopia, and the University of Dar es Salaam, introduced QA at institutional level through further collaboration with European universities, before the introduction of national QA processes. The South African Council for Higher Education was the first to introduce national QA processes through its HEQC in 2000. In 2005, the Inter-University Council of East Africa (IUCEA) embarked on a process to promote QA systems in public and private HEIs in East African countries with support from the German Academic Exchange Service (DAAD; Woldetensae, 2012). According to Sall (2012), the Council for Higher Education in Africa and Madagascar (CAMES) is the management body for external quality assurance for all 17 member states, which ensures that there is acceptance of qualifications and maintenance of common standards. There are other subregional groupings, for instance, Anglophone West Africa, Portuguese-Speaking, and the Arab-African and North Africa. All of these subregional bodies were set up to ensure the development and implementation of QA systems in their member institutions. The Association of African Universities facilitated the establishment of AfriQAN in 2007 with support from the World Bank Development Grant Facility. AfriQAN serves as a regional body, mainly for the capacity building of national QA agencies.

The African Quality Rating Mechanism (AQRM) was developed by the African Union Commission as part of the African Union's strategy for harmonizing higher education, and was adopted by the Conference of Ministers of Education of Africa (COMEDAF) in 2007. The objectives of AQRM were as follows: to revitalize and strengthen African HEIs so as to be globally competitive and locally relevant; to be used as a tool for benchmarking quality in HE; and to encourage HEIs to undertake self-evaluation and develop an institutional culture of quality. The aim is to have African HEIs set the standards for their institutions and to have these standards reviewed by experts through a self-assessment process.

Building a culture of excellence for QA

According to EUA (2003), cited in Gvaramadze (2008), the concept of quality culture describes 'shared values and collective responsibility of all members of higher education institutions'. In the EUA perspective, quality culture is an internal organizational culture with permanent enhancement mechanisms at two distinct levels. These are at the institutional level, which refers to all administrative and managerial strategies put in place in order to enhance the quality and coordination of members; this is also termed quality as an enhancement process. The other distinct level is at the individual/staff level, and refers to the cultural and psychological aspects of shared values, beliefs, expectations and commitment towards quality culture among individuals; this is also termed quality as a transformation process.

Building a strong culture depends on measures identified by each individual institution, often expressed in its vision and mission statements. This often indicates the direction in which the institution intends to go and the strategy it means to use to achieve that goal. Based on this direction, internal quality measures are designed to guide the attainment of such goals. According to Gvaramadze (2008), the basic principles guiding internal quality assurance strategies are:

- responsibility of HEIs for internal quality assurance
- encouragement of internal quality culture, diversity and innovation
- efficient organizational structures
- transparency
- accountability for public and private funding
- inclusion of general social and individual learners' interests in the quality of higher education.

The attainment of effective culture will also depend on efficient systems being put in place. There should be adequate tools and effective teams. All of the other processes should be actively communicated to all stakeholders. Commitment by all stakeholders is necessary, especially from top management. Arafeh (2012) observed that ensuring the necessary quality culture requires working at institutional, national and regional levels. He postulates that solid interaction and partnership with other actors, and accountability and transparency with regards to all related stakeholders, are important to achieve a strong culture.

Recommendations

Institutions of higher learning must appreciate that for an effective culture to be built, all stakeholders must understand and appreciate the vision and mission of their institution.

Again, it is important that the appropriate policies and guidelines are developed and communicated to all stakeholders. This will help guide them as to the direction in which the institution is heading.

Feedback from major stakeholders must be used for continuous improvement. Their feedback by way of satisfaction surveys, exit interviews and tracer studies must be incorporated in initiating and formulating new plans.

Also, to ensure effectiveness of the QA system, modern methods of supervision, monitoring and evaluation should be implemented. This is to ensure the elimination of barriers to facilitate efficiency and effectiveness.

Above all, a systematic approach should be developed to manage the implementation of TQM. There should be commitment from top management, and TQM must apply to all areas of the institution's operations.

Conclusion

In response to the increasing need for quality control, higher education institutions in Africa, just like in other parts of the world, have risen to the challenge by establishing appropriate measures and standards to ensure consistently effective and excellent performance. These quality assurance measures are, essentially, new versions of two main types, which are based on institutions being predominantly self-governing or regulated by external authority. The objectives for implementing quality assurance are manifold. KNUST in Ghana, for instance, has adopted the TQM approach in implementing quality assurance measures to ensure that operational inputs, processes and outputs are optimal. Efforts are being made by various regional bodies on the continent of Africa to create awareness and to develop and strengthen the capacity of institutions to implement quality assurance programmes. Policymakers must appreciate the changing trends in higher education and constantly share ideas to build and maintain a strong culture of excellence using quality assurance.

References

Arafeh, Labib (2012) 'Quality assurance situation and capacity-building needs in higher education in Arab-African and North African countries'. In G.B. Alabi and J.C. Mba (eds), *The Quality Assurance Situation and Capacity Building Needs of Higher Education in Africa*. Accra: Association of African Universities.

Gvaramadze, Irakli (2008) 'From quality assurance to quality enhancement in the European higher education area'. *European Journal of Education*, 43 (4), 443–55. Online. Academic Search Elite, EBSCOhost (accessed 6 October 2015).

Harvey, L. (2005) 'A history and critique of quality evaluation in the UK'. *Quality Assurance in Education*, 13 (4), 263–76.

Harvey, L. and Green, D. (1993) 'Defining quality'. *Assessment and Evaluation in Higher Education*, 18, 9–13.

Kinser, K. (2011) 'Multinational quality assurance'. *New Directions for Higher Education*, 155, 53–64. Online. Academic Search Elite, EBSCOhost (accessed 6 October 2015).

Mizikaci, F. (2006) 'A systems approach to program evaluation model for quality in higher education'. *Quality Assurance in Education*, 14 (1), 37–53.

Oyewole, O. (2012) 'Developing quality assurance systems in African Universities–AAU initiatives'. In G.B. Alabi and J.C. Mba (eds), *The Quality Assurance Situation and Capacity Building Needs of Higher Education in Africa*. Accra: Association of African Universities.

Sall, M.M. (2012) 'Quality assurance situation and capacity-building needs in higher education in seventeen French-speaking African countries'. In G.B. Alabi and J.C. Mba (eds), *The Quality Assurance Situation and Capacity Building Needs of Higher Education in Africa*. Accra: Association of African Universities.

Vught F.A and Westerheijden, D.F. (1994) *Towards a General Model of Quality Assessment in Higher Education*. Netherlands: Kluwer Academic Publishers.

Woldetensae, Y. (2012) 'Quality assurance situation and capacity-building needs in higher education in East African countries'. In G.B. Alabi and J.C. Mba (eds), *The Quality Assurance Situation and Capacity Building Needs of Higher Education in Africa*. Accra: Association of African Universities.

Section 2

The skills and values of
internationalization

Editors' introduction to Section 2

The skills and values of internationalization

The internationalization of higher and vocational education carries with it the potential to influence and enable the development of those skills and values that are central to its development. This section presents a series of papers that explore this theme and enable the readers to further understand the phenomenon we are witnessing.

A major and vital element in the internationalization process is the integration and development of 'intercultural skills'. **Najda and Shaw** in their paper explain the work they and colleagues at the British Council have undertaken on intercultural fluency – which can be developed through training to enable practitioners to operate effectively in intercultural situations. **Cunningham and Sandell's** paper explores further the importance for twenty-first century graduates of developing intercultural skills. **Schuessler's** paper on 'Masters beyond borders' is a demonstration of the importance of cross-border study for students and, as a result, the support it brings to the connecting of cultures.

The next two papers, the first by **Freshwater and Esterhuizen** and the second by **Middlehurst and Kennie**, explore different aspects of the importance of leadership qualities. Freshwater and Esterhuizen examine formal and informal leadership models, alongside institutional values and identity as international strategies are implemented. Middlehurst and Kennie's paper explores the way that leadership development can enable both leaders themselves and their institutions to operate globally and connect cultures.

Atherton's paper explores the contribution global dialogue can play in building an access agenda, and in ensuring equality. He argues that dialogue must have a crucial role if ever inequality is to be addressed globally. **Naidoo** discusses the ways that internationalization in higher education can contribute to the creation of well-being, and further explores the importance of well-being globally.

Wendy Jordan's paper has particular urgency in the current international political context where there is widespread unrest and disruption, with academics being dislocated in the context of all too frequent emergency environments. She highlights the restorative powers of higher education and, in asserting its central values, reminds us of their power and importance.

The final two papers, the first by **Arzhanova, Arefiev, Baryshnikova, Derman and Klyagin** and the second by **Ledger,** both take a specific global context and examine global skills development and cross-cultural competence. Arzhanova *et al.* look at the Russian context and explore the importance of internationalization. Ledger uses the example of the ASEAN Economic Community to demonstrate the importance of cross-cultural connections.

All the papers in this section have, at their core, a commitment to the development of skills and values through, and at the heart of, internationalization. Our understanding of the importance of these values is key to both our deeper understanding of internationalization – since it is at the heart of Going Global – and our perception of how we must act in taking this agenda forward.

Intercultural fluency:
A practice-led approach
Ruth Najda and Neil Shaw

The British Council is the world's leading cultural relations organization, with more than 80 years' experience of working across cultures in more than 100 countries worldwide. Intercultural engagement – 'connecting cultures', to reference a key theme of Going Global 2015 – is at the heart of the British Council's vision and values. In our intercultural fluency work we aim to capture the organization's considerable expertise of innovative intercultural collaboration; and translate this into an effective training approach that helps novice and experienced practitioners anticipate, better understand, and interact effectively in intercultural situations.

We believe that the importance of this work is difficult to overstate. Language skills are, of course, vital. But they are only part of the story. Lack of competence interculturally can lead to misunderstandings, mistrust, and resentment that can have a deleterious impact on working relationships, damaging the capacity of individuals and organizations to work together effectively. By contrast, enhancing the intercultural fluency of individuals and organizations can have a direct impact on their future success – on the likelihood of students embracing mobility opportunities; on the employability of graduates; on the effectiveness of multicultural teams; on the capacity of businesses to thrive in international markets; and on the capacity of academic institutions in different countries to collaborate innovatively and creatively. In a world ever more interconnected and interdependent, intercultural fluency is fast becoming the definitive twenty-first-century skill.

The British Council's approach to intercultural fluency is practice-led, and the starting point in developing a training offer to aid participants to improve their intercultural fluency was our own staff. An initial step was to hold a series of workshops in different locations (Scotland, Morocco, Belgium, Kazakhstan, Qatar and China) with expert practitioners, including our own staff. These practitioners represented a range of cultural origins and all had in-depth experience of working in a range of cultural contexts. In the workshops, participants were invited to share their experiences within a framework of established intercultural theory. The initial consultation phase was followed by a period of testing training courses with a variety of business and Higher Education groups. This user-driven methodology had a critical role in shaping the British Council's approach to intercultural fluency.

The term 'intercultural fluency' itself was coined to evoke the similarities with first and second language fluency. Just as we are fluent in a first language, we are fluent in at least one culture by virtue of being immersed in it since birth. When we learn a new language, our learning is inevitably influenced by our knowledge of our first language. In the same way, learning about new cultures depends on our existing knowledge about cultures. An important feature of the British Council training approach involves beginning with what is familiar and then moving to the less familiar.

One of the theoretical insights drawn on by the training developers when capturing the expertise of the expert groups and translating it into practice was the dichotomy between 'common wisdom' and 'reality of practice' (Huxham and Vangen, 2005). The notion of 'common wisdom' represents the principles that underlie good practice and the notion of 'the reality of practice' refers to the complex and shifting nature of the intercultural situations that we encounter. The aspects of theory and research identified as being most useful by the expert practitioner groups were combined with the principles outlined below (Table 1) to inform the British Council's training approach.

Table 1: The principles of intercultural fluency

Common wisdom Some of the principles that inform our behaviours as intercultural practitioners	Reality of practice The dilemmas that we are faced with in practice
1. We want to behave in ways where others are treated fairly and respectfully.	What if your view about what is fair is contrary to those of others? Which is more important – respect or fairness?
2. We all have intimate experience of culture. We are already cultural experts about at least one culture.	Can we view the cultures that we are most familiar with in objective ways? Can we see ourselves as others see us?

3. Generalizations about the characteristics of cultural groups with which we are not familiar can provide genuine insights. This process can help us to conceptualize 'otherness' and anticipate the cultural preferences of others.	Generalizations about what cultures are like can never give a complete picture. How can we be sure that generalizations about groups of people offer insights rather than inaccurate and biased views?
4. Cultures are made up of individuals who will have different preferences and views from the norm.	People make a difference in intercultural encounters. Is it better to see people as individuals rather than members of groups?
5. Experience of intercultural contexts is essential for effective practice.	Is experience enough? What particular qualities, understanding, and skills are needed to be effective? Can you be an expert in one cultural situation and a novice in another?
6. An effective practitioner should adapt and change to suit the preferred norms of the culture.	Should you always be the one to adapt and change? What about your own sense of identity? What happens if your most deeply held beliefs and values are compromised?

Capturing a set of principles underlying good practice in intercultural encounters was only one half of the story. Consideration had to be given as to how these principles can be put into practice. Culture is complex, mutable, and contested. The practical task facing us was to help participants in any global location deepen their understanding of the intercultural situations they face and hone their inter-personal and communication skills.

To this end, in conjunction with the expert groups, we developed a range of core tools that support reflective practice by providing an 'under the surface' understanding of intercultural situations.

One of these tools was a broad definition of culture. This definition places culture in a framework where basic needs, personality, and the wider world are essential parts of one whole. This definition has many sources, particularly the work of E.T. Hall (1966; 1976), G. Hofstede (2005), R.J. House (2004), E. Schein (2010) and H. Spencer-Oatey (2000). The definition is used as a tool to support analysis of the factors that may be present in an intercultural situation.

A guiding principle for our intercultural fluency training approach is the idea that our values, beliefs, and practices are the result of the interplay between the individual, his/her cultural environment and wider influences. It is the dynamics of how this interplay operates that complements the definition in our analytic tool (Figure 1).

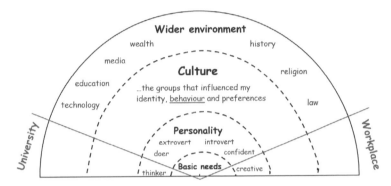

Figure 1: The 'influences' spectrum – culture and our other influences. How should gender and age be represented on the spectrum?

Culture is the set of values, beliefs and practices shared by a community that:

- is important to us
- influences our behaviour and preferences
- helps form our senses of identity and belonging.

Culture, according to this definition, sits within a range of influences that make us who we are at a particular moment in time. As well as culture, these include: basic needs, personality and the wider environment.

How does the definition of 'culture' help us better understand what might be happening in an intercultural team? For example, let's say you are the team leader of a new international team. You expect all team members to show initiative and express their opinions freely. This is not happening. Why not?

Is it because of *cultural influences*, such as team members with different

- expectations about ways of communicating
- expectations about displaying emotions or trying to control them
- expectations about authority and initiative
- ideas about time?

Is it because of *wider world influences*, such as:

- the different education systems that team members have attended
- the range of languages that are used in the workplace
- a split between junior and more senior staff that reflects wider regional or global inequalities and conflicts, e.g. post-colonial relationships?

Is it because of *personality*? Which members of the team are extroverts, introverts, confident, not confident, speakers, listeners, thinkers?

What's at stake for each team member if they get it wrong with you, their new boss? Is anyone's well-being or financial security under threat? When our *basic needs* are not satisfied then these become more important than anything else.

A second tool we developed with our expert groups is an enhanced 'cultural islands' metaphor. This was considered a more effective representation than other metaphors often used to make the concept of 'culture' accessible. These included the 'iceberg' that emerged from Hall's work (1966; 1976) and Hoftede's (2005) 'Software of the Mind' and 'onion' metaphors. In the enhanced 'cultural islands' metaphor, culture is compared to many connected islands in an ocean. Each island has some aspects above the surface and some below. These represent the aspects of an unfamiliar culture that are easily seen and heard and the 'under the surface' values, beliefs, expectations, and preferences that are harder to learn about and important for deep understanding. Examples of above the surface elements include body language and political and religious symbols; below the surface elements include, for example, legacies of the past, tolerance to difference, and attitudes to time. The islands are connected by the movement of people mixing cultures and ideas. The sea-bed and the surrounding ocean are universal features representing commonalities that we all share, such as the importance of family and friends or similarities reflected in religious, political and other beliefs.

This metaphor has been developed into a practical tool that participants first use with a familiar culture, linking what is 'under the surface' with what is 'above'. In Poland, for example, when analysing their own culture, participants on a training course connected the above-the-surface elements of 'people look very similar, i.e. 'White', large family gatherings are popular, popular ceremonies involve the church, e.g. weddings, funerals, communion' with the following below-the-surface elements:

- 'What your family does reflects on you and your status'
- 'People have a hierarchy of friends, with only a few close friends'

- 'Households have strong gender defined roles'
- 'People are very settled, so getting on with people around is really important'
- 'Legacies of the past including the relationship between colonizers and the Catholic church are important'.

Newcomers to Poland can readily observe that families are big and extended and that the role of the Catholic church is important. But the deeper factors bound up with this are initially hidden. The cultural islands tool played a key role in helping the group provide a snapshot insight about the importance of family, religious belief, historical legacies and homogeneity for Polish society. By analysing and acknowledging their own unique cultural context, participants could better understand how their cultural make-up and biases could influence how they might perceive attitudes and behaviours of people from other cultural backgrounds.

To test the effectiveness of our intercultural fluency training during the pilot phase the British Council developed a prototype impact assessment tool. This has been utilized with a range of corporate and Higher Education audiences internationally. It involves a pre-course and a post-course online survey to elicit responses to a series of statements – for example, 'I am aware that some aspects of my behaviour may be unusual or difficult for visitors to my country to understand.' The purpose of the first survey is to establish a baseline for the assessment of the impact of training courses. The purpose of the second, which was essentially identical to the first, was to assess the impact of the training course on the cultural competence of the participants.

In Kazakhstan, for example, we carried out impact assessment of our courses with 77 individuals – students volunteering at an Education UK Fair. Before and after the courses, they were asked 35 closed questions in the form of Likert-type statements, with a five-point scale for responses. By way of illustration of the impact suggested, when presented with the following statements, the percentage of respondents saying they 'agree strongly' increased from before to after the course as indicated:

- 'I am aware that some aspects of my behaviour may be unusual or difficult for visitors to Kazakhstan to understand.' *(Before: 6%; After: 28%)*
- 'I can identify behaviours that visitors to Kazakhstan may find unusual or difficult.' *(Before: 14%; After: 32%)*
- 'I am aware of the behaviours that visitors to Kazakhstan may find difficult or unusual in a work situation.' *(Before: 6%; After: 22%)*

- 'I am aware of how my own behaviour is influenced by my culture.' *(Before: 19%; After: 34%)*
- 'I try to make a good impression when meeting people from unfamiliar cultures.' *(Before: 4%; After: 12%)*

While we should be aware of the possibility that increased level of agreement can reflect the *expectation* of participants rather than their *experience* of such an increase, the results were compelling, with often a substantial and consistent increase in the level of agreements across all the items in the survey. This pattern of responses provides a strong indication that the participants had experienced a rise in their level of awareness in relation to intercultural communication, and in their confidence in conducting intercultural encounters.

Our assessments also include open questions to enrich the quality of feedback elicited. This mechanism has highlighted that participants see the 'definition of culture' as a helpful introductory aid, while the 'cultural islands' metaphor is frequently mentioned as being one of the most useful aspects of the courses.

We set out to develop a practice-led training approach to intercultural fluency, one that has a number of core tools, including our 'definition of culture' and a 'cultural islands' metaphor. The evaluations that have taken place so far indicate that the courses help novice and experienced practitioners anticipate, better understand and respond effectively in intercultural situations. The next step is to explore ways of more robustly assessing the intercultural competencies that our practice-led approach supports, further enhancing the credibility of a training offer that, in the most fundamental and important of senses, is designed to connect cultures.

References

Hall, E.T. (1966) *The Hidden Dimension*. New York: Anchor Press.

— (1976) *Beyond Culture*. New York: Anchor Press.

Hofstede, G. and Hofstede, J. G. (2005) *Cultures and Organisations: Software of the mind*. New York: McGraw-Hill.

House, R.J. (2004) *Culture, Leadership and Organisations* (Globe Study). London: Sage.

Huxham, C. and Vangen, S. (2005) *Managing to Collaborate: The theory and practice of collaborative advantage*. London: Routledge.

Schein, E. (2010) *Organizational Culture and Leadership* (fourth edition). San Francisco: Jossey-Bass.

Spencer-Oatey, H. (2000) *Culturally Speaking: Managing rapport through talk across cultures*. New York: Cassell.

Through the looking glass: What does intercultural competence look like in higher education?
Catriona Cunningham and Elizabeth J. Sandell

Introduction

The UK Higher Education Academy (HEA), the national body for learning and teaching in HE in the UK, advocates that internationalization is the responsibility of all of those in higher education at individual, curriculum and organizational level – we all have a shared, collective role to play in preparing twenty-first-century graduates to live in and contribute responsibly to a globally interconnected society. This paper argues that developing intercultural skills is central in this role and explores the impact of our work in interculturalism in institutional, national and international settings as evidence for the educational transformation they bring about.

Study abroad is often portrayed as a solution to the issue of how to foster global-minded individuals. However, depending on the institution and the discipline, it is not possible for all students to have international (that is, study abroad) experiences during their HE programmes. Alternatively, any student may have experiential intercultural opportunities that deliver similar outcomes to international mobility. Indeed, in their book on 'languaging', Phipps and Gonzalez argue that 'abroad is as much in the classroom or corner of the street as it is across some national border. So languaging and intercultural being are about dwelling-in-travel and translation' (Phipps and Gonzalez, 2004: 59). This is a rather lovely way of thinking about the movement across and between cultures happening in thousands of HE classes around the world. The openness that prevails is not necessarily geographical or even physical but is also about language as well as curiosity. The opportunity for individuals to talk with others among cultures has transformative and far-reaching potential, whether for outward student mobility, transnational education or collaboration and research across disciplines and languages.

The HEA framework

Following widespread consultation with the UK higher education sector, the Higher Education Academy (2015) has developed a framework for internationalizing higher education. The framework is the culmination of ten years of HEA funding and commissioned research into internationalization in higher education. It was created with experts working to internationalize HE and is therefore (in)formed by the principles of collaboration, sustainability, interconnectivity, inclusivity and flexibility. The central ethos is centred on values of respect and openness, with an emphasis on how individuals acquire the necessary cultural and linguistic skills and knowledge in interconnected classrooms (see www.heacademy.ac.uk/enhancement/ frameworks/framework-internationalising-higher-education).

Between 2014 and 2015, the framework has been piloted by 11 different higher education providers. Each institution or organization has worked on specific aspects of internationalizing the HE curriculum. Working collaboratively with these various HE providers, it has become clear that intercultural skills are at the very heart of this process, not only for students but also for academic and support staff. Results are observed when everyone works together across disciplinary boundaries to reflect – often critically – on how learning and teaching is intercultural as well as international. Examples included herein demonstrate the richness and potential at institutional and international levels.

Definitions of terms

The literature emphasizes how HE incorporates global perspectives into teaching, learning and research, builds intercultural competence among students, faculty and staff, and establishes relationships and collaborations with people and institutions representing other cultures. The definitions used here are from the HEA, created after broad consultation with experts throughout the HE sector and firmly embedded in the context of learning and teaching.

- *Internationalization*: for us this is a 'transformative and continual process and a sector-wide concern; where learning, teaching and research, and the interconnections between them, are centrally important'. To emphasize the ongoing nature of internationalization in higher education as a process, we use the gerund 'internationalizing'.

There is also focus on the student experience for everyone, regardless of geographical location, so that all students experience a 'high-quality, equitable and global learning experience'.

- *Interculturalism*: defined in the framework as 'taking place between cultures, or derived from different cultures'. We use it in the context of this paper as the achievement of shared goals among individuals or groups who do not share the same cultural origins or background. Cultural differences may be a result of any combination of factors including racial, ethnic, socio-economic, religious, gender and national differences.

- *Intercultural skills*: (1) understand culture as multilevel and multidimensional (personal, microcultures, mainstream national culture and organizational cultures); (2) understand barriers to effective relationships (verbal/language, nonverbal, stress, stereotyping and discrimination); (3) practise culturally centred communication (dialogue, conflict recovery, problem-solving skills); and (4) design and implement institution-wide competency.

Institutional impact

By focusing on the benefits that an internationalized class offers, the impact of intercultural awareness is tangible, as the examples below demonstrate. Intercultural competence is at the heart of global classrooms as a means through which to navigate power differences (Manchester Metropolitan University), to enhance staff awareness and development in this domain and help them internationalize their own programmes (University of Brighton), to research dominant teaching cultures (Bournemouth University), to bring the global to the local (University of South Wales), or to create an inclusive internationalized curriculum (University of Edinburgh) where *all* students are international students.

Manchester Metropolitan University

Drawing on the HEA framework, faculty and staff members at Manchester Metropolitan University wanted to carry out a self-audit of how disciplines and departments across the UK are embedding internationalization in the curriculum. They adapted the framework to their own institutional context and looked for local examples of internationalization in action. This flexibility and adaptability embodies the principles of the framework but also – arguably – of interculturalism itself.

(Case studies for each institution in this section are not available at the time of going to press but will be accessible on the HEA website in the near future.)

University of Brighton

At the University of Brighton, the team used the framework to create a developmental tool for staff, encouraging them to examine the language and design of their individual courses in order to gauge what they could change to incorporate an intercultural element into their teaching. The questions and suggestions are simple and yet carefully worded to ensure that course material is approached from a comparative perspective. This tool, used with staff, confronts many of the perceptions around why developing intercultural competence at staff and student level is difficult. For example, notions of not having enough 'space' in the curriculum are gently challenged. Here, interculturalism becomes about the benefits that multiple perspectives offer as well as the importance of faculty knowing the students, and students knowing one another. Interconnectivity is primordial to the HEA framework and the work at Brighton highlights the learning outcomes that can be gained from this kind of intercultural communication in class.

Bournemouth University

Bournemouth University is developing a global programme that is ambitious in its aim to ensure that every individual staff member and student in every programme is international in some capacity. This shift represents the importance the institution places on its role in developing global graduates as well as emphasizing the message advocated by the framework – that this is a *collective* responsibility. Led by senior management, this project was one of several on the programme that used the HEA framework as a means of evaluating where its staff members were in terms of the process of internationalizing the curriculum.

It also focused on an often-overlooked but hugely significant dimension of the international 'people' in the framework – the intercultural dimension of the staff. In an additional HEA-funded project, Bournemouth carried out research on the perceptions of its international staff to teaching and learning. This research, as well as providing a literature review on where the sector is in the process, is also an act of meta-intercultural awareness. As an organization, Bournemouth is therefore encouraging its own staff to talk about learning and teaching across its own cultural, disciplinary and linguistic borders. While the focus is often – rightly – on how we enable our students to become global citizens with the relevant intercultural skills, staff are integral here. In the UK, there is much to learn about pedagogical practices from across the world. As large numbers of international staff are integrated into UK institutions, are faculty and staff members interculturally equipped to learn from them, too? Bournemouth's approach raises this question for many in HE.

University of South Wales

The School of Art & Design at the University of South Wales used the framework in a different way. As a recently restructured school, there were lower numbers of international staff and students than at some of the other institutions taking part in our programme. In order to incorporate an intercultural experience, giving students the skills they needed to become global graduates, staff members used the disciplinary context and connections to enable virtual experiences in work environments both abroad and in Wales. Students were able to work in intercultural groups regardless of their own socio-cultural backgrounds. This project is not unique of course, and many programme leaders are turning to technology to enable their students to collaborate and gain intercultural skills, but what is striking is the way different staff members interpreted the framework and its emphasis on flexibility to embrace the ethos. This is an example of how internationalizing higher education is opening up productive ways of working both within and beyond the community.

University of Edinburgh

The University of Edinburgh was another institution taking part in the programme. Although faculty and staff members at Edinburgh have already developed the learning and teaching element of internationalization, they drew in particular on the 'inclusive' aspect of the HEA framework. Interculturalism is as much about learning about one's own culture as it is about being able to see others and how others see us (see Carroll, 2014). To overcome fear of the stranger, of the other, Edinburgh's project explored ways in which different disciplines in the School of Education could integrate both home and international students. They sought to break down the barriers that are so often prevalent in UK HE institutions (Carroll, 2014; Ryan, 2013). Their focus is upon both the formal and the informal aspects of the curriculum, reminding others of the importance of belonging.

International impact

The work that has been carried out in the UK using the HEA Framework in various contexts provides insight into how intercultural competence is being developed at institutional and national levels. The common themes advocated in the framework around collaboration, inclusion, flexibility and interconnectivity as well as long-term sustainability, appear in different forms. HE faculty and staff members are deeply involved in and excited about the potential internationalization and interculturalism offer to HE. It is, however, also interesting to explore the international impact of this work

Germany

In Germany, at a recent Deutscher Akademischer Austausch Dienst (DAAD; German Academic Exchange Service) seminar, those working in internationalization in HE in Germany came together – a combination of researchers, practitioners and international student officers. Participants looked at the HEA framework together and discussed more national perceptions and challenges around internationalization.

German research in the area drew on the same points of reference as the English-speaking world (Carroll, 2014). These common points of reference are reassuring because it implies that the Western world at least shares the same values, hopes and aspirations for what internationalization can bring to HE (Leask, 2004; Ryan, 2011). It also suggests that the work can be transnational. For example, the case study from Bournemouth can also be relevant in a German context. The big question of course is: would the converse apply? The barriers may be linguistic. In fact, many of the discussions here centred around language. In Germany, for a programme to be international it has to be in English. However, for academics such as Prof. Dr Uwe Koreik at the University of Bielefeld, this affects the quality and the potential of German research itself.

The perception of British universities as the very best may be a misperception. While the Anglophone model may still be seen as central – rightly or wrongly, individuals who are monocultural/monolingual may be less able to engage with those from different cultures – in countries such as the UK and the USA, where English is the lingua franca, this can actually be a disadvantage for students. Their chances of becoming global graduates may be limited because they do not participate in the international experiences that would be truly transformative. For an English-only speaker, even being in a German-speaking seminar for two days can reinforce the importance of intercultural skills – such skills provide the resilience to encounter the new, the unfamiliar and the unknown in order *to learn*.

United States

In the USA, many teacher preparation programmes are striving to incorporate teaching and learning strategies that impact intercultural skills: (1) knowledge about cultures and about cultural competency;

(2) experience and interaction with persons of cultures different from those of the faculty or students; (3) reflection about experiences; and (4) coaching about skills development. Faculty members have used various measures of skills development: cultural-mindedness, effective communication skills, problem-solving skills, dialogue, negotiation and conflict recovery, coaching, mentoring and teamwork.

Research in teaching and learning at Minnesota State University, Mankato, has examined the effectiveness of intentional active learning strategies on the cultural competency of more than 600 undergraduate students. For this study, the IDI version 3 (Hammer, 2012) was used as a measure of cultural competency. Results indicated that undergraduate students tended to minimize cultural differences at the beginning of their studies at university. The campus-based curriculum was redesigned to provide students with knowledge, experience, skills, practice and reflection around cultural differences and similarities.

After the intentional active learning interventions, subjects showed statistically significant positive gains in their cultural competency. The results were analysed according to varying inputs (lecture, research projects, service learning, reflection, coaching sessions, etc.). Analysis suggested that reflection and coaching were among the most important strategies to foster intercultural competence among university undergraduate students. Experience within another culture may result in an interesting and unique tourist experience, but it does not necessarily foster cultural competency. *Information* and *knowledge* about other cultures is not enough to establish cultural competency.

Conclusion

In this work, we wanted to spark discussion and to provoke our audience into exploring how we define interculturalism, what intercultural skills we can develop, and also how, realistically, we can measure effectively the development of these skills. We did not seek consensus in this debate, but what we did want was to exploit the opportunity of exploring global, national and local perspectives of what interculturalism looks like and how its power can be felt. We use the word 'power' with careful deliberation for in the many diverse and wide-ranging discussions taking place over the four days of Going Global, it was clear that the ability to talk across and between cultures has the creative force that can lead to innovation in higher education, but also in the way we lead our lives. Examples suggest that rather than universities acting as guardians or anchors for these networks, perhaps their influence and impact are more fluid and flexible, able to embed themselves in different ways in different contexts.

Encounters with the new and unfamiliar in a language that is often different or unusual (even if it is English) causes learners to 'slip and slide and lose their way' (Pirrie and Macleod, 2010). The transformative potential of intercultural encounters is found in the stories of culture shock, confusion, cognitive dissonance and brilliant 'ah-ha' moments. Each individual academic, student, programme provider or organization becomes 'lost in translation' (Hoffman, 1998).

We wanted to use the examples outlined above to illustrate the many ways in which intercultural competence can be developed in campus settings in higher education in different disciplinary, institutional, national and international contexts. Our aim was to demonstrate the impact of our work and the reach of interculturalism as a dynamic tool with transformative potential for our students and ourselves.

References

Carroll, J. (2014) *Tools for Teaching in an Educationally Mobile World*. London: Routledge.

Hammer, M. (2012) 'The intercultural development inventory: A new frontier in assessment and development of intercultural competence'. In M. Vande Berg, R.M. Paige and K.H. Lou (eds), *Student Learning Abroad*. Sterling, VA: Stylus Publishing. Ch. 5, 115–36.

Higher Education Academy (2015) 'Framework for internationalising higher education'. York: Higher Education Academy. Online. www.heacademy. ac.uk/sites/default/files/downloads/internationalising-he.pdf (accessed 13 November 2015).

Hoffman, E. (1998) *Lost in Translation: A life in a new language*. London: Vintage.

Leask, B. (2004) 'Internationalisation outcomes for all students using information and communication technologies'. *Journal of Studies in International Education*, 8 (4), 336–51.

Phipps, A. and Gonzalez, M. (2004) *Modern Languages: Learning and teaching in an intercultural field*. London: SAGE.

Pirrie, A. and Macleod, G. (2010) 'Tripping, slipping and losing the way: Beyond methodological difficulties in social research'. *British Educational Research Journal*, 36 (3), 367–78.

Ryan, J. (2011) 'Internationalisation of pedagogy and curriculum in higher education. Plenary at the 2011 Internationalisation of Pedagogy and Curriculum in Higher Education'. Coventry: University of Warwick. Online. https://vimeo. com/channels/243969 (accessed 13 November 2015).

— (ed.) (2013) *Cross-cultural Teaching and Learning for Home and International Students*. London: Routledge.

Sandell, E.J. and Tupy, S. (2015) 'Where cultural competency begins: Changes in undergraduate students' intercultural competency'. *International Journal of Teaching and Learning in Higher Education*, 27 (1).

Masters Beyond Borders
Melissa Schuessler

Introduction

The UK International Unit's Outward Mobility Strategy (2013) provides a clear vision of the importance of international experiences, and challenges institutions to remove barriers to outward mobility, including those involving quality assurance and credit recognition.

Much has been written about how students benefit from international experiences, but there is scant literature on how to facilitate and implement these types of programmes – especially at postgraduate level. The Outward Mobility Strategy addresses this in its 'Strategic Objective 3: Build capacity in UK higher education to facilitate outward mobility', which aims 'to provide guidance on interpreting and applying quality assurance frameworks related to student placements overseas'.

The integration of these types of programmes into the curriculum is vital to their success. Extra or co-curricular activities are not explicit on a transcript or in the programme degree title and are often recognized only through the attainment of an additional award given by the higher education institution. Though beneficial, this type of award has little merit to a potential employer who would prefer to see academic credit and recognition for such activity (Wilson, 2012). To facilitate this recognition, changes are needed to programme structures to evidence this learning experience on transcripts and degree awards.

The why

The aforementioned strategies and policy guidance provided us at Leeds University Business School the external rationale to support the creation of new master's programmes with international experiences. Internally, we at the business school turned our attention inwards and asked ourselves – what type of programme do we want to offer?

Like many institutions in the UK, we have undergraduate programmes in place that have an international variant that allows students to receive credit for a study abroad experience. At Leeds this is done through the addition of an extra year, turning a three-year programme into a four-year programme. A four-year undergraduate programme is in line with a number of academic systems at our partner institutions around the world.

Turning our attention to postgraduate taught programmes, the majority of our MA and MSc programmes are only one year in duration. This makes having an international experience as part of a degree programme difficult for two reasons: there is little space in the curriculum and such a duration is not in line with academic systems in other parts of the world, most of which offer two-year postgraduate taught programmes.

Despite the difficulties, we found that there was strong demand from our postgraduate taught students to have access to international experiences. Many students expressed that they were interested in study abroad while studying for their undergraduate degree but did not access the opportunity. While furthering their studies, students were beginning to understand and appreciate the benefits of this type of experience.

Student demand guided the initial consideration of a master's-level study abroad experience. In line with external policy and employer expectations, colleagues sought to provide a credit-bearing international experience to our master's programmes. As colleagues within the business school continued to think about this new initiative, other strategically important aims emerged as well.

Aligned with the University of Leeds's values and our strategic plan, three aims were articulated to support the creation a new postgraduate taught programme with study abroad.

1. To provide a credit-bearing international experience to postgraduate taught programmes.
2. To provide diversity in the classroom via incoming students, as a way of providing internationalization at home for students who were not able to go abroad themselves.
3. To improve the ranking of our programmes.

With the vision of the International Unit and the aims of the university and business school, colleagues and I set out to create a programme variant that included an additional semester of study abroad as a recognized, credit-bearing part of our postgraduate taught degrees.

This was challenging for the organizational structure of our institution. The creation of this programme pushed us to consider how the international dimension could be structured into the curriculum, how to evidence internationalized learning outcomes and how to operate a new programme. The operationalization of the outgoing component of the study abroad process was only half the task. Also new to our institution was the formal process of accepting incoming exchange postgraduate students.

The how

Support was secured from senior management and academic colleagues to create a new programme variant to allow for an additional semester of study at an overseas partner. The biggest challenge was working through the administrative functions to approve, formalize and put a new programme variant into operation.

We started with one programme in one school and allowed only a small number of students onto the scheme in the first year to allow us to work through any unanticipated issues that may have arisen.

Programme structure

With the aims above in mind, our first consideration was how to structure the programme. Rather than creating a new programme, we choose to create a variant to the current one. Similar to the undergraduate level, a programme variant allows students to opt in to the scheme once they are enrolled on the programme. It is not recommended that students apply directly onto programmes with study abroad options as a number of variables need to be considered over which the host institution has little control or influence. These include, among other things, any change to visa registration, both in the home and host country, as well as changes in entry requirements of the host institution. Opting into a study abroad scheme allows coordinators at the home and host institutions to work through any issues caused by the external environment.

Upon choosing to design a programme variant rather than creating a new programme, we had to next consider when to provide the opportunity. The programme was designed to be an exchange, so a time had to be chosen that would be appropriate for both incoming and outgoing students. We were very keen to have reciprocal exchange agreements with our partners where the fees are waived for the incoming students rather than study abroad agreements that supported outgoing mobility only and where students were charged a fee by the host institution. We were equally keen to have the incoming students in our postgraduate taught classrooms, providing their unique perspectives and offering potential for the internationalization of home students.

We found that the best time for the opportunity was to extend the current 12-month programme to allow for an additional semester of study in semester one of the following academic year. At taught postgraduate level, this time is traditionally spent waiting for exam and dissertation marks to be released before the winter graduation ceremony. Providing an opportunity during this semester meant outgoing students could retain their enrolled student status and incoming students were able to access modules at the start of a new academic year.

The programme variant for outgoing students is as follows:

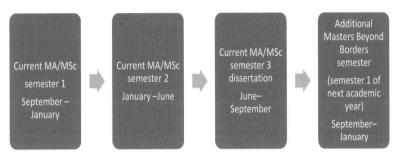

Figure 1: Programme variants

To maintain the credit-bearing element of the programme variant, a new module was created to support the international experience. Again, inspiration came from the undergraduate study abroad programmes where, at Leeds, a year abroad is awarded a year's worth of credit supported by a study abroad module within the school or faculty. Credit is awarded by the successful attainment of two elements: pass marks from the host institution as evidenced through a transcript, and the completion of an online learning assignment. This reflective assignment is marked and assessed by academic staff in the school or faculty. This is a 'pass for progression' module, meaning that students must pass their year abroad to receive the internationalized variant of their degree. If students do not pass their year abroad, they are allowed to progress to the final year but do not receive the internationalized variant of their degree.

Masters Beyond Borders required an additional postgraduate study abroad module to ensure credits were awarded as per our aims for the scheme.

Quality assurance and approval

Both the quality assurance team within the business school and the central quality assurance team were vital to the success of this programme variant.

Approval was required for both the variant to the programme as well as the new module. Institutions often have well-established approval processes in place for both of these functions, but for the programme approval process, specific international expertise was required. Professional international expertise was needed to dispense information on market and financial viability and to provide guidance on internationalized learning outcomes to ensure the acquisition of intercultural competence. Other important considerations for the programme variant included progress rules and a fallback award for an instance where a pass for the postgraduate study abroad module could not be obtained.

QA supported us through all academic compliance issues by providing high-quality advice and guidance. They also informed the external examiner about the new variant so the examiner would be able to administer both the existing programme and the new variant.

Operations and administration

Operationally, our most challenging obstacle for the creation of a study abroad master's programme was the need for an additional exam and the resources required for this.

In the business school, postgraduate exam boards were held once a year in November, following the submission of the dissertation in September. All course work and dissertations went to this exam board to allow for graduation in the winter degree ceremony. In the new Masters Beyond Borders scheme, our outgoing students would be overseas at this time on a credit-bearing part of the programme and the incoming students would be on their study abroad semester at our institution. It quickly became apparent that the success of this programme relied on the creation of an additional exam board after semester one. The amount of work to support an additional exam board should not be underestimated. Academic staff are required to mark at a different time of year, professional staff are involved in collating assessed marks and external examiners are needed to confirm marks outside of the agreed timescales. One by one, colleagues worked through these issues. During this time the strong support and leadership of senior management was essential to reassure staff that this work was in line with strategic aims.

Incoming students

Once the additional exam board was created to support the marks of the incoming students during semester one, all that was left to do was create a process for admitting incoming postgraduate exchange students and to sign the study abroad agreements for student exchange at this level.

Again, institutions often have processes in place for both of these actions. And again, inspiration and guidance came from the undergraduate study abroad scheme.

Colleagues in the central Study Abroad Office and colleagues in the Faculty Postgraduate Admissions Office were involved with setting entry requirements for incoming exchange students. The application process, admission and creation of study records was shared between these two offices.

Study abroad agreements with current partners were amended and approved via the normal committee approval process to add taught postgraduate level to the arrangement.

Impact

The evidence and impact of this new programme is still being measured. Colleagues are looking to quantify participation rates, programme ranking, new partnerships and the academic achievement of both incoming and outgoing students. Key Performance Indicators have been set to support how success is measured.

However, the immediate impact has been much stronger at an organizational level. Going through the process of operationalizing a new international initiative has highlighted how all staff are integral to its successful implementation in a very real and practical way. Senior staff kept collaborators focused on the strategic importance of the programmes, academic colleagues provided the curriculum with creativity and authority, while professional staff both within the business school and in the central function teams were crucial in ensuring that compliance issues were addressed as the programme was developed. Masters Beyond Borders is changing the culture of how internationalization is viewed at our institution.

Further evidence of the impact of this scheme is seen in the improvement in the relationships between the business school and our international partners. This activity allows for much deeper collaborations with our partners, many of which are already able to offer exchanges at the postgraduate level. This scheme provides further confirmation of our commitment to internationalization and serves as a platform for advanced collaboration.

Conclusion

More research is needed to examine the complexity and practicalities of implementing internationalized degree programmes in UK higher education. Such research will increase our effectiveness with regard to both our international partners and our students. Commitment and flexibility are key components but may be difficult to maintain when a number of external factors affect the structure and operations of higher education institutions in the UK and around the world. As international education increases in importance, a firm understanding of how internationalization operates in all areas and at all levels of the university organizational structure is vital to its continued success.

Furthermore, research in this area will support the internal policy needed to confidently ensure our institutions are equipped to implement international programmes and opportunities that will indeed connect cultures.

References

UK Higher Education International Unit (2013) 'UK Strategy for Outward Mobility'. Online. www.international.ac.uk/media/2468186/uk-he-international-unit-uk-strategy-for-outward-mobility.pdf (accessed 17 November 2015).

Wilson, T. (2012) 'A review of business–university collaboration'. Online. www.gov.uk/government/uploads/system/uploads/attachment_data/file/32383/12-610-wilson-review-business-university-collaboration.pdf (accessed 17 November 2015).

2.5

Connecting culture with leadership

Dawn Freshwater and Philip Esterhuizen

Introduction

In past decennia discussions regarding the prestige, elitism, tradition, and legacy of 'old' universities in relation to their 'younger' counterparts have been many and varied (Bargh *et al.*, 1996; Czarniawska and Wolff, 1998; Naudé and Ivy, 1999; Rolfe, 2003; Boliver, 2013; Raffe and Croxford, 2015). Such discourse relating to the role of structures and operations in institutions of higher education is fundamental to any discursive debates around organizational culture and leadership of those same institutions. As such, the role of the University cannot be overlooked when discussing globalization, internationalization and inclusivity, and specifically its contribution to evolving cultures. Indeed as Jo Johnson, the UK Minister for Universities and Science, observed at the Going Global event in London in 2015, the phenomenal growth of further and higher education has created countries with large and complex educational systems. Large systems that, according to the British Council study, in partnership with UNESCO and World Bank, attempt to translate radically different political, social and economic conditions in order to identify common characteristics. We would also add that the creation of large systems relates directly to the creation of large and diverse macro and micro cultures. Each with its own unique strategy to achieve internalization and to develop in a global arena.

Internationalization strategies in institutions of higher education have evolved rapidly, broadening and deepening universities' reach and significance across national borders, with the aim of addressing global problems, collaborating on a wide range of educational initiatives through consortia and focused networks. Top priorities for internationalization agendas are to position institutions for competitive advantage as well as mutual benefit, but also to promote intercultural exchange among staff and students emphasizing the promotion of innovation and impact on addressing global problems and challenges.

Whereas the status of older and established universities has been etched on, and ingrained in, social fabrics; polytechnics with their more recent 'elevation' to university status have intended to level the playing field and promote societal inclusivity (Raffe and Croxford, 2015), this in the context of an increasingly global and boundary-less world. If equity and inclusivity were one of the intended consequences of the massification of higher education, one might understandably question whether this has had the expected effect, or whether this attempt at equity has exposed yet another hidden hierarchy within a system; that of opaque hierarchy and power dynamics (Boliver, 2013).

This leads us to consider the impact and relevance of formal and informal leadership models, in the context of challenges and change, on the drivers of university business models, along with measures of international success. In turn, this raises questions regarding institutional values and identity as organizations develop and implement international strategies. This is often based purely on the sustainability of the business model, at the risk of losing the connection to the values and mission. Battilana in discussion with Nobel (2015) refers to this as duelling missions.

Duelling missions?

In the recent paper 'What to do when your organization has dueling missions', Battilana (2015) provides an interesting commentary on the difficulties of combining the social mission of a 'non-profit' institution, with the revenue model of a 'for profit' business. Referring to the concept of 'hybrid organizations' that have to simultaneously pursue commercial and social objectives, Battilana (2015) asks the question 'is it really possible to do well on the social dimension while engaging in commercial activities?' Interestingly, Battilana (2015) raises the challenge that many Higher Education Institutions currently face, and which speaks to the drivers for internationalization and *going global*. She states (2015) 'Hybrid organizations always face the challenge of how to allocate resources between their social and commercial missions', running the risk of mission drift as they focus more on profits, forgetting the important connection to their social mission. For us, this is a really significant point, and one that is well made when related to the issues of culture and leadership and their connection to both the social and commercial missions of the global institution.

Connecting culture with leadership: macro climate

For the purposes of this chapter we take a psycho-social perspective of culture that relates directly to the spaces between people. We employ Goleman's (2013) notion of leadership, that it to say, that the primal task of the leader is that of directing attention to where it needs to go. This is a powerful application, in our opinion, of Harvard policy analyst Joseph Nye's 'smart power' (Nye, 2013). Economic power and prosperity through student recruitment and military might in the form of research citations and awards are of course influential and essential forms of leadership in Higher Education Institutions. These form part of the formal power and the macro climate of the organization, and are regulated through economies of performance such as regulatory governance, standards and ethics (see Stronach, 2010 for a more comprehensive review of economies of power). However, as Stronach (2010) points out, the ecologies of performance are of equal power and import. Examples of ecologies of performance can include branding, values and symbols, and of course cultural empathy and cultural power. Both economies and ecologies of performance are critical to achieving a sustainable business model, and to ensure alignment with values. And as Battilana (2015) has signalled, an integrated approach to both the ecology and economy of the institutional performance is critical in order to ensure the equal privileging of both the social and commercial missions of the organization; an important aspect of connecting culture with leadership. These agendas, in the context of globalization promises and perils, have major implications for leaders at all levels who are being pressed to develop new skills sets that involve new ways of thinking, behaving, and managing across cultural and hierarchical boundaries. Universities are globally connected to cultures through their students, faculty and partners, with campuses being increasingly connected to and dependent on higher education communities around the globe. In such situations leading with congruence to achieve inclusivity is both demanding and required.

Connecting culture with leadership: micro climate

In general terms universities espouse visions of inclusivity and innovative thinking (Lynch, 2006), yet Boliver (2013) discusses the discrepancy in the number of offers made to students from ethnic minority backgrounds by prestigious universities and those institutions seen to be more accessible to less advantaged groups. This would appear to be a bi-directional dynamic as a survey from the National Union of Students (2011) showed that students from ethnic minority groups believe more discrimination to be associated with prestigious universities and therefore apply to institutions known to be ethnically diverse. The circular, cause-effect, motion suggested here is also discussed in work by Naudé and Ivy (1999), Ivy (2001) and Hemsley-Brown and Oplatka (2006) indicating that marketing strategies vary across institutions and tend to target specific, potential clients. In the United Kingdom, while governmental policy dictates the operationalization of equal opportunity at local and institutional levels (May and Bridger, 2010; Equality Challenge Unit, 2013; Wray, 2013), it would appear to offer institutions flexible margins within which to recruit students. One could suggest that a mission statement regarding equity and inclusivity could be mirrored by, and operationalized through, the staff employed within an institution. If this is taken to be a valid argument, then the statistics provided by the Equality Challenge Unit (2013) necessitates a reflective pause. The 2013 statistical report identifies that 44 per cent of all academics were women and 4.1 per cent of all academic staff were Black. One could think that this correlates with the representation of students across universities. In other words, the question posed by Williams (2015) is worth considering as to whether staff recruitment and retention strategies have undisclosed agendas skewed towards maintaining a dominant discourse and whether there is a question of tokenism by employing a nominal representation from marginalized groups and, therefore, ensuring insufficient critical mass to challenge. Williams argues that societal shifts in 'political correctness' result in less overt discrimination but increase more subtle and insidious forms of discrimination. Work by Norton and Sommers (2011) and Nobel (2013) conducted around the concept of 'colour blindness' to racial identity, found those participants claiming not to notice ethnic characteristics displayed less socially acceptable behaviour such as avoiding eye contact with someone from a different ethnic background. Also, in this regard, 'colour blind' individuals did not recognize racial disparities and could not understand the perceived experience of those who felt marginalized. This phenomenon is also identified in work by Esterhuizen and Freshwater (2015) inasmuch as those who are part of an institutional dominant discourse did not, in fact, recognize the existence of a power dynamic. Failure to recognize the perceived marginalization of another is tantamount to negating their identity and raises the issue that, by attempting to ignore the issue, one is ignoring the core being of 'the other'. Although this is not seen as being overt discrimination, surely negation of an individual is equally profound. Gallagher (2003) and Harper (2012) challenge the construct that personal 'colour blindness' reflects tolerant and progressive thinking, suggesting rather that it maintains and legitimizes ethnic privilege. However, the same argument can be used for all individuals perceiving marginalization due to their identification with any of the 'protected characteristics' such as race, religion, gender, mental health, sexual identity and sexual orientation. Returning to the initial point of staffing, Sue (2010) proposes that institutions should be focused and intentional in their commitment to diversity, aspire to recruit and retain staff that represent societal diversity, and provide ongoing education for staff. However, organizational self-awareness is equally vital to embrace and sustain diversity and Sue highlights the importance of confidence to recognize institutional bias and interrogate a dominant discourse present within an institution.

In defining the subtleties of what are termed micro-aggressions, Sue (2010) suggests three categories of micro-aggressions, namely micro-assaults, micro-insults, and micro-invalidations. He suggests that micro-insults and micro-invalidations are subtle, ambiguous and unconscious whereas micro-assaults are conscious and intentional and micro-aggressions are a form of sexism or racism but are often unclear and difficult to recognize. Sue (2010: 5) goes on to define micro-aggressions as ' ... the brief and commonplace daily verbal, behavioural, and environmental indignities, whether intentional or unintentional, that communicate hostile, derogatory, or negative racial, gender, sexual-orientation, and religious slights and insults to the target person or group'. Basford *et al.* (2014) indicate from their empirical study that the more overt micro-aggressions are, the more significant the impact will be on the individual. Although this relationship would seem obvious, the researchers suggest overt micro-aggressions impact negatively on the victim's work outcomes and that women are more often affected. Importantly, Basford *et al.* (2014) identified from their research that both men and women recognized micro-aggressions against women. These findings have implications for changing organizational culture as self-awareness is a pre-condition for changing behaviour. In terms of changing and challenging organizational culture, Bolden *et al.* (2008: 366) highlight the importance of distributing leadership across individual, group and organizational levels, arguing that 'social capital' and 'social identity' are links between 'individual agency and organizational structure'. These, together with the organizational and individual self-awareness previously mentioned, are key elements of inclusive leadership (Esterhuizen and Freshwater, 2015).

Understandably, specific objectives stated behind a university's marketing strategy may not go further than attempting to identify students with the best potential of success, and discriminatory practice cannot be overtly identified, however proactive and reactive dynamics appear in maintaining an institutional status quo. Connecting culture with leadership at a micro-institutional level invariably leads to a degree of incongruence between the espoused institutional narrative and the actual practice being made visible. The inclusive leader is one that does not deny the incongruence with values that exist at some level in any organization, but reflects carefully on the opaque power dynamics and hidden hierarchies that lead to patterns of behaviour that perpetuate the incongruence. As March and Weil (2005) observe 'The leader at the top of his or her organisation symbolizes its unity and shared culture, while at the same time encouraging local diversity to a greater or lesser degree.' We assert that the importance of identifying patterns, which reveal themselves through behaviours, is a fundamental aspect of inclusive leadership that links the values of macro culture with the actions in the micro culture of an institution.

Strategic imperatives for inclusive leaders and organizations

The role of the leader is not to make sure that people know exactly what to do and when, it is to make sure the organization knows itself (Goleman, 2013). To this end, institutions need to have internal and external processes to stimulate and facilitate self-correction in relation to the compromising of values. To critically reflect on the lived experience of the institutional values as enacted by and through leadership, and specifically through the discharge of its internationalization strategy is, as described by participants in our recent study, a strategic imperative (Esterhuizen and Freshwater, 2015). Inclusive leadership not only requires cultural sensitivity, it also requires a diversity of thought leadership for diverse solutions. What does this mean for institutions in their global pursuit? Robert Quinn, executive director of the Scholars at Risk network, claims that institutions should not shy away from talking about their values with both potential and existing international partners and networks. Quinn is explicit in his views on how universities should include formal agreements on values as they initiate international partnerships, and agreements that clearly detail such fundamentals as basic human rights and respect. This sort of imperative in turn makes the identity of the organization distinct, a clear representation and presentation of both the value proposition and the culture. In his publication *The Soul of Leadership* Chopra (2011) states that the journey a leader takes is one of expanding awareness. Inclusive leadership is not simply based on inclusive values, rather it is a socially complex skill, in both its reach and strategic scope. Connecting culture with leadership demands humility, insight and awareness, this in the service of delivering a unified and integrated approach to going global, which in turn ensures the sustainability of an education sector that is known, trusted and understood.

References

Bargh, C., Scott, P., and Smith, D. (1996) *Governing Universities: Changing the Culture?* (Society for Research into Higher Education). Buckingham: Open University Press.

Basford, T.E., Offermann, L.R. and Behrend, T.S. (2014) 'Do you see what I see? Perceptions of gender microaggressions in the workplace'. *Psychology of Women Quarterly*, 38 (3), 340–9.

Battilana, J. in Nobel, C. (2015) 'What to do when your organization has dueling missions'. HBS Working Knowledge. Harvard Business School Link. Online. http://hbswk.hbs.edu/item/what-to-do-when-your-organization-has-dueling-missions

Bolden, R., Petrov, G. and Gosling, J. (2008) 'Tensions in higher education leadership: Towards a multi-level model of leadership practice'. *Higher Education Quarterly*, 62 (4), 358–76.

Boliver, V. (2013) 'How fair is access to more prestigious UK universities? *The British Journal of Sociology*, 64, 344–64.

Chopra, D. (2011) *The Soul of Leadership*. London: Random House.

Czarniawska, B. and Wolff, R. (1998) 'Constructing new identities in established organization fields: Young universities in old Europe'. *International Studies of Management & Organization*, 28 (3), 32–56.

Equality Challenge Unit (2013) *Equality in Higher Education: Statistical report 2013*. London: Equality Challenge Unit.

Esterhuizen, P. and Freshwater, D. (2015) 'A Delphi Study: Towards a clear definition and operationalization of "inclusive leadership" (in a global context?)'. In Stiasny, M. and Gore, T. (eds) *Going Global: Inclusion, innovation, impact*. London: Institute of Education Press.

Gallagher, C.A. (2003) 'Color-blind privilege: The social and political functions of erasing the color line in post race America'. *Race, Gender & Class*, 10 (4), 22–37.

Goleman, D. (2013) *Focus: The hidden driver of excellence*. London: Bloomsbury

Harper, S. R. (2012) 'Race without racism: How higher education researchers minimize racist institutional norms'. *Review of Higher Education*, 36 (1), 9–29.

Hemsley-Brown, J. and Oplatka, I. (2006) 'Universities in a competitive global marketplace: A systematic review of the literature on higher education marketing'. *International Journal of Public Sector Management*, 19 (4), 316–38.

Ivy, J. (2001) 'Higher education institution image: A correspondence analysis approach'. *International Journal of Educational Management*, 15 (6), 276–82.

Lynch, K. (2006) 'Neo-liberalism and marketisation: The implications for higher education'. *European Educational Research Journal*, 5 (1), 1–17.

March, J.G. and Weil, T. (2005) *On Leadership*. Oxford: Blackwell.

May, H. and Bridger, K. (2010) *Developing and Embedding Inclusive Policy and Practice in Higher Education*. York: Higher Education Academy.

National Union of Students (2011) *Race for Equality: A report on the experiences of Black students in further and higher education*. London: NUS.

Naudé, P. and Ivy, J. (1999) 'The marketing strategies of universities in the United Kingdom'. *International Journal of Educational Management*, 13 (3), 126–36.

Nobel, C. (2013) 'The case against racial color blindness in the workplace'. Online. www.forbes.com/sites/hbsworkingknowledge/2013/01/20/the-case-against-racial-colorblindness-in-the-workplace.

Norton M. I. and Sommers, S.R. (2011) 'Whites see racism as a zero-sum game that they are now losing'. *Perspectives on Psychological Science*, 6 (3), 215–18.

Nye, J. (2013) *The Future of Power*. New York: Public Affairs.

Raffe, D. and Croxford, L. (2015) 'How stable is the stratification of higher education in England and Scotland?' *British Journal of Sociology of Education*, 36 (2), 313–35.

Rolfe, H. (2003) 'University strategy in an age of uncertainty: The effect of higher education funding on old and new universities'. *Higher Education Quarterly*, 57 (1), 24–47.

Stronach, I. (2010) *Globalizing Education, Educating the Local: How method made us mad*. London: Routledge.

Sue, D. W. (ed.) (2010) *Microaggressions and Marginality: Manifestation, dynamics, and impact*. Hoboken: Wiley.

Williams, A. (2015) 'Modern-day racism in the workplace: Symbolic diversity or real change?' *From Science to Practice: Organizational Psychology Bulletin* (special issue: *Enriching the workplace by scientifically integrating psychology and organizational life*), 1 (1), 6–10.

Wray, M. (2013) *Developing an Inclusive Culture in Higher Education: Final report*. York: Higher Education Academy.

Connecting cultures and forging futures through global leadership development

Robin Middlehurst and Tom Kennie

Globalization as a context for transnational collaboration

The dynamic of globalization in the twenty-first century, experienced in diverse ways across the world, is a major driver for connecting cultures as we seek to forge positive futures for all societies and communities. While the origins of globalization remain contested among scholars and media commentators, few would argue that today's global connectivity in trade, financial flows, transport, communications and ideas is having major economic, social and environmental impacts across the globe. Giddens, in discussing *The Consequences of Modernity* (1991), captures some of these impacts in his definition of globalization as 'the intensification of worldwide social relations which link distant localities in such a way that local happenings are shaped by events happening many miles away and vice versa' (p.64).

International organizations such as the World Economic Forum and Millennium Institute, which monitor opportunities and risks associated with globalization, point to positive features such as increasing cultural diversity, economic and technological advances and educational and health benefits. They also warn of the negative impacts, including climate change and environmental degradation, shortages of food and water, and interracial and religious conflicts. Of critical importance to the achievement of beneficial outcomes from globalization and the amelioration of negative consequences is the ability of sectors, systems, governments and organizations to work together to address the already identified – and as yet uncertain – global challenges that face us. In their most recent analysis of 'The State of the Future', the Millennium Institute authors emphasize the urgent need for collective international effort: 'Our challenges are transnational in nature, requiring transnational strategies ... Humanity needs a global, multi-faceted, general long-term view of the future with bold long-range goals to excite the imagination and inspire international collaboration' (Glenn *et al.*, 2015: 1).

Universities have a central role to play in addressing the impacts of globalization as anchor institutions in their localities and as major international knowledge producers and brokers across regions and sectors. Institutions are already addressing some of the challenges that come with globalization through their research and teaching, and through the scale and scope of their increasingly collaborative internationalization strategies. The need for international collaboration is clearly stated – for example, by the Worldwide Universities Network (WUN), a consortium of 18 universities working together on joint research and teaching initiatives. WUN's rationale for collaboration echoes the analysis of the Millennium Institute: 'The major issues facing our planet are of a magnitude that no one institution or organization can address on its own. They require the pooling and sharing of knowledge across institutions, across disciplines and across continents' (WUN website).

The phenomenon of globalization is changing government and societal expectations of the role of universities; they must now be both local and global in their missions and activities. For example, contributing to local and regional development in sub-Saharan Africa, southern India or in the Arctic region will now often involve international perspectives and connections, while contributing to the international competitiveness of a country or region such as Australia or China, Europe or ASEAN, will necessarily bring institutions into a global arena. The increasing importance of internationalization for regions, countries and higher education institutions (HEIs) is clearly visible in responses to the International Association of Universities' (IAU) regular global surveys, which began in 2003. In their most recent survey, 75 per cent of the 1,336 institutional respondents from 131 countries in every world region stated that they either had or were developing a policy for internationalization (Egron-Polak and Hudson, 2014: 16).

However, building the capacity and capability for successful, productive and sustainable transnational and cross-cultural university initiatives is not straightforward because higher education systems have been designed and have evolved mainly to serve national and local needs. New structures and mechanisms, new processes and ways of working, new behaviours and methods of communicating are needed to challenge, stimulate and support individuals and groups to connect across cultures and forge different futures. The IAU's recent survey notes that internationalization initiatives are being driven in large measure by the senior levels of leadership in the institutions surveyed. It is therefore timely and useful to focus on the ways in which leadership development activities can contribute to building the capabilities and capacities of leaders and their institutions to engage globally in order to address global challenges. In the following section, three global leadership development initiatives involving the authors are outlined.

Global leadership development: Three models and a new diagnostic tool

Changing the world through dental leadership: The senior dental leadership programme

This leadership development initiative was created in 2007 to address the major public health challenge of early childhood caries. At the heart of the Global Child Dental Health Strategy, launched in 2006 at King's College, London, has been the need to build a network of senior dentists around the world who would advocate for child oral health and create preventative programmes in their home countries with the aim of reducing the epidemic of dental cavities in under-five-year-olds. The Senior Dental Leadership (SDL) programme, celebrating its tenth anniversary in 2016, has been the vehicle to deliver the strategy and its goals. The platform of support for the programme demonstrates the power and value of collective global engagement, building as it does on a university partnership between King's College, London, and Harvard University in the USA, combined with the top global dental corporations Colgate Palmolive and Henry Schein. This combination has provided a prestigious academic base and the leverage has been made possible by sharing the reach of the partners' corporate social responsibility activities.

The SDL programme is focused around a shared global vision of a cavity-free world for children. The initial conference held in London served as a catalyst for what is now an annual six-day event, held alternatively in London and Boston, which brings together distinguished leaders in dentistry from all over the world, including chief dental officers, policymakers and respected academics. The programmes have provided crucial support, ideas and networks that have enabled delegates to go on to build numerous successful long-term programmes to improve access to dental care and ultimately the oral health of disadvantaged children. Initially attracting 14 delegates from 11 countries, the programme has grown in breadth and depth, bringing in 24 more countries from all world regions with increased levels of sponsorship and with broadening goals.

Sessions within the programme have focused on horizon-scanning and scenario-planning, change management and leadership, with case studies on workforce development, mid-level providers, women in dentistry and building a stable financial model for dental education and dental care. There is a mix of delegate presentations and external contributions. Over time, more space has been given to facilitate the creation of legacy projects and initiatives within countries, to build regional leadership support networks and to discuss how to build and sustain effective leadership networks. The programmes have been a rich source of new ideas and relationships, but have also been a means of bringing tangible resources to those who need them. For example, a delegate from Cambodia on SDL-5 was able to set up a three-year project with ten partner organizations aiming to treat over 60,000 children in and around Phnom Penh, while a delegate from Malawi in SDL-6 was able to access resources to refurbish two dental surgeries through linkages made within and subsequent to the programme.

As the SDL programme reaches its ten-year milestone, there are still more ambitious goals to be reached as the 2005 mission of the chief dental officers around the world has a target date for the end of the next decade: that all children in the world born from 2026 will be cavity-free in their lifetime. This global leadership development initiative has demonstrated how a focused agenda, supported by creative, talented, committed and resourceful individuals working together across boundaries, can build capacity and capability to address globally recognized challenges. The programme provides an environment, a platform and a springboard that 'energizes everyone, catalysing new ideas and initiatives' (comment from the Dean of the Dental Institute, King's College, London, contributing to SDL-6, 2012).

Global Engagement: Global Challenges leadership programme

The Global Engagement: Global Challenges initiative is on a smaller scale and does not have the targeted focus or the combined resources of the SDL programme. Instead, the programmes offer a platform for senior leaders from different countries and institutions to develop their own international strategy or set of international activities through sharing ideas, developing knowledge and skills and creating new networks as vehicles for future collaborations. The developmental agenda concentrates on raising awareness, gaining perspective, developing insight and understanding at three different levels on how:

- another country is addressing national and international higher education challenges that are similar or relevant to one's own
- other institutions from different countries are addressing specific challenges arising from globalization and the internationalization of

higher education with implications for teaching, research, enterprise or university operations more broadly

- individual leaders and leadership teams are seeking to address the global challenges in their own contexts.

These programmes are also six days long, involve 12–16 invited participants, and are aimed at senior institutional leaders and policymakers principally from the UK and Europe, but open to all countries. The programme design has emerged from 15 years' experience in delivering 32 top management programmes for UK HEIs, with an international week (in the Far East, Middle East, parts of continental Europe and the USA) as an integral and important part of the programme. In common with the SDL programmes, the aim is to provide challenge and support for leaders – in this case, those leading HEIs and higher education policy agencies.

The Global Engagement: Global Challenges programmes are focused on particular themes such as higher education's engagement with business and communities; the shifting public purposes of higher education and institutional responses to new expectations; universities' engagement with regional, national and international imperatives; and new business models for higher education. Beginning in 2014, three programmes have been initiated with different partners: in Chicago (with the British Consulate); in Melbourne and Adelaide (with LH Martin Institute, University of Melbourne); and in Philadelphia (with the University of Pennsylvania).

To date, 45 senior institutional leaders from seven countries, representing a wide variety of types of institution – from small specialist to large comprehensive HEIs – have participated in the programmes, with some individuals choosing to come to more than one programme and country. The programmes are organized around visits to institutions and policy agencies in one or two locations in the chosen country, each designed to illustrate how the particular themes of the programme are being addressed in practice and highlighting success criteria, barriers to implementation and lessons learned. Each session and visit is carefully structured and facilitated to ensure that participants are able to discuss, question, reflect and learn from engaging with their peers (both other delegates and those who host visits) and a variety of resources are offered in support of each theme and programme. Exploring and assessing governance, leadership and management processes, actions and styles provides a common thread that runs through the programmes.

As these programmes are still relatively new, initial evaluation data only have been collected about the programmes rather than information about their longer-term outcomes. These data suggest that the principal benefits to participants have included: seeing and discussing different approaches to global engagement in the range of institutions and organizations visited; the breadth of interactions with hosts and fellow delegates in a variety of senior roles in institutions with diverse missions; the insights gained by observing another country's higher education system in ways that hold up a mirror to one's own system; and the opportunity to shape thinking about institutional strategies for global engagement supplemented by useful links and networks.

Leading globally engaged universities: An initiative of the International Association of Universities

The International Association of Universities (IAU) was founded in 1950 as a global association of HEIs and university associations. Its mission is to strengthen HEIs worldwide by providing a global forum for institutional and association leaders to discuss, examine and take action on issues of common interest. In 2015, it had 630 member HEIs from every region in the world as well as more than two dozen national and regional associations. It also has affiliations with specialized organizations and a growing number of individual associates. While the IAU has a long history of producing scholarly publications and research reports, providing grants, offering advisory services and opportunities to participate in projects focused on internationalization issues, it has developed an increasing role in advocacy and in facilitating collective action to address issues of concern to members arising from globalization and its impacts. Internationalization is a priority theme for the IAU and in promoting its '4th Global Survey', the IAU goes further in arguing that effective and modern HEIs must be 'internationalized' (Egron-Polak and Hudson, 2014).

The latest initiative of the IAU is designed to further its advocacy and collective action through the design of a global leadership development programme. This new programme, launched in Malaysia in November 2015, is focused on building capacity and capability for global engagement across the leaders of its member institutions. A central plank of the programme is peer-to-peer learning that engages and assists individuals to assess their own capabilities and their institutional strategies in the light of internationalization developments in other countries.

Some elements of this programme are shared with the models described above. For example, the first 20 delegates are drawn from 18 different countries across all global regions; a variety of public and private

HEIs are represented by leaders in different senior academic and professional support leadership roles; the programme is being held in one global region (Kuala Lumpur, Malaysia) to shine a light onto local, global and institutional challenges in that country and region while enabling delegates to reflect on their own institutional and national contexts; workshop sessions and visits to institutions involve practical examples of strategies to address common internationalization issues as well as opportunities to build networks and collaborative projects beyond the programme. However, this programme is more closely focused on building specific individual insights and capabilities associated with 'leadership for global engagement'. To achieve this, two different diagnostic tools are being used: one that is well established, designed to explore teamwork and collaborative working, in this case with a particular emphasis on cross-cultural working; the second a new diagnostic tool created to help individuals explore key elements of globally engaged leadership and their particular responses to relevant leadership attitudes, behaviours and practices. The new diagnostic tool is briefly outlined below.

Globally engaged leadership: A new diagnostic

This self-assessment diagnostic is designed both to help individuals review their effectiveness and impact in operating as a globally engaged leader and to identify key themes for future development. Globally engaged leadership can relate to institutional, professional and disciplinary roles and responsibilities at different levels and encompasses leadership activities that require engagement with others across geographic and cultural boundaries. The questionnaire is in four parts:

- first, the context in which the individual operates (the environment and nature of challenges faced)
- second, the breadth and depth of experience of globally engaged leadership
- third, self-orientation in relation to mindset and world view
- fourth, assessment of effectiveness in managing a range of different leadership situations that require cross-boundary and cross-cultural working.

The diagnostic has been developed and validated by occupational psychologists working with higher education specialists, each with wide experience of leadership and global engagement. The dimensions of the diagnostic seek to create a rich picture for each individual. Dimensions relating to the reach and strategic scope of the individual's working context include:

- building a global reputation
- integrating global best practice and innovation
- facilitating a globally enabling environment.

In relation to role, dimensions include:

- boundaries
- levels of complexity
- ambiguity and autonomy
- motivations for global engagement
- the level of social complexity of role and context (focusing on boundary spanning, stakeholder divergence, power and influence and cultural differences).

Dimensions of the experience profile include supportive and challenging experiences, while those relating to leadership mindset and world view are assessed on scales of simplicity–complexity and positive–negative attitudes. Finally, effectiveness across different leadership situations includes reviewing positives, gaps and risks across dimensions of tactical versatility, which include:

- clarifying complexity
- open-minded engagement
- energizing purpose
- collaborative co-creation
- cultural intelligence
- boundary-spanning
- negotiating difference
- reflective learning and ego-maturity.

The four sections of the diagnostic offer cumulative insight into globally engaged leadership for the individual; these insights can then be discussed and interpreted through one-to-one dialogue with facilitators (and peers, if desired). Following extensive piloting, this new diagnostic will be used within the programmes described above.

Conclusion

Globalization is bringing a range of opportunities and challenges to all societies, and universities and colleges are expected by their stakeholders to play a central part in helping their communities to navigate these challenges successfully. A growing imperative in order to deliver on these expectations is an ability and willingness to engage transnationally in ways that connect cultures and spark creative ideas, networks and projects that address local and regional needs. Leaders of higher education institutions, at many levels, need to build their own – and their faculty and staff's – capabilities and capacity to engage and lead transnational projects and programmes. Carefully designed leadership development opportunities that address the intellectual, relational and affective dimensions of global engagement can assist in growing the capabilities and capacities needed to connect cultures and forge positive futures for our institutions and the purposes and people they serve.

References

'Changing the world through dental leadership: The Senior Dental Leadership Programme 2007–present' (2014). Online. www.gcdfund.org/communications (accessed 16 November 2015).

Egron-Polak, E. and Hudson, R. (2014) '4th Global Survey on Internationalization of Higher Education'. Paris: International Association of Universities.

Giddens, A. (1991) *The Consequences of Modernity*. Oxford: Blackwell.

Glenn, J.C., Florescu, E. and the Millennium Project team (2015) 'Executive Summary: 2015–16 State of the Future'. Online. www.millennium-project.org/millennium/publications.html (accessed 16 November 2015).

World Economic Forum (2015) 'Outlook on the Global Agenda 2015: The future of education'. Online. http://reports.weforum.org/outlook-global-agenda-2015/wp-content/blogs.dir/59/mp/files/pages/files/outlook-2015-a4-downloadable.pdf

2.7

Access and equality in higher education: Building the global dialogue

Graeme Atherton

Introduction

The question of who participates in higher education (HE) is seen predominantly as a domestic issue best addressed (if addressed at all) by national or local policies. But, like so many social challenges facing the world, the reality in the early twenty-first century is that it is a local problem with global dimensions. From the richest to the poorest countries, who participates in higher education is defined by inequalities in social background. It is dominated by those with wealth and power.

This paper will examine the role of global dialogue in understanding and addressing these inequalities. It will outline the case for this dialogue, drawing on the discussions of experiences in England and Mexico from Going Global 2015. It will then look at how to facilitate this dialogue and argue that the opportunities to build a worldwide dialogue exist, presented in particular by UNESCO's new global development goals (www.globalgoals. org). But both ambition and strategic thinking will be required to realize this opportunity.

The constant inequality

The available data shows without question that participation in higher education across the world is unequal (European Commission/EACEA/ Eurydice, 2014; OECD, 2014). However, the nature of these inequalities is related to the circumstances of individual countries. While inequality by socio-economic background appears to be a common denominator for each country, particular inequalities differ in importance (Clancy and Goastellec, 2007) – for example, in South Africa race dominates the agenda, while in India it is caste. The presence of such differences does not however ameliorate the case for a global approach to this local problem. Higher education perhaps even more than other areas is becoming increasingly interconnected. This interconnectivity provides the infrastructure for mutual and shared learning to address problems with significant degrees of commonality, such as widening access. The fundamental forces underpinning participation inequalities while refracted through a local lens increasingly begin from the same point. There is a growing body of work pointing to the globalized nature of economic inequality. Finally, the marginalization of particular social groups is echoed by the marginalization of equality and those who aim to deliver on it, in both institutional and policy contexts across the world. In higher education globally it trails behind research, teaching and internationalization in terms of strategic and practical importance. In many parts of the world, as a concern in itself (separate from extending participation per se), it is at a formative stage. The positioning of equality as an issue therefore makes global collaboration and dialogue a must in the field.

England, Mexico and Going Global 2015

Going Global 2015 illustrated this clearly in the session 'Skills for success in HE: Mexico in a global context', which featured research looking at the factors affecting HE progression in England and Mexico. While there were some distinct differences in focus across the two countries in terms of issues affecting progression, with the need for independent learning skills when entering HE a distinct issue where England was concerned, the dialogue initiated at this session revealed the potential for broader global dialogue in this area. Mexico is a country that has experienced rapid expansion in its HE system in the past two decades. Over 150 new higher education institutions were created in the 2000s (Ruiz-Flores *et al.*, 2014). England has a far more established infrastructural base. However, when it comes to access by under-represented groups in HE, the differences are not so extreme. Research shows that in Mexico, children of parents who completed a college education are five times more likely to continue their education than children with parents who completed only primary studies (Dellepiane and Paniagua, 2015). In England, the difference in HE participation between those who receive free school meals in school (who are from low-income backgrounds) and those who do not is 17 per cent (Department of Business, Innovation and Skills, 2015). So while Mexico's levels of inequality in participation are greater, such differences are still profound in England. Looking at the root causes of these differences, though, there is some clear common ground. The British Council report 'Skills for higher education in Mexico', launched at the session, recommends in relation to Mexico that:

... upper secondary enrolment rates should also be addressed through support, mentoring and early intervention programmes. We recommend that the incidence of intervention programmes in Mexico is increased in order to reduce some of the huge disparities in skills gaps between rich and poor students and that they are also run at a much earlier age.

(British Council 2015: 3)

This recommendation only echoes much of the thinking that dominates in England at the moment and the position of agencies who take the policy lead in this area such as the government-funded but independent Commission for Social Mobility, and the Office for Fair Access (OFFA, 2014), whose role it is to hold to account universities in the areas of access to higher education. As was discussed further in this session, underpinning these ideas regarding early, extra-curricular support is the need to consider how to build on the cultural capital that learners from lower-income backgrounds have in order to equip them to reach the levels necessary to enter HE and then go on to succeed when they enter. The space appears to exist, looking at these two countries, for the sharing of practice and knowledge. It is not confined to just these countries, however.

In the forthcoming publication *Access to Higher Education and Nationhood*, which looks at the issues underpinning inequalities in HE participation across 13 countries drawn from each continent in the world, Atherton argues that 'addressing cultural capital disjunctures appears at the centre of what drives disparities in HE participation across the world'. The book contains examples from countries such as South Africa, where attempts to increase participation and completion among black students post-apartheid are bedevilled by the conflict between the cultural capital of the students and many older institutions constructed under apartheid. Returning to South America and Colombia, the book contains examples of how students from poorer and rural areas benefit from exactly the kind of extra support that the British Council report above recommends for Mexico. Finally, back in Europe, Germany – widely acknowledged as one of the most successful economies in the world with an extremely strong education and training system – faces its own challenges in terms of how to give older learners the opportunity to enter higher education through 'second chance' routes.

Making access and equality matter globally

The objective of advancing access and equity globally should in principle be relatively straightforward to articulate. Research by Calderon estimates that there will be over 400 million students globally by 2030 (Calderon, 2012). As argued above, all of the available evidence suggests that these students will continue to come predominantly from more advantaged groups. Addressing this imbalance would seem to be a goal that could be supported across national boundaries. However, the degree to which any imbalance across groups should be reduced by this point would seem rather more contestable. What sort of shift is realistic and how should this be decided? Furthermore, while it is undoubtedly fundamental that *who* enters HE should be something to try and change, it can also be argued that equal, if not greater, attention should be placed on the success of learners in terms of *when* they enter HE.

The mechanism by which access to higher education could become a global as opposed to a local issue needs some careful thinking. It requires dialogue but also a 'theory of change'. The critical question is: how exactly would working globally add value to what happens locally? The first indicator of how to address this issue is to focus on adding value locally, that is, enabling those in different countries and regions to produce change. Looking for an appropriate theory would lead one to the work of Christakis and Fowler and their 2009 book *Connected: The surprising power of our social networks and how they shape our lives*. In it they look at the growth of social networks. They argue that such networks are becoming increasingly important in the twenty-first century as a basis for the organization of societal relationships and a way of explaining social phenomena:

> Society has generally divided into two camps: those who think individuals are in control of their destinies, and those who believe that social forces (ranging from a lack of good public education to the presence of a corrupt government) are responsible for what happens to us. However, we think that a third factor is missing from this debate ... we believe that our connections to other people matter most, and that by linking the study of individuals to the study of groups, the science of social networks can explain a lot about human experience.

> (Christakis and Fowler 2009: 5)

This network-based theory of change implies that rather than developing coherent global projects that adopt relatively uniform ways to address concerns regarding equality in HE, it is preferable to establish networks through which local people can drive change in their own areas. This is not to say that new global projects are not welcome. One can look at the impact of these projects in fields of global social concern such as health and education – for example, the projects funded by the Gates Foundation (www. gatesfoundation.org/What-We-Do). However, with a challenge as pervasive and deep-rooted as inequalities in participation in higher education, the project approach may not be the best route to pursue.

Where to start the dialogue?

Amitia Etzioni is a renowned sociologist who has developed ideas around networks, dialogue and change in the context of communitarianism. He argues that to propel an issue to the forefront of policy and public attention in the twenty-first century dialogue is crucial. He has developed the idea of the 'megalogue':

> Megalogues involve millions of members of a society exchanging views with one another at workplaces, during family gatherings, in the media and at public events. They are often contentious and passionate and, while they have no clear beginning or end, over time they lead to changes in culture and people's behaviour. Societies are constantly engaged in megalogues but typically only one or two topics dominate these at any given time. Recent major issues include the legitimacy of the Iraq war and, in the US, gay marriage. In earlier decades, women's and minority rights were topics of such discussions.

> (A. Etzioni 2009)

Is it too ambitious to suggest that access to higher education could one day take the form of a megalogue? To an extent, such a megalogue has already developed in the context of primary schooling and the need to address the scandal of over 60 million children worldwide who do not receive or complete primary schooling. But developing the megalogue will certainly be a challenge where access to higher education is concerned. The 'global higher education access community' is in reality a fragmented group. Outside of a small group of nations – the US, UK, Australia and possibly Canada – a coherent cadre of professionals working specifically on access to higher education does not really exist. It is necessary then to look for particular 'touchpoints' that can articulate the access challenge to a more diverse audience of stakeholders drawn from inside and outside academic communities. In looking for these touchpoints there may be three areas from which to begin.

Improving what we know

While the available evidence does all point to systemic and universal inequalities in participation, the available evidence is limited. Data is collected on a pan-country basis by UNESCO and OECD. The data is good, but a lot of information is not captured. The focus of the research by these two bodies is on socio-economic group or gender. Attempts are not being made to capture information on participation by ethnicity, religious affiliation, language, disability etc. in a systematic way. Such work would enable a focus on equity to also interface with the field of higher education rankings. The position of both HEIs and countries in global rankings, such as those produced by the *Times Higher Education*, are having an increasing impact on the behaviour of policymakers and institutions. There is some ongoing work in this space that attempts to build the global knowledge base and the conversation around it. The 'Drawing the Access Map' study is being led by the National Education Opportunities Network (NEON) in England with support from the Centre for Excellence in Equity in Education at the University of Newcastle (Australia) and Pearson PLC. This study will consist of a survey examining the data available on HE participation by social background in 50 countries and produce case studies of six. It will report in early 2016.

Engaging students

The voice of students as equal partners in any global equity agenda is essential. We have seen in Germany how students can drive greater equity, as their actions forced the German government to abolish tuition fees in 2014. Global efforts to extend equity need more than politically organized student movements, though. There has to be systematic work to capture the experiences of students who have prospered in a range of ways through HE. The issues of who and how many participate in HE are in principle separate, but in reality they are intertwined. Expanding the system is usually an essential part of widening access to it. The emerging problem that hampers the case for equity, however, is the phenomenon of high level of graduate unemployment/under-employment especially in Asia (Sharma, 2014). Confronting this issue from the student experience position will engage a broad constituency from within HE.

Going beyond HE

Finally, those outside of HE have to be engaged. The aims should be to place access and equality in higher education alongside extending primary and secondary educational participation as an issue of global importance. NGOs, employers, foundations and policymakers sit on a spectrum, from those who may share a common commitment to greater equity in the development of knowledge societies but are operating in a different field, to those who are disengaged entirely from the question. However, this will involve some discussion of the values that orientate equity efforts (and even higher education overall). Most of those working in equity in higher education in the countries where the idea has the strongest hold – the UK, USA, Canada and Australia – come at this question from a strong social justice perspective that can be traced back to socialist/social democratic ideals. Such ideals may not be compatible with the increasing role that the private sector is playing in HE, especially in the developing world.

Conclusion

This article has argued for the virtue of dialogue in the field of access to higher education. Events such as Going Global provide the platform to develop dialogues of this nature, but as is also argued above, the community that can lead and shape a dialogue on access is not very well developed. However, a window of opportunity is certainly opening up for access and equity. The new United Nations Sustainable Development Goals launched in 2015 specifically refer for the first time to access to lifelong learning. It is not entirely clear yet how UNESCO intends to contribute to achieving this goal. Nor can it achieve any of the new 'Global Goals' alone anyway. Building a global dialogue on inequalities in access to higher education may be a big challenge, but it may also be necessary if inequalities in access to HE are ever to be really addressed on a global scale.

References

Atherton, G. (ed.) (forthcoming, 2016) *Access to Higher Education and Nationhood*. London: Palgrave Macmillan.

British Council (2015*) Skills for Higher Education in Mexico: Executive summary.* London: British Council.

Calderon, A. (2012) 'Higher education in 2035: The ongoing massification'. RMIT.

Christakis, N.A. and Fowler, J.H. (2009) *Connected: The surprising power of our social networks and how they shape our lives*. New York: Little, Brown.

Clancy, P. and Goastellec, G. (2007) 'Exploring access and equity in higher education: Policy and performance in a comparative perspective'. *Higher Education Quarterly*, 61 (2), 136–54.

Dellepiane, M. and Paniagua, G. (2015) 'Affordable higher education in Mexico: Implications for career advancement and social mobility final evaluation report – April, 2015'. Mexico City: C230 Consultores.

Department of Business, Innovation and Skills (BIS) (2015) 'Widening participation in higher education 2015'. London: BIS.

Etzioni, A. (2009) 'Hey big spenders'. *Prospect*, September 2009. Online. www.prospectmagazine.co.uk/features/hey-big-spenders (accessed 23 November 2015).

European Commission/EACEA/Eurydice (2014) 'Modernisation of higher education in Europe: Access, retention and employability 2014, Eurydice report'. Luxembourg: Publications Office of the European Union.

OECD (2014) *Education at a Glance*. Paris: OECD.

OFFA (2014) *National Strategy for Access and Student Success in Higher Education*. London: BIS. Online. www.offa.org.uk/wp-content/uploads/2013/03/National-strategy-interim-report-January-2013.pdf

Ruiz-Flores , J., Ramírez-Diaz, J.A. and Benítez-Zavala, A. (2014) 'Equity in access, retention and graduation in higher education in Mexico'. *Journal of Education and Human Development*, 3 (4), 217–27.

Sharma, Y. (2014) 'Rising unemployment: Are there too many graduates?' *University World News*, 14 February 2014 (No. 307).

Beyond national competition: Transnational higher education for global well-being

Rajani Naidoo

It is clearly very important for universities to contribute to their cities, regions and countries. However, many of the major issues facing humankind such as the destruction of the environment, rising inequality and violence across borders can be solved only by countries and universities working together. In this sense, the question of how higher education contributes to global well-being becomes very important. While definitions of global well-being are both socially constructed and contested and change across place and time, it is generally accepted that in order to live well as a global community, crucial dimensions that shape human flourishing, including personal choice and development, freedom from hunger and violence, access to quality health care and education, environmental security and political choice, should be broadly available within and across countries and should meet the needs of the present generation without jeopardizing future generations.

An important way in which higher education can contribute to global well-being is through transnational higher education, which can lead to creative synergies across borders and cultures for innovation and mutual benefit. Contemporary conditions offer many opportunities. First, higher education has expanded exponentially worldwide. An important development has been the reversal of the view that investment in higher education would bring limited benefits to developing countries. The publication of the World Bank report 'Higher education in developing countries: Peril and promise' (World Bank and UNESCO, 2000) reflected the international consensus on the crucial role of higher education in enabling low-income countries to 'leapfrog' intermediate developmental stages and escape peripheral positions in the global economy (Castells, 2001). The high participation rates of the United States, Japan and Western Europe have been overtaken by countries such as South Korea. In addition, higher education expansion has extended to emerging economies including

Lithuania and Hungary, and to resource-rich Middle Eastern countries like Saudi Arabia and the United Arab Emirates. The governments of India, China and Brazil have embarked on highly ambitious plans underpinned by strong financial resourcing to strengthen and grow their higher education systems (Wildavsky, 2010). Second, advances in information and technology communication have enabled instantaneous interaction through the ability to generate, utilize, access and transmit information rapidly across the globe. Third, the university as an institution, as well as students, academic faculty, managers and leaders are all increasingly globally mobile (Shields, 2013). These conditions create optimal conditions for higher education to contribute to global well-being.

Challenges to global well-being

At the same time, there are major challenges. The first is that higher education has been positioned as a key actor in various types of competition between countries. As an important site for the production and dissemination of economically productive knowledge and highly skilled knowledge workers, higher education has become a key contributor to each country's competitive edge in the global economy. Higher education is also implicated in the race for influence through which states assert their own preferred political, economic and cultural models onto the world stage (Naidoo, 2011). In the United States, Richard Riley, a former US Secretary of Education, has called on higher education to promote the country's diplomatic interests with the rest of the world (NAFSA, 2003). China has deployed what commentators have called soft power (Humphrey and Messner, 2006) to set up 272 Confucius institutes in universities in around 88 countries to disseminate Chinese culture. Thus, although universities attract students and faculty from across the world and establish branch campuses in other countries, there is a danger that responsibility appears to be felt primarily to the country; and within the country, to the economy.

The intensification of global economic competition together with the enhanced global mobility of research and development activities and skilled researchers gives rise to fierce status competitions between higher education systems, which sit in parallel to economic competition. These come with their own set of rules, established by those institutions and systems already judged to be 'the best' on an international scale and include government-sponsored contests, generally termed 'excellence policies'. These are strategies to identify and fund universities that are, or have the potential to be, world class. In addition, status competitions in higher education have been reinforced by global rankings. Countries including those in Europe,

Asia, Africa and Latin America strive for membership in the stratum of the most elite universities currently dominated by the United States. They exert an influence on all institutions, even those that have little capacity to feature in such rankings. All of these contests come with their own sets of rules and mechanisms to measure success – and none of these includes global well-being.

Transnational education can offer many advantages. As the work of Roger King (2009) shows, reputable foreign providers in contexts of good regulation can alleviate pressures for access and help build capacity to meet growing demand. Melanie Walker (2015) has also indicated that transnational higher education can challenge closed horizons of thinking and create generative teaching and research partnerships. At the same time, unequal partnerships may lead to tensions in relation to the question of who sets the research agenda and distributions in leadership. The transformation of higher education into a global commodity may lead to developing countries with little regulation becoming mass markets for the dumping of low-quality education programmes. Rather than gaining access to powerful forms of knowledge, many students in developing countries may therefore receive an education that has been reduced to narrowly defined competencies. Such initiatives are likely to stunt indigenous capacity in higher education and maintain global hierarchies (Naidoo, 2010).

Rankings also have both positive and negative consequences for global well-being. They open up debates on the strengths and weaknesses of individual universities as well as higher education systems. However, at the same time, rankings do not measure like with like, and the size of a country, the amount of gross domestic product spent on higher education and even whether English is spoken as a first language all matter. Nevertheless, as Simon Marginson (2009) illustrates, rankings lead to global templates that militate against the diversity of institutions both nationally and globally. The label of 'world class' becomes essential, and governments concentrate resources on elite research-intensive universities to the detriment of capacity building in the system as a whole. The universities that take on the most disadvantaged students in society are therefore both reputationally and financially penalized. Rankings also pit universities against other universities in a global race to achieve goals that exclude some of the most important functions of higher education (Enders, 2014), including how a university contributes to global well-being. The global templates that result from world rankings, which align closely with the characteristics of elite American and European institutions, exert an influence on all institutions, including those located in diverse national contexts with highly differentiated missions.

In this way, global rankings potentially contribute to the erosion of local missions and indigenous knowledge and culture.

Creating innovative synergies in transnational higher education

Given all of the above, what are the best ways forward, to collaborate across national borders and cultures in order to develop creative synergies for innovation rather than reproducing unequal relations of power?

First, there needs to be an acknowledgement that higher education is situated in a multipolar world of shifting power. China, for example, has challenged global governance, which places developing countries at a disadvantage, and has deployed Confucius centres worldwide. Brazil is hugely influential with its non-aligned stance and high level of south–south activity. South Africa, a part of the BRICS alliance, is a powerhouse in sub-Saharan Africa. At the same time, transnational corporations are entering the higher education sector and gaining influence over policy and regulation in their own interests. It is therefore very difficult to divide the world into the powerful higher education of the global north and the powerless higher education of the south. There are high-status, well-resourced universities in poorer countries that are detached from their surroundings and intimately connected to global power nodes of higher education. There are also poorly resourced institutions in rich countries that are detached from power and confined to their locality. In other words, we are witnessing what I have termed the combined and uneven development of higher education worldwide (Naidoo, 2016). This holds out the possibility of new forms of imperialism but also new forms of cooperation. It also presents the possibility for knowledge and innovation to be generated from many different geographic sources and for knowledge flows to become multidirectional.

Policy also needs to be developed to protect higher education from the most corrosive effects of commodification through rules and sanctions, but also to steer market forces through incentives so that institutions contribute to wider goals of well-being. An important area to investigate is the extent to which policy and regulatory frameworks aim to foster collaboration, competition or functional differentiation between domestic, foreign, public and private providers. This is a particularly important question given current understandings that public and private goods may be interdependent and that the production of one kind of good provides the conditions necessary for the production of the other. In this context, a discussion on which aspects of higher education should be protected from market forces and collectively funded by a range of countries for global well-being is crucial.

Research on how transnational education impacts on aspects such as employability is widespread but there is less focus on the impact on culture. While transnational education may erode indigenous culture, there is a need to avoid a binary logic contrasting Western and non-Western culture, or modernity with tradition. This would deny the very real multiplicity of the local and the global in people's lives. Equating knowledge in a simplistic manner with culture will also result in the sector being unable to evaluate knowledge (Naidoo *et al.*, 2015). However, there are fascinating 'natural experiments' such as the medical school in KwaZulu-Natal that applies scientific methods to explore both indigenous and Western medicine. The concerns around culture also extend the other way – does the culture of a university founded on academic freedom change when it erects a branch campus in a country where academic freedom is restricted?

Global well-being can also be enhanced by scrutinizing the education provided to students in all countries. There is a need to resist the pressure to see higher education purely as a space for consumption or a lever for economic development. Philosophers including Martha Nussbaum (2007) have pointed to the danger of seeing education purely in terms of employment and short-term economic benefit. She points to the erosion of the liberal arts and humanities worldwide and argues that there is a danger of producing students who are merely technically trained in the narrow sense of the word. She argues that higher education may be contributing to the development of individuals who are not able to empathize with the suffering of near and distant others and who are unable to identify with the most serious threats faced by democracies.

While there is general agreement with these views, one concern may be that these exhortations appear to have (at least implicitly) an elitist view of a golden age of education. In contemporary times, the living and the learning conditions of students vary greatly both across and within countries. In many institutions, students are lone parents living in financially precarious situations and working in full-time employment. They are often physically exhausted and time-poor and have to engage in education in small bite-sized pieces at irregular intervals. A greater instrumentality is also forced upon all students because there is greater competition for fewer graduate jobs. The challenge therefore is how to take the important principles of education that arose out of the elitist conditions of a period of time spent in funded full-time education and implement these under changing conditions of national and global inequality.

Higher education trailblazers for global well-being

The university is a multifaceted, multifunctional organization that can contribute to the national economy and to social development and which can and should have the freedom to focus on blue skies research. Within this, there is enough space and a huge level of commitment and motivation to contribute to global well-being.

In this sense, it is extremely important to turn the spotlight onto higher education initiatives for global well-being, which are often invisible because they do not feature in rankings or excellence policies. The International Centre for Higher Education Management at the University of Bath has invited submissions to an internet portal to identify higher education trailblazers for global equity. An important example is the Cuban transformation of medical education, one of the most elite professional education programmes, into one that maintains very high quality while recruiting the most disadvantaged students from all over the world. Cuban-trained doctors return to their countries of origin or engage in humanitarian work worldwide. A further example is the Ford Foundation Fellowship Programme, which was designed to promote social justice, community development and access to higher education. As the single largest programme ever supported by the United States Ford Foundation, the International Fellowship Programme supported talented individuals from marginalized social groups in low-income countries to enter high-quality higher education institutions worldwide, and encouraged them to use their leadership skills and knowledge to work towards positive social change in their home communities and countries. A final example is an ambitious research programme involving scientists from 14 European and South American research institutes that was launched to explore what may happen to the Amazon over coming decades as a result of climate change and deforestation. The research programme focused on the impact and effectiveness of public policies and measures to prevent Amazon degradation. These initiatives are inspirational and show how viable it is for transnational higher education to contribute to global well-being.

References

Castells, M. (2001) 'Information technology and global development'. In J. Muller, N. Cloete and S. Badat (eds), *Challenges of Globalisation: South African debates with Manuel Castells*. Cape Town: Maskew Miller Longman.

Enders, J. (2014) 'The academic arms race: International rankings and global competition for world-class universities'. In A.M. Pettigrew, E. Cornuel and U. Hommel (eds), *The Institutional Development of Business Schools*. Oxford: Oxford University Press. 155–75.

Humphrey, J. and Messner, D. (2006) *Unstable Multipolarity? China's and India's Challenges for Global Governance*. Berlin: German Development Institute.

King, R. (2009) *Governing Universities Globally: Organizations, Regulation and Rankings*. Cheltenham: Edward Elgar.

Marginson, S. (2009) 'University rankings and the knowledge economy'. In M. Peters, S. Marginson and P. Murphy, *Creativity and the Global Knowledge Economy*. New York: Peter Lang. 185–216.

NAFSA (2003) 'Securing America's future: Global education for a global age. Report of the Strategic Task Force on Education Abroad'. Online. www.nafsa. org/uploadedFiles/NAFSA_Home/Resource_Library_Assets/Public_Policy/ securing_america_s_future.pdf (accessed 16 November 2015).

Naidoo, R. (2010) 'Global learning in a neo-liberal age'. In E. Unterhalter and V. Carpentier (eds), *Whose Interests Are We Serving? Global Inequalities and Higher Education*. Basingstoke: Palgrave Macmillan. 66–90.

— (2011) 'The new imperialism in higher education: Implications for development'. In R. King, S. Marginson and R. Naidoo (eds), *A Handbook on Globalization and Higher Education*. Cheltenham: Edward Elgar. 40–58.

— (2016) 'The competition fetish in higher education: Varieties, animators and consequences'. *British Journal of Sociology of Education*, 37 (1), 1–10 (special issue, 'The competition fetish in higher education: Sociological perspectives').

Naidoo, R., Adriansen, H.K. and Madsen, L.M. (2015) 'Dynamic African universities: Struggling for a transformational curriculum in apartheid South Africa'. In H.K. Adriansen, H. Jensen, and L.M. Madsen, *Higher Education and Capacity Building in Africa: The geography and power of knowledge*. Abingdon: Routledge.

Nussbaum, M. (2007) 'Education for global citizenship: The importance of the humanities'. Paper presented at a Conference on The Future of the Humanities, Center for Philosophical Studies, Pontifical Catholic University of Peru, Lima, 27–9 August.

Shields, R. (2013) 'Globalization and international student mobility: A network analysis'. *Comparative Education Review*, 57 (4), 609–36.

Walker, M. (2015) 'Transnational Education: New Imperialism or Global Wellbeing'. Fishbowl presentation curated by Rajani Naidoo. British Council's *Going Global* conference, 2 June.

Wildavsky, B. (2010) *The Great Brain Race: How global universities are reshaping the world*. Princeton: Princeton University Press.

World Bank and UNESCO (2000) 'Higher education in developing countries: Peril and promise'. Task Force on Higher Education in Developing Countries. Online. www.tfhe.net/report/overview.htm (accessed 16 November 2015).

Higher education in emergency environments
Wendy Jordan

This paper draws on three case studies that were given at Going Global 2015 in London by HE Professor Osman Babury, Deputy Minister for Academic Affairs, Ministry of Higher Education, Afghanistan; Dr Helena Barroco, Emergency Support for Syrian Students; and Clare Banks, Assistant Director, International Institute of Education, who has worked with higher education professionals in Myanmar since 2013.

Introduction

Higher education is the engine for progress in society; it advances the economy, generates knowledge, research and innovation, and builds the intellectual capital of a nation. It promotes and protects freedom of thought and ideas, and the belief that universities are part of a global intellectual community. Any country robbed of this vital part of its education system will sustain incalculable losses in terms of both its short-term recovery and its long-term development. Emergency environments do not only pertain to political crises: health epidemics, hurricanes, tsunamis and industrial disasters are all disruptive forces, often with long-term implications. Universities can help to ensure the safety and integrity of the community as providers of assistance and resolvers of problems. In developing countries and fragile states, it is critical to understand the vital role of higher education as no country can sustain youth development and economic growth without a high-quality higher education system.

In a troubled and conflict-ridden world, academic assistance is emerging as a huge unmet humanitarian need. Those who are displaced as a result of the war in Syria and migrants from other states where terrorists have declared war on education include academic staff and students, so the education ecosystem is being eroded at all levels. This matter is generating rising concern, and some key agencies are working together to rebuild systems where the conditions allow. Universities are not only communities themselves but are part of the local communities in which they are based, and the impact of a long-term crisis can break down this sense of community.

Before examining the case studies, this paper looks at the common elements revealed by each. The first is the need to engage with partners and stakeholders with sufficient power and influence to enable rebuilding. The second factor is the necessity of operating at an international level, opening up possibilities and opportunities for entry into the globalized world of higher education. The third element is that responses must be appropriate to the timescale and issues.

While universities can become major casualties in emergencies, they can also perform in such situations. They can, for example, provide a refuge and medical facilities. They should also be integrative, and find solutions to problems. Prior to the emergency they can:

- develop plans for rapid responses
- formulate strategies and plans for recovery
- keep ongoing communication flowing – when links and partnerships are established, information and knowledge grows
- help ensure the safety and integrity of the community.

Afghanistan

The first case study deals with Afghanistan. Events in the country over the past 30 years have had a profound effect on the HE system, resulting in damage to infrastructure, the closure of some institutions, loss of faculty staff and students, major loss of quality, deterioration in the quality of facilities and teaching, the end of almost all research, and the isolation of faculty members from contacts in their field and the rest of the world. For individuals the consequences can include a breakdown of the sense of community and a need for individuals to focus on survival skills, mental health problems, depression and anxiety disorders. Some 40 per cent of the student population has been affected by depression, anxiety and PTSD, mostly related to war and conflict experiences. The political implications include risk of takeover by warlords, political interference, intimidation, arrests and violence. The psychological impact is often invisible but has a profound effect on a population caught up in war. Figure 1 shows the results of a school-based survey indicating the most distressing lifetime events.

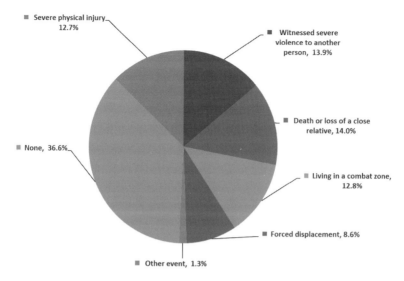

Figure 1: The most distressing life events

Source: Catherine Panter-Brick *et al.* (2009)
'Violence, suffering, and mental health in Afghanistan:
A school-based survey'. *The Lancet*, 374 (9692), Figure 4.

One response from the Ministry of Higher Education was to set up mental health centres at Kabul and Al-Biruni universities. Women and children were particularly affected.

The universities adopted a rapid response survival strategy. They developed underground activities to sustain their work, including teaching in mosques, hidden schools for women, saving books, documents and scientific works. They also kept up relationships with partners abroad, established lobbying activities to save HE and to attract moral and material support. They began rebuilding and carrying out repairs to the damaged infrastructure and prepared a plan to recover faculty and staff and expand HE provision.

For their long-term recovery, the universities are following up on the strategic and transformational agenda set by the ministry. The major aims are to re-establish the academic community, resume research, set high-quality priorities, revise curricula to restore mental and ethical strength, develop a new legal framework, gender equity, establish partnerships, develop international cooperation, and establish extracurricular activities for students. Resilience is a fundamental quality that HE institutions need to develop.

Myanmar

The second case study, 'Connecting with the World', deals with rebuilding HE in post-conflict Myanmar.

The Institute of International Education (IIE) has long protected students and scholars and responds to emergency situations in relation to higher education. Founded in 1919 after the First World War, its mission remains to promote peace and mutual understanding through educational exchange. Most recently it has worked in the post-conflict space in Myanmar. The universities and ministries identified the need to have international education offices on campuses as a first step to achieving a broader range of development goals. IIE initiated a distance learning course for HE professionals in universities and the ministries.

This project demonstrates how willingly the global academic community acts as a key player in helping other countries to internationalize their HE sector. A total of 35 volunteer mentors were linked to the course participants by email and Skype, in order to give them feedback on course assignments. Communication technology has revolutionized the ability to deliver projects across continents.

The course curriculum was developed by IIE in collaboration with leading international educators. The 20-week course was delivered in a hybrid distance learning model, taking account of local technology capabilities. It covered the strategies and skills required to run an international office:

- the basic role of the international office within a university
- developing institutional agreements
- hosting a foreign delegation
- facilitating student and faculty exchange.

Some 56 education professionals from 31 different universities and seven regions participated in the course. This is the summary of the initial outcomes:

- 100 per cent of the 56 participants completed the course
- 98 per cent of participants reported that they would use the ideas, strategies, skills and knowledge gained in their current work
- 84 per cent reported that their participation in the course increased their level of confidence in facing new challenges at their university
- participants reported significant increases in knowledge regarding the following:

  ⮞ cross-cultural communication skills

> ⟩ comfort and familiarity with technology
> ⟩ knowledge of the various components of international higher education.

Participants demonstrated a deep appreciation of the mentorship component of the course and a strong desire to continue to build upon their newly formed relationships.

The last point demonstrates the value of linking organizations and individuals in a common purpose and shows how cross-cultural links are esteemed.

The success of the pilot has secured funding from the Henry Luce Foundation and will build on the first course. Those who completed the first course desired to continue their learning, and the proposals for the next phase of this project are to:

- coordinate a second 'Connecting with the World' course for a new cohort of participants
- develop an advanced course for 'Connecting with the World' graduates that provides the next level of knowledge about managing international offices
- facilitate a Myanmar International Education Administrators network comprised of course graduates
- provide selected participants with short-term job-shadowing opportunities outside of Myanmar.

The elements of this e-course, which was specifically designed to serve Myanmar's strategic needs, will end the academic isolation that results from a war-torn and politically stifled society.

Syria

The third case study deals with the Global Platform for Syrian Students. This initiative is promoted by Jorge Sampaio, the former President of Portugal, and led by Dr Helena Barroco. It is dedicated to providing access to universities in safe-haven countries to alleviate the plight of students and academics displaced by the ever-worsening situation in Syria. Many students are in refugee camps without access to HE. The university partners involved have waived their tuition fees and the Global Platform awards scholarships for living costs. So far, the scheme has funded 100 students who have resumed their studies. There are 1,700 candidates waiting to be placed, with 500 places available in universities – despite fee waivers, however, no funds are available to send more students.

The vision of this rapid response programme is to take a holistic, student-centred approach, to work in partnerships, and be cost effective. Its aims are to:

- prevent the loss of a generation of university graduates
- prepare the future of Syria by investing in the higher education of forthcoming leaders
- shape the future by preparing leaders to build an inclusive society through education on dialogue, tolerance, resilience and hope and reconciliation
- save young people from despair.

Looking to the future

In each of the case studies, the commitment from the academic communities to rebuild their systems demonstrates their resilience and determination to protect their intellectual capital and bring on the next generation. It is clear that international partners and major stakeholders have a key role in this and the response of the international academic community is magnanimous and uplifting; however, as is shown here, academic assistance is a huge unmet humanitarian need. To this end, in July 2015 the York Accord was created. This is an agreement to address how best to protect and rebuild higher education during and after conflict.

Clause 9 states:

> We commit to fostering and strengthening the collective will to protect and rebuild higher education during and after conflict. We believe that through collective participation and actions, the impact of conflict on higher education can be mitigated and challenges turned to opportunities for rebuilding.

The accord also addresses the need to develop a global rapid response mechanism as an integral part of humanitarian aid; however, therein lies a major challenge, as a new funding model is needed, so that higher education is given the priority it requires to help restore peace and prosperity. As Professor Babury noted in his presentation, universities can and should be part of the response to emergencies and offer safe havens.

In Figure 2, Dr Barroco has proposed that HE should be prioritized in the international agenda and seen as an integral part of restoring societies – not as detracting from the immediate needs of a disaster. Rebuilding HE is part of restoring communities and economies.

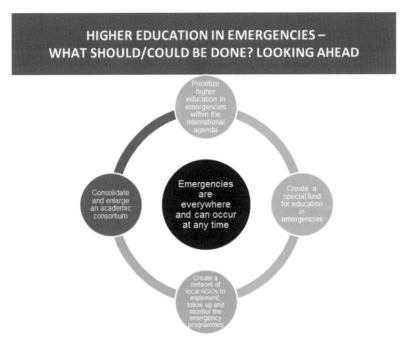

Figure 2: Rebuilding higher education

Source: Dr Helena Barroco.

Conclusions

In conclusion, the higher education sector is capable of making an immense contribution in terms of restoring peace and prosperity following natural or political disasters. This paper has focused on three countries. Each demonstrates that HE itself needs protecting and rebuilding. They have also shown that they have the resilience to continue in the most difficult circumstances. For Myanmar, coming out of isolation, engaging internationally is a major component of its academic development. However, these examples have also shown that emergency responses are fragmented; many organizations and agencies are at work and they make huge investments of time to raise money and navigate the global academic world. The proposal in Figure 2 for a unified system with an ongoing remit, plus the commitment made in the York Accord, must be explored further. Designing and managing a global fund that can remain nimble and which does not become hampered by bureaucracy will require a high degree of trust among all of the parties involved. The foundation exists as universities are already working across cultures and continents. The challenge for the HE sector is to draw all of these aspects into alignment, to gain acceptance by international aid agencies that assistance for the sector is as necessary as is support for basic education.

Acknowledgments

This paper has drawn heavily on the material supplied and presented by the speakers at Going Global and my thanks to them for making such cogent presentations. In addition, the York Accord has clearly articulated the dangers still facing universities and academics and offers a channel of support. My thanks to Dr John Law for bringing together the speakers in London and his assistance in the production of this paper and to all those who have brought this acutely pressing issue to a wider readership.

The higher education system in Russia: Reform process and dynamics of internationalization

Irina Arzhanova, Pavel Arefiev, Marina Baryshnikova, Dmitry Derman and Alexander Klyagin

This paper was prepared by the team of experts from the National Training Foundation as part of a larger research project titled 'A comparative analysis: Challenges and opportunities for large higher education systems'.

The implementation of this large-scale project has allowed us to evaluate the dynamics of the national higher education system within a broader international context, as well as to compare recent trends with other countries' experiences. Despite the specifications of particular countries and research approaches, the international team of experts has identified common features and development trends among modern higher education systems.

Even as early as the preliminary meeting of experts in New Delhi, all of the participants expressed a general view that the report does not sufficiently address an important avenue of higher education development – that is, the internationalization process. The same conclusion was drawn during the expert meeting in London at the Going Global conference.

It is important to emphasize that the topic of internationalization was not initially considered one of the leading issues in the structure of the report, though it was partially included in several parts of the common research. However, the cross-cultural format of the comparative study as well as the pressing character of the issues dealt with have made internationalization the subject of a special debate and turned it into a possible direction for future joint work.

What is internationalization?

Internationalization of higher education systems represents such a difficult and complex subject that it deserves special attention. It is not a coincidence that this issue was researched by various national and international organizations, including the OECD, which has applied its research methodology in Russia.

It is interesting to note that in recent years, despite the lack of a stated government strategy of internationalization, growing attention to and support for international cooperation programmes at the federal level indicate the priority of this issue within a national Russian context and a shift of governmental policy towards encouraging internationalization or at least considering it through evaluation at university development level.

However, studying internationalization is not limited to the simple counting of foreign students and professors, foreign language programmes, double degree programmes or other resources, introduced to foster international cooperation. These factors merely represent indicators, and give a first impression on how successful the internationalization process in a particular university may be. It is much more important to address the processes that lead to the **creation of a learning environment**, including quality of education and university management, which enable the achievement of high levels of international cooperation.

The same processes also ensure the competitiveness of a university on the domestic market. High-quality education is a guarantee of high enrolment rates and a professional team of professors and well-known researchers, as well as access to more substantial resources. But, in terms of the international competitiveness of a university, most of the processes, actions and results are 'success factors' or simply come under the category of 'must have' elements: for instance, the existence of an effective structural unit maintaining international relations, a sound internationalization strategy, educational programmes in a foreign language, an informative and promotional campaign abroad, internationally recognized 'names' among the professors and researchers, etc.

The same approach should be used not only for a particular higher education institution, but also when assessing the general level of internationalization demonstrated by the national higher education system. Is there a declared state strategy of internationalization? What resources are allocated for its support? How is the internationalization process encouraged and evaluated at the state level? How are its results presented to the wider international community?

Such an understanding of the internationalization process requires attention to the institutional environment in the national higher education system. As the history of the Russian education system represents a process of major institutional shifts, leading to increasingly complex public systems and organizational structures in the field, the aim of this paper is to examine **how the newest trends in the Russian higher education system correspond to the concept of internationalization as the national institutional context evolves.**

Institutional structure of the Russian higher education system

Given the fact that the educational system was imbedded into the planned economy, the collapse of the USSR led to an expected crisis in Russian education in the 1990s. As had often happened throughout Russian history, the internal crisis became a driver for the re-evaluation of the approach to reforming the system of higher education, taking into account the global trend of transitioning to a post-industrial stage of development.

Starting from 1992, Russia converted to a multilevel system of higher education and standardization. The federal law 'On Education' that came into force in 1992 introduced the concept of an educational standard in Russia. Article 7 of the law was dedicated to state educational standards.

Starting from 2003, the system of higher education in Russia received an impetus to integrate with the European educational space as part of the Bologna Process.[1]

Over the brief period from 2006 to 2013, Russia succeeded in performing an **optimization of the university network,** creating a nucleus of leading institutions (noted classical universities, national research universities, federal universities), as well as integrating the university network into the territorial and production complexes by setting up a subgroup of federal universities. This transformation stage was accompanied by a legal framework reform (a new federal law 'On Education in the Russia Federation' from 29 December 2012, #273-FZ), and a set trajectory for the further development of the country's education system.

At the federal level, the **Ministry of Education and Science of the Russian Federation** is responsible for developing and implementing the state policy and for the normative legal regulations in the field of education. The ministry determines the enrolment procedures and the final end-of-study assessment; it also sets federal educational standards and educational activity procedures and ensures the development of and keeps a register of model educational programmes. It is the founder of approximately half of public universities in the country (around 48 per cent of universities;[2] the founders of the remaining public universities are other state governmental bodies, at federal level, or regional authorities, at sub-federal level) and has the power to appoint the presidents of educational institutions within its jurisdiction.

In terms of financing higher education, the Ministry of Education and Science of Russia distributes the admission quotas and target enrolment figures for citizens using funds from the federal budget. It also acts as the state customer of federal target programmes[3] in the field of education. These two sources of financing ensure more than half of the financing for the higher education system in the country (55.3 per cent in 2013).[4]

Therefore, state institutions in the system of Russian higher education are the founders of public higher education institutions that **distribute state orders for educational and scientific services, determine the framework of the educational process and control its quality**. Nonetheless, despite this rather large number of functions within the higher education system performed by state agencies, higher education institutions have a sufficient amount of autonomy.

An important initiative is the transition of leading Russian higher education institutions into a new legal organizational form – autonomous institutions. This legal form gives the university more flexibility in using and allocating funds, including funds from extra-budgetary activities; it also simplifies procurement procedures and envisions the creation of a supervisory board with the number of state agency representatives not exceeding a third of the total number of supervisory board members. At the end of 2013, 43 universities in Russia (7.4 per cent of the total number of state universities) had the status of autonomous institutions.[5]

Another innovation that increases the autonomy of universities is the possibility of independently determining part of the content of educational programmes – up to 50 per cent for bachelor's programmes, and up to 70 per cent for master's programmes,[6] set out in the new federal state educational standards.

Despite the fact that the development of the higher education institutional system in Russia was historically dominated by the state, current institutional trends prove an emerging balance between state–private actors. The country's state education policy is **focused on enhancing the autonomy of state universities and on reducing the normative barriers** that prevent universities from flexibly responding to the changes in the educational service market.

Specificities of the university network in Russia and the internationalization process

An institutional feature of the higher education system in Russia as a country with mass higher education is a significant level of systemic diversification. It is characterized by the presence of both strong, internationally recognized universities and a large number of institutions that focus only on the national and even regional levels. Thus, it is logical that the approaches to the development and evaluation of the internationalization process should be differentiated as well.

The Ministry of Education and Science of Russia adopted this kind of approach, which included a range of initiatives – from strategic projects such as the '5–100' project (see below), with a required confirmation of universities' international competitiveness in the global rankings to annual performance monitoring. The latter evaluates a set of factors – geographical location, structure of the educational programmes, average entry score, employment of graduates, compatibility of education with the needs of the labour market etc. Based on these criteria, management decisions are made about the future of a particular university. As a result, several elements of the national higher education system emerged.

Currently, all educational institutions are classified as 'educational organizations of higher education', though there are several categories or types of educational organizations:

- leading classical universities of the Russian Federation
- federal universities
- national research universities.

The *leading classical universities* of Russia are Lomonosov Moscow State University and Saint Petersburg State University. These two universities are at the forefront of Russian education. They are traditionally ranked the highest among the country's universities by international ratings (according to QS World University Rankings 2014/2015 – places 114 and 223, respectively[7]). They have maximum organizational autonomy, as well as autonomy in research and educational activities. Their activity is regulated by a separate law of the Russian Federation: these universities have the right to implement educational programmes based on their own standards and to organize additional admission exams; their presidents are appointed by the President of the Russian Federation himself. Each university was given RUB 5 billion to implement its development programmes (with a duration of ten years). This category was formed in 2009.

Federal universities began appearing in 2006 through the merging together of several regional universities.[8] Each newly created federal university compiled a development programme that was then reviewed and approved by the Government of the Russian Federation. The main focus of the development programmes was to participate in the social and economic development of the regions in which the federal university was located and the neighbouring regions, and to provide the labour markets of these regions with highly qualified personnel. Additional financing to the amount of RUB 1 billion per year was allocated to implement these development programmes (the duration of the programme is ten years, with the first five years funded from the state budget). There are currently nine federal universities, and another one, Vernadsky Crimea State University, is in the process of creation.

Federal universities are meant to become the intellectual centres at the level of Russia's federal districts (several regions united administratively – there are currently nine federal districts in Russia), thus territorially diversifying the country's system of higher education, which is largely concentrated in two cities, Moscow and Saint Petersburg.

The *national research university* category was normatively consolidated in 2008. The majority[9] of the universities were given this category following a competitive selection of their development programmes. This ensured the group had a relatively high quality level right from the project launch. The main goal was to create a network of leading research universities at a national level on the basis of Russia's strongest universities (with the exception of Moscow State University and Saint Petersburg State University, which already enjoyed additional support).

The strategic mission of universities within the national research university group is to support the dynamic development of the country's science and technology sector, and to provide it with the required human resources, balanced in terms of headcount, training areas, qualification and age structure and taking into account the required renewal rate and the forecasted structural changes in science and the economy. The project to support national research universities (hereinafter referred to as NRU) presupposed the provision of additional financing to implement the development programme created in order to participate in competitive selection. The duration of the programme is ten years, with the first five presupposing financing from the state budget.

In 2013, the Ministry of Education and Science of Russia initiated the '5–100' project[10] in order to develop world-class universities. The goal of the project is to increase the international competitiveness of leading Russian universities and to have five of them included in the Top 100 of international ratings by 2020. Programmes were introduced to grow competitiveness, and 15 universities were selected overall to participate in the project. Of the 15 winners, 11 have the status of NRU, and three are federal universities. Recommendations from the project's international council played an important role in the competitive selection process.

Despite the fact that there were no special categories normatively established for the project winners, the project can also be viewed as strategic for the country's higher education.

Conceptually, it continues and develops the ideas that were at the basis of the NRU support project, **setting the participants more ambitious targets of increasing international competitiveness and attracting more resources to tackle the challenge.** The average volume of additional financing for a university under the programme in 2014 was RUB 725 million. Moreover, this project presupposes a number of management innovations (for projects through the Ministry of Education and Science of Russia): for the first time, an international council of experts plays an important role in a strategic project and also new, participating projects that failed to pass the intermediary assessment lose the financial support[11] of the state.

Conclusion

Over the past few years the Ministry of Education and Science of Russia has initiated a number of comprehensive strategic projects to form and support different elements of the higher education structure. A goal of internationalization is also integrated in the main process of structural changes and is influenced by the overall institutional dynamics.

The leading role of the state's strategic actions – such as the creation of the '5–100' project – remains persistent. However, different elements of the higher education system emerge, and as the balance of state–private actors changes, more autonomous higher education institutions are able to form their own methods of achieving the goal of internationalization within a given structure of incentives.

This dual institutional development will continue to influence the future of the internationalization process in Russia's higher education system.

Thus, the support the British Council granted to this international comparative study, the results of which were presented and discussed at the Going Global conference 2015, has laid a good foundation for the continuation of scientific research on major issues of shared concern with a long-term perspective. The internationalization of universities and/or their national orientation is a topic that deserves further study both in individual countries and in the framework of large-scale comparative projects.

Notes

[1] On 19 September 2003, at a meeting of ministers of education in Berlin, Russia joined the Bologna declaration on developing a single European higher education environment.

[2] According to the list of subordinate organizations (https://is-mon.ru/i/report/orglist/ – in Russian).

[3] Federal target programmes are a widely used tool of programme and objective financing in the Russian federation. The majority of strategic educational projects described below are implemented as part of federal target programmes.

[4] According to official statistics published on the site of the Ministry of Education and Science of Russia (http://opendata.mon.gov.ru/ – in Russian).

[5] According to official statistics published on the site of the Ministry of Education and Science of Russia (see URL in note 4).

[6] See N. Drantusova and E. Knyazev (2014) 'The European dimension and institutional transformation in Russian higher education'. *Educational Studies*, 2, 109–31.

[7] See www.topuniversities.com/university-rankings/world-university-rankings/2014.

[8] Immanuel Kant Baltic Federal University was the only one created without a merger, and was based on Immanuel Kant Russian State University.

[9] During the pilot stage of the project, two universities were assigned to the national research university category without competitive selection.

[10] See http://5top100.ru (in Russian).

[11] Based on the results of the first year, it was decided to stop financially supporting the development programme of one of the universities.

ASEAN cross-cultural skills development
Jonathan Ledger

Introduction

Furthering the Going Global 2015 World Café discussion 'ASEAN Economic Community: What now for tertiary education?', this paper seeks to demonstrate how organizational cultures develop when connecting people and ideas through international partnerships and how this leads to borderless innovation that continually anchors and sustains innovation and creativity for further growth for all involved.

This paper will:

- seek to show that connecting people and ideas across cultures produces internationally significant innovation and look at the nature of that innovation
- highlight the evolution of cross-cultural connections and networks of innovation
- demonstrate the impact on structures and operations of skills and education partners.

Background

The establishment of the ASEAN Economic Community is set to have a huge direct impact on education and employability opportunities within the region and on international engagement from ASEAN. In technical and vocational training and education (TVET), a number of regional trends are already emerging in anticipation of increased education harmonization. These reflect the mix of developed and emerging economies in the region.

It is important to set the context, using the example of a Vietnamese client that operates as a joint stock company and that was, until recently, 100 per cent state owned. As a corporation operating in a socialist republic, trading processes and social expectations are almost the complete opposite of those experienced in the UK. The Vietnamese corporation at the heart of the partnership is keen to drive radical change that encourages more effective use of staff resources and business growth. Senior management ambitions have a strong desire to pierce the heart of long-established practices to produce a global operating model that sets it apart from its competitors, without killing off the 'body' in which it operates.

Borderless partnership

One pioneering skills programme between Proskills UK and Vietnam's leading building materials manufacturer has built on the UK-wide and regional expertise of policymakers, employers, and technical and vocational education providers to develop and deliver practical initiatives that are not only creating higher-level skills, but are bringing about innovation through training delivery and whose resulting business impact is reaching much further than originally anticipated. Throughout this process, all of the partners have imported learning across borders from other regions and developed models of collaboration within the ASEAN region – and then used this to update their learning to be reapplied back outside the region.

Proskills UK Group supports employers, training providers, colleges and governments across the globe to bring about systemic change using vocational training, education and competence assessment. Currently, Proskills is working on a number of long-term industry-based projects from Europe to Asia and is proud to be the joint winner of the British Council's prestigious International Skills Partnership of the Year 2015 award for this work in Vietnam. This is the second time in two years that Proskills has won this award.

This particular skills partnership aims to create a transnational skills development programme supported and underpinned by robust, high-quality skills processes originally developed in the UK, but transposed for use by business in Vietnam. The work with an employer in Vietnam aims to develop new national occupational skills standards, supporting the vocational teaching curriculum as well as competence assessment, capable resource development and the implementation of new skills system approaches within five business sectors.

In turn, this combined approach was designed to feed directly into the development of the National Qualifications Framework, both in

Vietnam and in the wider ASEAN region through the ASEAN Reference Framework. In creating this model, the UK aims to share credible expertise with an economy and culture very different from its own and that of Europe in general. This transitional journey aims to create a new dynamic approach to cultural changes in skills perspectives and to demonstrate how business can be at the forefront, effectively contributing to its own skills and capabilities as well as those of the nation, the wider region and beyond. The final aim of the work is to develop a transitional model that can be moved to any country in the world in a contextualized and locally applied manner.

Business impact

The direct impact of this borderless skills programme in terms of measurable numbers is easy to ascertain:

- 120 members of staff in-country have contributed to the development of the new standards and curriculum
- 500 staff have been consulted on these skills standards
- 30 staff have received trainer and assessor training in 15 sites across the country
- five sets of new occupational standards and matching curriculums over five levels have been created.

Top-down innovation: more importantly, involvement in the innovation and creation process has been led from the top and has permeated its way throughout the affected business units and beyond into another 40 company divisions – incorporating staff ranging from the CEO through to operational employees at all levels on the factory floors.

Nurturing pilot: the newly developed National Occupational Skills Standards (NOSS) have been accepted by the Vietnamese agency responsible for standards of use across the industry in Vietnam, recognizing their international transferability. The training and assessment approaches have provided a nurturing pilot to demonstrate the new transposed methodology, ensuring best fit and practical use.

Wider reach: an unexpected and immediate impact is that the 'common' standards, which include health and safety, have already been adopted by the wider group of businesses. These are seen as having a profound business impact and are applicable to all areas of the corporation's scope.

Figure 1: Integrated cross-cultural skills innovation

Broad impact: the common standards will impact on:

- health and safety
- environmental issues
- materials usage
- wastage
- leadership and management
- staff morale and staff turnover
- recruitment and training processes.

Activities creating lessons for all

Leaping the first cultural barrier: language

When we talk about language, there is a tendency to assume we are talking about the different dialogues of nations. Instead, by language I mean here the terms used to describe the structures, policies, processes, delivery methodology and more. It can also be used to describe the aspirations that a country, industry or employer seeks to realize.

The partners spent a lot of time understanding each other's language and used this as part of the process of alignment, which is critical to the success of the partnership. This removed much, if not all, of the miscommunication that can result from the use of differing terms. It provided a mechanism whereby cultural differences were identified and bridged at the outset. Where cultural differences were not bridged, they were identified, understood and planned for. Cultural differences are not just about the way each society and its individuals behave and react in their own nations, but how this permeates through their policies, structures and implementation methods. Culture is a catch-all description for the beating heart of a nation, the fabric that weaves a society as one cloth.

One key term, potentially the most important in this instance, is that of 'TVET' itself. TVET is traditionally more of a phraseology used to indicate a work-based or hands-on programme of training and practice. When working across borders, experience has shown time and time again that it is generally better to start from a position of 'skills development' because this is increasingly being used by employers and is gradually replacing the supply-led system language of 'technical and vocational education and training' (TVET). 'Skills development' demonstrates a significant shift in emphasis away from supply-led systems that dictate the mode of learning and the pathways to be followed.

Instead, 'skills development' places emphasis on the acquisition of skills in demand by employers in the workplace – be these soft, generic or technically specific skills, and regardless of where, when or how they are acquired. This change of emphasis alters the relationship between training provision and the industry, allowing for a greater range of types of learning environment, increased flexibility of content and improved engagement by relevant stakeholders. It allows employers and industry to be much more in control of policy, strategy and skills delivery, and of course to bear an increased portion of the cost, while using educational expertise of delivery partners to support the innovation and growth of the most appropriate support and delivery system, contextualized to realize aspirations.

Facilitating innovation across borders

The partnership made use of a core programme of UK-based expertise that was transportable across the globe in a unique, multicultural way. Using the essence of its long-developed skills council, combined with its National Skills Academy, Proskills was able to demonstrate a flexible approach to skills and competence in faraway nations delivered in a contextualized manner and implemented with great success.

It was essential for all parties to really get under the skin of and truly understand the way in which each other's skills system operated currently, and to discern how this might be best used to shape the system going forward.

Working in partnership with the Vietnamese employer, an initial detailed mapping process was undertaken of the Vietnamese corporation's five current sets of building materials-related skills standards. This was linked with both a functional and occupation analysis of the existing 67 business job roles so that those of parity could be accurately matched and fully contextualized for local corporate use. The same analysis was completed with the five sets of curriculum, with content being mapped against the newly developed standards and then contextualized to ensure that they would deliver the knowledge and skills required. Coupled with this activity was a huge ongoing programme of training and assessment resource capability development, involving not only 'train the trainer' and 'train the assessor' programmes, but lots of in-country coaching and mentoring to ensure robust and fair competence decision making.

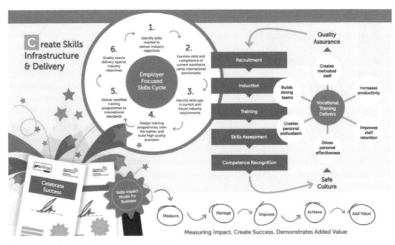

Figure 2: Borderless skills model

During the initial analysis and mapping exercise, much time was spent with Vietnamese staff exploring and developing an understanding of cultural contexts and how that transpires through working practices. The cultural context of working practices – the opposing socialist business principles – brought about the opportunity to immerse staff in an exploration of what was required to maintain a successful business, rather than what the current practice and situation was. Effectively this process began to remove inward-looking views and created outward mobilizing structures and methodology to compete in a regional and global economy. Understanding the background to the business and social context of individual and corporate skills requirement was to prove absolutely essential for the enablement of transitional development.

By working in total partnership with the company and its staff in this detailed way, as well as taking into account the national and regional system requirements, it led to the development of a robust new NOSS for building materials and a reduction in cultural divide.

Cultural transition

The cultural sharing of actual and perceived differences has been challenged, discussed and built into the programme through wide-ranging consultations within and outside the organization at a local and national level. There has been a lot of practical discussion with the management of the Vietnamese corporation as well as the factory management and operating staff to ensure that all perspectives are understood, recognized and respected.

Most critically, this was not a UK-created programme, but rather a facilitated transitional process that applied the best learning from within the partner's countries and from other countries. By developing a true understanding and a purposeful bridging of cultural difference, the Vietnamese team created their own impact by developing a skills system that they know they can sustain moving forward.

The curriculum has been further developed in partnership using the expertise of a UK-based further education college, thus extending the reach of the partnership activity. The curriculum has been developed, tested and approved for use by the Vietnamese building materials industry expert technical panel and is now live and being used in the current pilot programme.

Innovation also came through the Vietnamese corporation's integration of the newly developed skills processes throughout the core of the company's human resource systems, while retaining its robustness in terms of competent business performance on the factory floor. Real challenges emerged that in many cases forced alterations in long-established business processes. Invariably, this first meant a cultural shift in all staff perspectives – sometimes immediate and revolutionary in nature, sometimes gradual and evolutionary.

When two groups of people from different countries come together to work jointly on what could be considered opposing sides, there is inevitably a point at which the connection becomes the centre of creation and innovation, with the challenge of culture shift taking place through the resulting implementation.

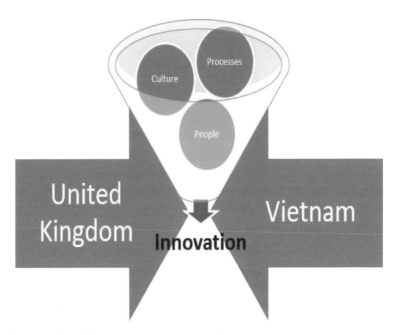

Figure 3: Combining cultures generating innovation

Organizational development

A partnership like this has had a profound effect on the way the network of skills partners think, work and deliver. For example, organizations within the partnership have changed their international operating structures to better mirror the way in which the Vietnamese corporation works so that a common way of working becomes a natural process, rather than a special event.

The administrative and logistical processes through which the skills partnership is managed and implemented have been challenged and changed to balance the cultural needs of the overseas partner. In its simplest form, this emerged as a change in the way documents were produced and formatted; at its most complex, the process flows and language used in contracts were enhanced. This in turn has provided some very effective process reductions, improved process flows and increased appreciation of individual needs and wants. Even the personal safety and security of those staff involved in the overseas delivery have been enhanced because of the innovative way in which this project has developed and been delivered.

Lessons learned from the creation, implementation and management of this project have been extracted and added into programmes operating in other parts of the ASEAN region and across the globe into which they fit and are applicable. This will no doubt give rise to further development outside Vietnam and re-importation at a later stage – thus continuing the global development cycle.

During this development cycle, the Vietnamese partners spent time in the UK with Proskills and its delivery partners. It was seen as essential for Vietnamese corporation staff to experience first-hand the operating environment in which the offered experience originates and the benefits reaped by UK employers. This UK tour gave Vietnamese participants a real insight into the ways in which UK businesses use skills development to improve, grow and sustain business through the skills of their employees. It also helped to demonstrate differences in productivity between the two cultures in the workplace. Most importantly, all of the Vietnamese delegates were given opportunities to have in-depth discussions with operational and managerial staff so that they could go beyond the mechanics of running the business and start to understand the cultural and 'unsaid' thought processes that occur.

Conclusions

Cultural change through innovation and business development does not in any sense diminish the challenge of ensuring that the productivity of everybody, whether relatively low-skilled or high-skilled, continuously improves or is at least sustained. The following conclusions can be drawn.

- **Don't stop at good:** from the outset of this partnership, the preparation has been second to none. Dedicated teams have worked together to ensure that both sides are completely understood and that where they exist, perceived and real barriers have been removed, overcome and challenged. In order to take the good facets of any project and make them better, a continual review process has been employed so that the skills partnership creates the best possible impact and cultural change possible. Just ticking the 'preparation box' is no longer enough. When something good has been created, review it carefully to make it even better; manage it further to make it the very best that can be achieved.
- **Engage employers:** the use of skills as the bedrock of productivity gains requires the delivery of skills to make a measurable positive difference to business and enable employees to be the best they possibly can be. This is not only a corporate or governmental ambition, but an individual aspiration. Employers who demand the highest-value skills and training possible from skills providers, and colleges who deliver the

very best technical capability, do so with the need to create innovation through global cultures.

- **Create symbiosis:** cultural understanding and exchange do not come about merely by working with an international organization. Culture is developed by consciously considering and enabling all staff from all organizations to work symbiotically together. So dynamic and explosive is the cultural impact, it requires the consultant partner to accept from the outset that the partners and client will all have a direct and indirect, expected and unexpected impact on the way it does business tomorrow, both within the UK and overseas – and not just in Vietnam, but in all of its global operations.

- **Revisit the brief:** throughout the process of international partnership, it has proven essential to continually revisit the original project brief and client ambition to ensure that the cultural impacts support the delivery of the ambitions in an acceptable way.

- **Align thinking:** the organizations involved in this project have become 'twinned' and gone on to develop more strands of activity to boost business performance through skills. This long-term, self-sustaining distance partnership would not have been possible if the cultural bridge had not been traversed in a way that enabled both organizations and countries to align their thinking, methodologies and delivery models. The smelting pot of cultures, views and expression that is naturally provided by the vast array of people involved in such a project can only provide an opportunity of change and growth that is to be welcomed and exploited.

For more information on this project

- To view the video clip about this project, see here: www.proskills. co.uk/vietnam-moves-towards-sector-based-skills/.
- To read more related articles about this project, see here: www.proskills. co.uk/new-thinking-and-a-cultural-change-in-vietnam/ and www. proskills.co.uk/competence-testing-and-curriculum-development-in-vietnam/.

Section 3

Knowledge, technology
and innovation in
internationalization

Editors' introduction to Section 3

Knowledge, technology and innovation in internationalization

This final collection of papers, Section 3, all focuses on particular case studies and examples of knowledge transfer, technology and innovation in internationalization. The authors offer their experiences with reflections on how internationalization as a process – and even a 'state' and a context – all provide a vehicle for innovation, or are the very vehicle by which innovation and knowledge transfer can be shared and thereby enriched.

Mirza and Lawrence write about education reform in the Kingdom of Bahrain, and highlight internationalization as one of the most significant reforms. The role internationalization has played in the strategy to improve the skills gap has been of major significance. **Cometti**, focusing on vocational and professional education in Brazil, highlights the innovative models employed. The role internationalization has played has been significant for Brazil. With a focus on Japan, **Kitamori's** paper explores innovative ways of developing PhD education, and ways of enabling and encouraging PhD students to become innovative themselves. Education–industry links are key to this, but so too are the international links the author has developed through the Going Global platform. International contexts have enriched and inspired new ways of developing PhD holders 'to become the bearers and creators of innovation' (Kitamori). **Tan,** in exploring the Hong Kong context where he is based, offers us an insight into the work of the Knowledge Transfer Office at Hong Kong Baptist University. This plays a major role in steering and enabling innovation at the University. He draws comparisons from the international context and the learning his institution has derived from this. The next two papers, by **Mark Thorley** and by **Christina Slade** have each a focus on creative industries. Thorley explores the way that catalysing creativity and innovation in, specifically, the music industry is made much more productive and even exciting through an international platform. The result is not only international links, but graduates who are, as a result, fitted for global careers. Slade's paper is on the importance of the creative industries to her university, Bath Spa, which works internationally to make links with partners across national boundaries, to ensure that students following creative education programmes have the preparation for the international context in which they will need to work, against an international backdrop. The final paper in this section is by **Hearn, Achampong, Van't Land, and Manners.** It explores the strength that international universities' networks can bring to the higher education context, providing what are, effectively, 'experimental laboratories' in which ideas, new knowledge and solutions can be generated. These networks are clearly acting as catalysts for innovation, knowledge transfer and development.

The discussions arising out of and inspired by the Going Global conferences have inspired innovative thinking about how internationalization can drive innovation, knowledge transfer and change. The examples in this section show how this can happen.

Creating a national innovation and skills ecosystem through international bridges

Cameron Mirza and Annamarie Lawrence

Introduction

The Kingdom of Bahrain has seen various waves of education reform since the country became a pioneer of public education in the Gulf Cooperation Corporation (GCC) thanks to its offer of free schooling to citizens in the 1930s. Of all the stages of education reform in the GCC, internationalization is one of the most significant (Knight, 2013; Donn and Al Manthri, 2010). This chapter will look at the role of internationalization in developing Bahrain's national innovation and skills ecosystem and highlight the impact across a number of stakeholders within it.

In discussing the impact of internationalization and innovation systems, it is important to define what these terms mean. Leading academic Jane Knight defines internationalization as a dynamic process of incorporating international/intercultural elements to the education experience (Knight, 1997). This includes, but is not limited to, the cross-border transfer of people, programmes, processes, curriculum, knowledge, ideas and quality standards across regions or national borders (ibid.). This definition encompasses the internationalization at all levels of innovation and the skills ecosystem and allows the integration of the various actors within the system. The national systems approach to innovation is described by Lundvall (1992) as including social institutions, macroeconomic regulations, financial systems, education and communication infrastructure. The OECD describes it as an interaction that facilitates the flow of technology, information and knowledge across actors in the system, which form complex relationships to produce, distribute and apply knowledge (OECD, 1997). The OECD also states that international knowledge transfer is an important part of any innovation system.

Along with its Gulf neighbours, Bahrain has stated a clear desire to become a knowledge economy and move its reliance away from energy resources as the main source of income for the country. This desire is at the core of the country's economic reforms. While the population of Bahrain is 1.2 million, only half of this number are Bahraini nationals, with the remainder made up of expatriates employed to fill the jobs Bahraini nationals are unable to fulfil. Bahrain has experienced challenges in ensuring graduates from higher education have the skills needed for the job market. This skills gap negatively impacts on all international indicators of innovation, including graduates who are capable of generating innovation and quality of scientific institutions.

Under the governance of the Ministry of Education, the Higher Education Council (HEC) was formed in 2006 to regulate and promote the higher education agenda in Bahrain. The HEC is playing a critical role in addressing the skills gap and enhancing innovation through coordinating various aspects of the ecosystem and formalizing the interactions between actors within the system. In 2014 the HEC published Bahrain's first National Higher Education Strategy. The national strategy was developed after extensive consultation with all stakeholders within the innovation and skills ecosystem. This provided an opportunity for a wide variety of stakeholders to contribute to the future role of education and research in innovation for the country. The key themes of the National Higher Education Strategy include: quality enhancement, skills for the future, strategic access, becoming a regional hub for higher education, technology in education and entrepreneurship. Strategic priorities are outlined under each of the themes, and various aspects of internationalization are included within each of the priorities as the HEC looks to international best practice and benchmarks to implement the strategy. Work is well underway on the implementation of many of the strategic priorities. While it is too early to clearly measure the impact of this work into tangible outputs at any meaningful level, there is hard evidence that internationalization has had an impact, contributing to Bahrain's progress in building a national innovation and skills ecosystem.

Creating an innovative and skilled workforce

Following the 2014 GCC regional economic forum, consultants Ernst & Young (2014) published a report stating that 29 per cent of employers in the GCC feel that the education system prepares students with the necessary technical skills and training for the workplace. This means that at least 71 per cent of employers are not happy with the skills of graduates. In the same report, 64 per cent of students feel that their education system is preparing them adequately for the world of work; this means that more than a third of all students believe that the system is failing them. The overall message of this report is that there is a clear disconnect between higher education and employers in Bahrain, which is further compounded by employers wanting to engage Bahraini graduates as their first choice. There have been a number of previous studies into this 'skills gap' among GCC graduates, many of which state the same conclusion, that 'critical thinking' or 'problem-solving' skills are one of the key areas lacking among graduates (Donn and Al Manthri, 2010; Jones and Punshi, 2013). However, when it comes to skills that may lead to innovation, critical thinking and problem solving are fundamental. With this in mind, GCC education policymakers have made the skills gap issue one of their key priorities. Many discussions are taking place among education professionals in the GCC as to why graduates lack these skills. Some would highlight the use of very traditional rote-learning teaching and learning methods prevalent within the Bahraini primary and high school sector as one of the reasons.

The HEC in Bahrain's efforts to improve this skills gap are focused on four key areas: improving access to a diversified higher education sector, improving the overall quality of the higher education sector, improving student performance and skills and increasing the use of technology in higher education. Internationalization has been a key part of the strategy for reducing the skills gap. In 2008 HRH the Crown Prince of Bahrain established Bahrain Polytechnic, a public higher education institution set up to address the skills gap. International expertise was used to help set up the Polytechnic and to ensure international models of best practice in university–industry collaboration. The success of the Polytechnic is seen in local capacity-building through internationalization. A deliberate knowledge transfer programme between international staff and Bahraini staff has produced evidence of best-practice higher education/industry integration.

Part of the role of internationalization has been to create a more diversified higher education sector. This has been done in a pragmatic way by developing joint programmes with overseas universities, supplemented by a few international branch campuses. For the purpose of this discussion, our definition of an international branch campus is a foreign institution setting up a physical presence in countries to offer programmes of study. There are various models of branch campuses with differing models of ownership and levels of integration and autonomy between the parent university and the branch campus (Lane, 2011). The use of international programmes and branch campuses as a strategy for knowledge transfer and skill development is a deliberate effort to allow students access to high-quality international teaching and curricula and the opportunity to study abroad as part of their study experience. It is hoped that this taste of an international faculty and curricula will allow students access to modes of teaching and learning that enable them to develop critical thinking skills alongside their subject knowledge or technical skills.

Another initiative to better align graduate skills and industry needs is the establishment of a national employer-led steering committee, with representation from both Bahraini and international companies. This committee has helped develop the nation's first national graduate skills guide, which outlines job forecasts, key skills required and qualifications for 15 key sectors in Bahrain. This has allowed universities to take a more integrated industry-focused approach to curriculum design and the skills development of students. At national policy level, the committee allows the HEC to ensure education supply aligns with future employment needs. Another key initiative is to make it mandatory for universities to have their own strategy geared at ensuring students are employable, with a clear plan of how employability will be embedded within the curriculum.

It is mandatory that all new international programmes within Bahraini higher education institutes demonstrate that they are linked to labour market needs. The overseas university must have rigorous quality assurance procedures in place to ensure that the student experience is not compromised. International programmes and branch campuses have been established with a large percentage of teaching staff from the parent university rather than from local employees to ensure international best practice is embedded in quality teaching and learning standards. The desire is for international staff who teach at local campuses to create formalized systems for mentoring Bahraini staff in order to transfer knowledge of best practice. There are some very good institutional examples of knowledge transfer occurring as a result of this internationalization.

Improving the quality of higher education has been instigated using policy instruments. One example is the introduction of accreditation through the British Accreditation Council. In addition, the Bahrain Qualifications Framework was established in tandem with the Scottish Qualifications Framework. This is supported by providing local education professionals with capacity-building training from international partners, including aspiration partners such as Massachusetts Institute of Technology (MIT). Practical workshops have been offered and supported by the British Council in order to raise capacity in the sector. The benefit of utilizing internationalization for capacity building is mentioned by Stephan Vincent-Lancrin in the OECD 2007 report 'Cross-border tertiary education'.

Vincent-Lancrin states that utilizing international professionals as part of a capacity-building strategy is particularly useful where local education supply does not meet education demand, as is the case in Bahrain.

Improving student performance has been accelerated by focusing on improving teaching skills and revising student assessment. In 2015, Bahrain launched its first professional standards framework, which was developed in partnership with the Higher Education Academy UK. This framework is based on three key pillars: core skills, core knowledge and professional values. The launch of the framework signifies a clear shift in approach – that by building teaching capacity it should have a positive impact on student performance. Student assessment has also been made more robust through local universities offering joint degree programmes with international partners who take responsibility for benchmarking and assessing students.

The Global Innovation Index (GII) 2015 ranks Bahrain at number 59 out of 125 countries for its levels of innovation. However, when looking closer at the rankings, Bahrain does not score well on research, especially high-impact research. In 2014 Bahrain ranked 119 globally for research output (Scopus). This poor ranking is not conducive with the knowledge economy aspirations of Bahrain, and reform is therefore required to improve the country's research outputs. This research ranking is measured by several indicators that include patents, capacity to innovate, knowledge-intensive workers and innovative entrepreneurs.

In 2014 the HEC released its National Research Strategy, alongside its previously mentioned National Higher Education Strategy. The focus is to build a sustainable framework through leveraging international partnerships, which may impact on five key areas of work. These key areas cover:

- research collaboration between industry and higher education
- upgrading the quality of scientific research
- increasing the supply of science and technology students
- enhanced use of technology in education
- developing innovative entrepreneurs.

However, given the current global economic conditions, gaining additional public funds for research is unrealistic. Therefore, the HEC has looked at various models of industry–university collaboration for research. A successful example of this is the Royal College of Surgeons Ireland's (RCSI) Bahrain-based branch campus. RCSI Bahrain was established in 2004 to train doctors. In 2015 RCSI formed a research partnership with the John Hopkins Healthcare Company owned by the Saudi Aramco oil company.

The John Hopkins Healthcare Company is located in the Kingdom of Saudi Arabia, about an hour's drive from the Bahraini border. With John Hopkins University being a world-class name in the field of medical research, the relationship with the RCSI Bahrain campus provides significant opportunity for capacity building among Bahraini and Saudi health-care professionals and researchers. This type of collaboration provides a significant opportunity to leverage the existing relationship of each institution for further international joint research projects. Such access for Bahraini and Saudi research professionals is a great example of how internationalization can be used for capacity building and to improve innovation outputs from the countries.

Legislation has also been used to ensure that research is prioritized. Universities now have to appoint deans of research and are encouraged to reward and recognize research through promotion and a reduction in teaching hours. Capacity building through international partnerships has further provided an impetus for change, including initiatives to develop a university self-assessment toolkit in partnership with Stanford University. There has been dialogue with the Research Council UK to help establish a transparent process for managing a central research fund for which universities can apply. While traditionally Bahraini universities tended to work in silos, there are now examples of excellence in research collaboration. One such is the Royal College of Surgeons and the Arabian Gulf University pooling finances and expertise to undertake collaborative medical research. This increase in collaboration is being supplemented by the development of a National Research Impact Framework based on the UK Research Evaluation Framework. As in the UK, this tool may be used by universities applying for funding to demonstrate institutional research impact and expertise. This will allow a more targeted use of funds and ensure maximum output from national research funding.

Internationalization is also being utilized to help create a knowledge-intensive workforce through increasing the supply of students in STEM-related subjects. In making these programmes attractive to students, local universities are partnering with overseas universities such at George Washington in the USA or South Bank in the UK. Offering these international joint degrees has attracted a small increase in the number of students choosing to study STEM in Bahrain, from 9 per cent in 2013 to 12 per cent in 2015. In addition to joint degrees, Bahrain is now strategically using overseas scholarships by prioritizing students who wish to study STEM subjects abroad. The final aspect in closing the innovation gap is the promotion of an enhanced use of technology in higher education, supported by the development of a credit-bearing module in entrepreneurship in partnership with the Ministry of Higher Education Oman. This module will be made available from 2016 to all students in higher education.

Impact at a national level

When the significant national strategic document 'Bahrain Vision 2030' was published in 2009, terms such as 'entrepreneurship' and 'innovation' were generally used only within a specific context and were not necessarily a normal part of daily language in education and the public and private sectors. With a number of international conferences on various focused aspects of innovation and entrepreneurship being hosted in Bahrain during the past five years, the general rhetoric has changed, however, and now includes concepts of innovation and entrepreneurship. In the public sector there is significant reference to innovation, not only when discussing education and research, but also when looking at ways in which the public sector can utilize technology such as creating 'smart cities' within Bahrain. Hosting international innovation and entrepreneurship experts, for both consultation work and conference presentations, has helped to raise awareness of the need for better coordination within the system for mutual benefit. The traditional approach of ministries being treated as silos competing for budgets has given way to ministries requesting funding for cross-ministry projects that support the development of innovation and skills formation. One example of this is the Ministry of Social Development working with Bahrain Development Bank, the Ministry of Labour and educational institutions to offer home-based business access to funding, markets and entrepreneurial skills and training.

There is some evidence that internationalization has already had a national impact in terms of capacity building to support innovation and skills formation in the field of health-care science. In 2006, the Royal College of Surgeons Ireland's Bahrain branch campus added nursing education to its programmes, in addition to its medical training. Best practice in health-care education that was brought from the parent campus in Ireland has had a demonstrable impact in Bahrain's health-care industry. Prior to the college offering its nursing programme, the number of Bahrainis choosing nursing as a profession was very low – meaning the health-care industry needed to look to expatriate nurses to fill the gap. Traditionally, nursing was deemed as an undesirable career choice for Bahrainis for cultural reasons. The Ministry of Health partnered with RCSI to change the perceptions of nursing as a career choice and undertook a promotional campaign among school leavers. As a result, the number of Bahrainis applying to study nursing has increased by 150 per cent (Cowman, 2014).

The gradual improvement of Bahrain's innovation ecosystem was evident in the internationally respected key indicator of the Global Competiveness Index produced annually by the World Economic Forum. This index is often used as a key metric by international industry and universities when evaluating potential partnerships for trade, investment, relocation and research.

The following table outlines the innovation index within Bahrain's ranking of the Global Competitiveness Report.

Table 1: The World Economic Forum Global Competitiveness Report's 2014 and 2015 for the Kingdom of Bahrain

Bahrain's innovation rankings out of a total of 144 countries		
Parameter within the 'innovation' index	2013–14	2014–15
Capacity for innovation	82	65
Quality of scientific research institutes	114	102
Company spending on R&D	99	85
University–industry collaboration	121	90
Government procurement of advanced tech products	24	23
Availability of scientists and engineers	69	58
PCT patents and applications per million population	56	69

There is an improvement in seven out of eight indicators of this year's rankings. What is of particular significance is the steep rise in the university–industry collaboration. This shows a tangible impact in terms of the work of the HEC to ensure all higher education institutions integrate industry into their curricula and create better alignment with its needs.

Although the fall in the 'Availability of scientists and engineers' parameter is detrimental to the development of an innovation economy, the rise in all other indicators is firm evidence of progress in the development of the skills and innovation ecosystem. While the framework is being built and progress is being made, it is now a question of when that delivers a sustainable and innovative economy through national, organizational and cultural readiness with collaborative internationalization at its core.

Conclusion

The knowledge management guru Karl Wiig (2007) states that people are society's knowledge agents, who develop through formal and informal education; Lundvall (1992) says that it is the coordination of people within the system that allows knowledge to turn into innovation. The work of the HEC in the Kingdom of Bahrain is focusing both on developing the skills for citizens to become Bahrain's future knowledge agents and taking the lead coordinating role of all the actors within the broader skills and innovation system. It is hoped that the long-term outcome of this work will see a future generation of Bahraini innovators and knowledge agents who make a positive impact in terms of economic success and society's knowledge development.

References

Cowman, S. (2014) 'Editorial'. *Journal of Advanced Nursing*, 70 (11), 2417–18.

Donn, G. and Al Manthri, Y. (2010) *Globalisation and Higher Education in the Arab Gulf States*. Didcot: Symposium Books.

Ernst & Young (2014) 'Perspectives on GCC youth and employment'. Riyadh: Ernst and Young Saudi Arabia.

Global Innovation Index (2015) Online. www.globalinnovationindex.org/content/page/GII-Home/ (accessed 14 October 2015).

Jones, D. and Punshi, R. (2013) *The Paradox of Plenty*. Dubai: Motivate Publishing.

Knight, J. (1997) 'Internationalisation of higher education: A conceptual framework.' In J. Knight and H. De Wit (eds), *Internationalisation of Higher International Education in Asia Pacific*. Amsterdam: European Association for International Education/IDP Education Australia.

— (2013) 'Crossborder education in the Gulf countries: Changes and challenges'. In G. Donn and Y. Al Manthri (eds), *Education in the Broader Middle East: Borrowing a baroque arsenal*. Didcot, Oxford: Symposium Books.

Lane, J.E. (2011) 'Importing private higher education: International branch campuses'. *Journal of Comparative Policy Analysis: Research and Practice*, 13 (4), 367–81.

Lundvall, B.-A. (1992) *National Systems of Innovation. Towards a theory of innovation and interactive learning*. London: Pinter.

OECD, World Bank (1997) 'National Innovation Systems'. Paris: OECD.

OECD, World Bank, Vincent-Lancrin, S. (2007) 'Developing capacity through cross-border tertiary education'. In *Cross-border Tertiary Education: A way towards capacity*. Geneva: OECD. 47–102.

Wiig, K. (2007) 'Effective societal knowledge management'. *Journal of Knowledge Management*, 11 (5), 141–56.

World Economic Forum (2015) 'The Global Competitiveness Report 2014–15'. Online. http://reports.weforum.org/global-competitiveness-report-2014-2015/ (accessed 28 September 2015).

3.3

Federal Institutes: A new Brazilian model of vocational, scientific and technological education

Nilton N. Cometti

The beginning: A timeline of vocational and professional education in Brazil

The Federal Network of Vocational, Scientific and Technological Education celebrated its 106th anniversary on 23 September 2015. It comprises 38 federal institutes, two federal centres for technological education, the Pedro II College and 23 technical schools linked to the University.

In little more than 100 years, in 2014 the Federal Network has reached more than 1 million youth and workers who have attended courses in engineering, general education, technical qualification, technology, teaching licences and apprenticeship. The service extends to postgraduate programmes.

The official history of education in Brazil begins with the signing of Decree number 7,566 by President of the Republic Nilo Peçanha on 23 September 1909 that created 19 schools of apprentices and craftsmen. However, well before that, during the colonization of Brazil, crafts were being taught to the indigenous people and slaves (Brazil, 2009).

More than a century after being established, the professional and technological Federal Network has undergone various transformations. In 1937, the schools of apprentices and craftsmen were converted into industrial high schools. That year, the Brazilian constitution specifically addressed technical, professional and industrial education, establishing in article 129: 'The pre-vocational and vocational education for the lower classes is, in education, the first duty of the State ... '

In 1941 vocational education, then considered to include mid-level and high schools, gave way to industrial and technical schools, and students trained in technical courses were allowed to enter higher education in the same area of their training.

In 1959 the institutions came to be known as Federal Technical Schools, with autonomy over teaching and management. In 1971 the Law of Guidelines and Bases for Brazilian Education was published mandating that all high school curriculum must be technical and professional. As a result, the Federal Technical Schools significantly increased enrolment and deployed new technical courses.

In 1978 three Federal Technical Schools (Paraná, Minas Gerais and Rio de Janeiro) were transformed into Federal Centres for Technological Education – CEFETs. This change gave the institutions another assignment, creating operation engineers and technicians, a process that extended to other institutions over time.

In 1996 a second Law of Guidelines and Bases for Brazilian Education was sanctioned that provides vocational education in a separate chapter from basic education. It surpasses approaches to welfare and social prejudice contained in the first professional education legislation of the country by making a critical and qualified social intervention to become a mechanism for social inclusion and democratization of social assets.

From 1909 to 2002 140 *campi* were built, forming the Federal Professional Education Network in Brazil.

In 2005 the Federal Network Expansion Plan of Vocational and Technological Education launched its first phase of construction with 64 new *campi*.

During 2006 the Secretariat of Vocational and Technological Education – SETEC – of the Ministry of Education, in partnership with the National Forum of Professional Education State Management, held the first National Conference on Vocational and Technological Education.

In 2007 the Federal Vocational and Technological Education Network launched the second phase of the expansion plan, aiming to build over 150 new *campi*, creating 354 units in total by the end of 2010, covering all regions of the country, offering training courses, technical education, higher education and postgraduate, attuned to local and regional development needs.

In 2008 amid growing pressure for CEFETs to turn into technological universities, the Ministry of Education created 38 Federal Institutes of Education, Science and Technology, as the great innovation for professional and technological education. Its creation came with new goals and objectives that would guide professional and technological education at a federal level to this day.

In 2011 it was announced that 208 new *campi* would be built by 2014, totalling 562 *campi* in the Federal Network of Professional Education, Science and Technology (Brazil, 2014).

Federal Institutes are born: an innovation in vocational and professional education in Brazil

The creation of the Federal Institutes in 2008, with Law number 11,892 of 29 December 2008 (Brazil, 2008), was a milestone in terms of innovation in Brazilian Education, especially with regard to professional and technological education. With the creation of the institutes, vocational and professional education gained a specific focus in the national system, covering institutions that are obligated to maintain a minimum of 50 per cent of places for technical courses and at least 20 per cent of places for training teachers. Additionally, their task of offering vocational and technological education is closely targeted to meet the demands of society and the productive sector as a whole. On the other hand, the Federal Institutes are responsible for offering professional education at all levels, including professional training courses, technical courses in high school, and college courses, undergraduate (bachelor, teaching licence and technology) and graduate (specialization, masters and doctorate). In addition to the proposed vertical integration of education, Federal Institutes are able to award grants to conduct applied research, occupying an empty space at national level, outside the academic nature of research conducted by higher education and research institutions.

The major innovation occurred in the model of delivery of courses that is closely related to social inclusion through the provision of specific comprehensive programmes such as Thousand Women, PROEJA or the expansion of minority access to the various courses offered.

With the expansion of the Federal Network through the Federal Institutes, vocational education has achieved high coverage, covering all Brazilian states and 75 per cent of geographical micro-regions.

The Federal Institutes are responsible for the majority of the enrolments at different levels of the Federal Professional and Technological Education Network. In 2002 there were approximately 70,000 enrolments. In 2010, as seen in the figure below, it surpassed 400,000 registrations. In four more years, they exceeded the barrier of 1 million registrations realizing 1,040,580 enrolments in 2014. This was an extraordinary leap, because in four years registration for technical and higher education more than doubled.

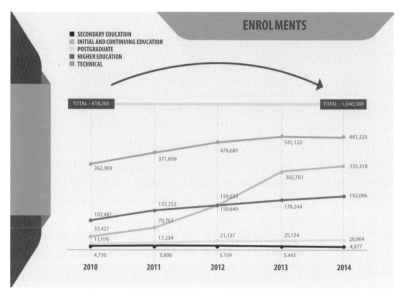

Source: SIMEC, Ministry of Education, Brazil, 2015.

The Brazilian vocational and professional education system and the Federal Institute vocational and professional education model

The current Brazilian professional and vocational education system is established in the Law of Guidelines and Bases, number 9,394 of 20 November 1996 (Brazil, 1996). The table below shows that it permeates all levels of education, from basic education to postgraduate.

Professional qualification, indicated in the table as initial and continuing education, does not properly constitute a level, because it can be offered to everyone, from workers with no education to professionals needing training.

Technical courses at the secondary level effectively take three forms: integrated high schools that are enrolled in the same institution with only one registration, concomitant, when the technician course is held in the same period as the normal course but in a distinct environment and time, and subsequent, when the student has already graduated from high school. In the Federal Institutes, which prioritize integrated technical courses, this level has a requirement for 50 per cent of positions by law.

With the vertical integration of education, the Federal Institutes are obliged to supply at least 20 per cent of places for teacher training. All other professional education offerings, including other undergraduate and graduate, can occupy up to 30 per cent of places.

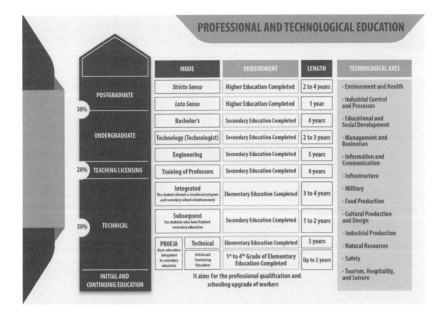

MODE	REQUIREMENT	LENGTH	TECHNOLOGICAL AXES
POSTGRADUATE 30%			
Stricto Sensu	Higher Education Completed	2 to 4 years	- Environment and Health
Lato Sensu	Higher Education Completed	1 year	- Industrial Control and Processes
UNDERGRADUATE Bachelor's	Secondary Education Completed	4 years	- Educational and Social Development
Technology (Technologist)	Secondary Education Completed	2 to 3 years	- Management and Businesses
Engineering	Secondary Education Completed	5 years	- Information and Communication
TEACHING LICENSING 20% Training of Professors	Secondary Education Completed	4 years	- Infrastructure
Integrated The student attends a vocational program and secondary school simultaneously	Elementary Education Completed	3 to 4 years	- Military - Food Production
TECHNICAL 50% Subsequent For students who have finished secondary education	Secondary Education Completed	1 to 2 years	- Cultural Production and Design
PROEJA Basic education Integrated to secondary education	Technical	Elementary Education Completed	3 years	- Industrial Production - Natural Resources
Initial and Continuing Education	1st to 4th Grade of Elementary Education Completed	Up to 2 years	- Safety
INITIAL AND CONTINUING EDUCATION	It aims for the professional qualification and schooling upgrade of workers		- Tourism, Hospitality, and Leisure

Source: Brazil, 1996.

The Federal Institutes (Brazil, 2008), at the moment of their creation, also became an innovative model in their organization since they are providers of basic and professional higher education, *pluricurriculares* and *multicampi*, differing from the centralized model and mono campus hitherto existing. This configuration allowed speed and flexibility in the administrative and pedagogical processes, and permitted them to expand very rapidly in a short period of time, virtually tripling in size in just ten years.

Among the characteristics of the Federal Institutes, we can highlight:

1. offering vocational and technological education at all levels and modalities, forming and qualifying citizens aiming at professional activities in various sectors of the economy, with an emphasis on local, regional and national socioeconomic development
2. developing vocational and technological education as an educational and research process of generation and adaptation of technical and technological solutions to social demands and regional peculiarities
3. promoting vertical integration of basic education with vocational and higher education, optimizing the physical infrastructure, the cadres of personnel and resource management
4. guiding their training offer for the benefit of the consolidation and strengthening of clusters, social and cultural sites identified based on the

mapping of socioeconomic and cultural development potential within the scope of action of the Federal Institute

5. forming themselves into a centre of excellence in the provision of teaching science in general and applied sciences, particularly by stimulating the development of critical thinking, focused on empirical research

6. qualifying themselves as a reference centre in support of science education provision to the public education system, providing technical training and educational upgrading for teachers of public schools

7. carrying out and encouraging applied research, cultural production, entrepreneurship, cooperation and scientific and technological development.

The characteristics of the Federal Institutes allow them to fulfil several objectives, innovative from the standpoint of a new institutional framework:

1. ministering mid-level technical professional education, primarily in the form of integrated courses for graduates of elementary school and the public from adult education

2. conducting initial and continuing training of workers, aimed at capacity building, improvement, specialization and updating professionals at all levels, vocational and technological

3. carrying out applied research, stimulating the development of technical and technological solutions, extending its benefits to the community, with emphasis on the production, development and dissemination of scientific and technological knowledge

4. delivering superior technology courses, undergraduate, bachelor's, and engineering postgraduate, master's and doctoral courses that contribute to promoting the establishment of solid foundations in education, science and technology, focusing on the process of generation and technological innovation.

Innovation policy in the Federal Vocational and Professional Education Network

Technological innovation has become essential to sustaining and extending the current trajectory of economic and social development of Brazil. However, Brazil has faced significant difficulties with its balance of trade in recent years. The balance of trade in electronic products and semiconductors still shows a major deficit, and there is a common view that the lack of projects for IC and manufacturing plants is a serious problem for the innovation of new products (Andres and Silva Filho, 2014).

To significantly increase the productivity and competitiveness of the Brazilian economy and at the same time continue the policy of income distribution, massive investment is needed in research, development and innovation (R, D and I), especially in areas considered as defining the strategic direction of the country. Accordingly, the federal government has set as a priority under the National Strategy for Science, Technology and Innovation – ENCTI 2012/2015 – (Brazil, 2011a) the promotion of innovation in enterprise, the adoption of a new standard of public funding for scientific and technological development, strengthening research, scientific and technological infrastructure, and training in human resources.

The creation of the Brasil Maior Plan in 2013 also constitutes a key strategy for innovation in the country. Conceived as a national investment policy in industrial, technological and foreign trade, its basic objectives are to sustain inclusive economic growth, maintain the country's growth in the global economic crisis, promote productive consolidation of Brazilian industry and induce technological development and innovation in the productive sectors of the country. In 2014 the Inova Empresa Plan was launched with major investment to support and promote innovation in companies of all sizes and sectors of economic activity in Brazil.

As part of this set of measures to strengthen R and D in Brazil, the federal government created the Brazilian Company for Industrial Research and Innovation, Embrapii. Its creation was inspired by the successful international experience of stimulus to industrial innovation through close cooperation between innovative companies and research institutions. These institutions are committed to the search for technological solutions for innovative products, processes and services.

Among the highlights of Embrapii's partnership with renowned research and technological development institutions is the creation of Centres for Innovation in the Federal Institutes. These specialized units aim to improve productivity and competitiveness of domestic industry, based on the development of applied research and innovation. They have the following duties: developing R, D and I projects, providing technological services that contribute to business innovation, and training human resources in technology-based areas. Teachers and students of the Federal Institutes and scientists of external companies or research institutions act at the poles.

In 2015 it began the implementation of the first five Centres for Innovation in the Federal Institutes (Brazil, 2015), as shown below:

Federal Institute	Field
Bahia	Medical equipment
Ceará	Embedded Systems and Digital Mobility
Espírito Santo	Metallurgy
Fluminense	Environment Monitoring and Instrumentation
Minas Gerais	Smart Automotive Systems

The Centres for Innovation were designed to establish a synergy between the recognized technical and scientific competences of the Federal Institutes, and the knowledge acquired by companies on a day-to-day basis, to find solutions, totally innovative or incremental in character, which, over time, translate into gains in productivity, business competitiveness and the strength of the economy.

The creation of the Federal Institutes brought great innovation in the roles of existing institutions that came together to form the Institutes, as well as in those newly created. The development of vocational and technological education has come to be treated as an educational and research process of generation and adaptation of technical and technological solutions to social demands and regional peculiarities, promoting the production, development and transfer of social technologies, notably those aimed at conservation of the environment. In this context, the Federal Institutes should perform and stimulate applied research, cultural production, entrepreneurship, co-operation and scientific and technological development. In line with these objectives, the Federal Institutes were set up to be centres of excellence in the provision of teaching science in general and applied sciences, in particular by encouraging the development of critical thinking, focused on empirical research.

All purposes and objectives of the Federal Institutes focus on the development of its activities in connection with the labour market and social segments, with emphasis on the production, development and dissemination of scientific and technological knowledge. The generation of knowledge and technological solutions in the Federal Institutes adds to its new capability to minister postgraduate master's and doctorate courses. In this they must contribute to the country to promote the establishment of solid foundations in education, science and technology, aimed at the process of generation and technological innovation.

From 2013 the Department of Vocational and Technological Education (SETEC) of Brazil's Ministry of Education started a strong innovation policy for the Federal Professional and Technological Education Network in line with national innovation policy and founded on two main pillars: applied research and the training of cadres.

In the field of applied research and innovation in 2013 we started to publish a series of calls for financial support for the development of research projects, technological development and innovation to be carried out in the Federal Institutes, but with the obligation of meeting external demand, including companies, industries, co-operatives and production associations. This bill reaches its third edition this year.

In the field of training, in addition to strengthening the functions of the professional networking master's, training of servers, SETEC has been implementing teacher training programmes in other countries, sending groups of professors abroad to attend a three-month immersion programme. Its aim is to get involved with the technological education institutions that perform applied research in order to acquire expertise in the relationship of the institution to the production sector. Some groups of professors were already involved in the programme in countries such as Canada and Finland. Now, we aim to expand it to the United Kingdom, United States, Australia and Germany. The first groups who have returned have developed action plans to replicate the knowledge acquired from their institutional colleagues.

The impact of the Federal Institute model on Brazil's development

The creation of the Federal Institutes caused a profound change in professional education in Brazil. In addition to the great results obtained in the National Program for Access to Technical Education and Employment (PRONATEC), launched in 2011 (Brazil, 2011b) by offering 8 million jobs in education and the creation of an innovation policy in the Federal Network, the largest impact of our programmes was social inclusion and the integration of the academy with the production sector. Technological development and innovation made Brazil improve with the creation of the new institutional model of the Federal Institutes, which could generate knowledge and develop technologies associated with the development of human capital, fundamental to economic and social growth.

The Federal Institutes have been fundamental for the formation of the students, as well as for gaining experience with production, technological development, and the culture of innovation, and bringing this culture to the companies with which they will act. The great merit of using this technological education model closely linked to applied research and innovation is the increased chances of graduates in the labour market of getting good jobs, the rise of new entrepreneurs creating start-ups, and the technological improvement of companies close to the Federal Institutes.

Brazil's internationalization

According to the WIPO Statistics Patent Report (WIPO, 2014), Brazil appeared among the top ten countries in the world in the year 2007. After that Brazil never came among the top ten, with an increasing loss in productivity and competitiveness worldwide. In 2011, the Brazilian government launched the National Strategy for Science, Technology and Innovation (Brazil, 2011a), with the proposal of encouraging science and technology in the country, increasing the participation of companies in R and D funding, improving human capital qualification and disseminating and popularizing science and technology. One effect of this plan was the creation of the programme Science Without Borders, which in the last three years has sent more than 100,000 students abroad, mainly to English-speaking countries such as the US, UK and Australia, and countries with rapid scientific growth and technology such as China and South Korea. In 2012, for instance, Brazil offered little more than 3,700 international scholarships per year.

The results of Science Without Borders show that students returning from abroad find it easier to get internships and jobs after graduation.

The Ministry of Education, through the Professional and Technological Education Secretariat, has invested in sending professors for immersion missions for three months in vocational education culture and innovation in countries with recognized professional education at a high level, such as Finland, Canada and the United States. Programmes are also set to be pursued in Australia and England, in partnership with the British Council. The results of the first 150 professors who returned from the internship abroad are very promising, and they have conducted training programmes for colleagues, and conducted seminars and workshops for the multiplication of acquired knowledge and skills.

Finally, the Ministry of Education has participated in the promotion of vocational education in the BRICS countries (Brazil, Russia, India, China and South Africa), bringing improvements to the framework and standards of vocational education in order to incorporate good practices of vocational and technological education by universities and Federal Institutes.

References

Andres, F. and Silva Filho, O.S. (2014) *CI@PracticeDay Workshop, 2014*. Sapporo: NII.

Brazil, Planalto (1996) Law Number 9,394, Brasília, 20 December 1996. Online. http://www.planalto.gov.br/ccivil_03/Leis/L9394.htm (accessed 6 December 2015).

Brazil, Planalto (2008) Law Number 11,892, Brasília, 29 December 2008. Online. http://www.planalto.gov.br/ccivil_03/_ato2007-2010/2008/lei/l11892.htm (accessed 6 December 2015).

Brazil, MEC (2009) 'Histórico da Educação Profissional'. Brasília: MEC. Online. http://portal.mec.gov.br/setec/arquivos/centenario/historico_educacao_profissional.pdf (accessed 6 December 2015).

Brazil, MCT (2011a) *Estratégia nacional de ciência, tecnologia e inovação 2012–2015: Balanço das atividades estruturantes 2011*, Brasília: MCT. Online. www.mct.gov.br/upd_blob/0218/218981.pdf (accessed 6 December 2015).

Brazil, MEC (2011b) 'O que é o Pronatec?' Brasília: MEC. Online. http://pronatec.mec.gov.br/institucional-90037/o-que-e-o-pronatec (accessed 6 December 2015).

Brazil, MEC (2014) 'Expansão da Rede Federal'. Brasília: MEC. Online. http://redefederal.mec.gov.br/expansao-da-rede-federal (accessed 6 December 2015).

Brazil, MEC (2015) 'A EMBRAPII divulga o resultado da Chamada Pública 02-2014'. Brasília: MEC. Online. http://embrapii.org.br/a-embrapii-divulga-o-resultado-da-chamada-publica-02-2014/ (accessed 6 December 2015).

WIPO (World Intellectual Property Organization) (2014) *World Intellectual Property Indicators*. Online. http://www.wipo.int/ipstats/en/wipi/ (accessed 6 December 2015).

University–industry collaboration: A novel model to advance PhD education on innovation

Takehiko Kitamori

Human resources are the most important national resource for knowledge-based economies. Statistics show that the GDP of a nation is highly correlated with the number of PhD graduates working in its science and technology sectors. Despite this, however, global trends worryingly indicate that unemployment is on the increase among PhD graduates. One reason for this seeming contradiction is that although the established PhD training methodology is very effective in giving students mastery of a specific subject area, which remains a valuable attribute, it does not necessarily equip graduates with an understanding of the roles that they can play in the modern industrial context and of the skills needed in order to create innovation.

Solving this issue, then, requires the active participation of industry as well as of higher education institutions. University–industry collaborations will need to broaden their scope beyond the traditional realm of research and development to encompass collaborative involvement in innovative forms of PhD delivery. This, in turn, will challenge the higher education sector to reconsider the nature and aims of PhD education, and indeed of universities themselves. Furthermore, in this era of globalization, universities play a key role as pivotal hubs, enabling excellent students from all over the world to congregate and share perspectives and experiences on current social, industrial and economic challenges from different countries. Therefore, there is increasing pressure on higher education institutions to equip students with the skills to be internationally competitive. Providing students with opportunities to work and excel in multi-cultural internationally minded teams will be an important focus for many universities in the coming decades.

This paper considers the meaning of innovation and the challenges of educating PhD students to become global innovation bearers under the current model. It introduces the example of a new international internship scheme developed in partnership by leading global research universities and industry, and looks at the benefits of closer university-industry collaboration on PhD education for all stakeholders. In closing, it considers some ways in which initiatives such as this one, which enables the exchange of ideas across institutional cultures as well as across geographical ones, could influence the broader development of PhD education.

The existing gap between PhD education and innovation

What is innovation?

It is almost a truism that higher education institutions are required to create innovation via their research, as well as to train their students to be innovative, in order to contribute to a knowledge-based economy. However, we need to start by clarifying what we mean by the term 'innovation'. It is not merely the discovery or invention of something new, intriguing or even with potential. It is only once such an invention is developed into a product, marketed and has an economic impact, that it can truly be termed an innovation.

The failure to bridge the gap between invention and innovation is particularly acute here in Japan. Our country has received several Nobel Prizes in science and technology, particularly in the twenty-first century, yet there are still few examples in which this research has been successfully introduced to the market. For example, Koichi Tanaka won a Nobel Prize in chemistry for his research using a mass spectrometer known as MALDI; but the company for which he worked, Shimadzu, sold only one such machine before his award. It was a German company, Bruker Daltonics, that converted it into a marketable product and went on to sell thousands of units.

Of course, there have been cases even in Japan in which Nobel Prize-winning discoveries have been economically successful, such as the blue LED. However, the MALDI case exemplifies typical difficulties in converting research breakthroughs into the creation of new markets. It demonstrates that simply locating researchers inside industry is insufficient for innovation creation; we need to pay closer attention to the content of the training such researchers receive. PhD training in many countries, including Japan, has tended to focus only on the first stage of the innovation process, the generation of an original idea. In order to work within industry, however, PhD graduates need to understand the entire process of developing this idea into a concrete product that opens up a new market, as well as the range of skills this process requires: not only expertise in research and development, but also transferable skills including strategy, product positioning, design, production, quality control and sales. PhD students should realize that there are career openings for them within all of these roles; they will then be able to select the most appropriate positions in which to use their talents, and ultimately to spearhead innovation leading to greater economic impact.

The different research cultures of PhD education and industry

There is another significant difference between research culture in universities and that in industry. PhD programmes at universities are a highly individual process: PhDs are never awarded to a group. Research topics differ from student to student, and they are supervised on a one-to-one basis. Within industry, however, research and development is carried out within the context of a group working towards a common goal. Moreover, because of the complex problems that are now being addressed by industry, these groups are often made up of members from quite different fields. One of the main concerns expressed by industrial partners about PhD education has been the narrow mindset of graduates, and their lack of understanding of industry's systems and goals.

Functioning effectively in this type of research context requires a whole range of different skills, beginning with teamwork and leadership. Often, however, PhD students who have no industrial experience are not even aware of the differences between these research cultures, still less equipped to deal with them. Indeed, these differences are often further enhanced in international organizations, where R and D is often undertaken by diverse multicultural and multilingual teams.

Researchers need to be able to identify key problems in their fields of expertise and to solve them individually, while at the same time being aware of the team's overall mission, and of the importance of their work to its final success. They also need an understanding of the industrial and social contexts in which their research is taking place. Furthermore, they need to be able to communicate the results of their research, and the processes by which they arrived at them, to their team members, as well as to management. Industrial partners tell us that verbal communicative ability is more important than written, but traditional higher education programmes at all levels still emphasize the latter. As a result of this process, researchers come to understand what leadership is. The team leader needs to understand and co-ordinate the overall progress of the team, including research in areas in which he or she is not a specialist.

The need for a paradigm shift

Given the contradictions inherent in the different research cultures, foremost among which is the different value placed on the innovation process, one of the major issues with which the providers of PhD education must grapple is how to prepare their students to work in industry. It is a challenge for which there is no simple solution; one that requires the higher education sector to re-evaluate the theoretical foundations and the concrete aims of the training that it offers to the next generation of researchers. Looked at from another viewpoint, however, it offers the sector a unique opportunity to overhaul its PhD education to ensure that it remains fit for purpose.

In today's highly competitive job market, international work experience is widely considered as a ticket to a successful career. However, universities alone can no longer offer their research students a truly world-class education that will prepare them to work not only in any country, but in any setting. Collaboration with industry in different sectors and countries is essential in the development and implementation of initiatives to broaden the scope of PhDs. However, past university-industry collaborations have tended to focus purely on research and development. The mobilization of university and industry partners to co-create better, experience-based learning programmes, which provide students with hands-on exposure to different working environments and enable them to develop the skills to be effective beyond the bench, remains a relatively under-explored concept.

PhD education through university–industry collaboration

Creating opportunities to exchange ideas

At the University of Tokyo, we have been thinking for several years about how to work together in imaginative and creative ways with our international industrial partners. These considerations led us, together with the IBM Watson Research Center and MIT, to establish the Deans Forum, a global consortium of leading engineering schools and industrial research laboratories. Since 2011, a members' working group consisting of world-leading research institutions including the University of Tokyo, MIT, UC Berkeley, ETH, KTH, Imperial College London, a representative of the French Grandes Écoles, and the University of Cambridge, meets on a regular basis to discuss common issues in education, research and management. This partnership has enabled those of us in the higher education sector to learn more about the actual needs and experiences of industry in these areas.

Together, we have held theme-associated workshops revolving around cutting-edge innovation, including resilience engineering and brain-inspired computing. These workshops have been similar to traditional research and development-based university-industry partnerships, but have been more multidisciplinary, involving collaboration at an organizational level.

However, we are now looking to develop the model further. The reform of PhD education to better meet the needs of our knowledge-based economy is an issue of paramount importance to both academia and industry, and one for which the active involvement of both sectors is required in order to reach any solution; indeed, this was one of the principal factors motivating the establishment of this consortium. Our experiences of working together thus far, especially on the brain-inspired computing workshop that was proposed by IBM, have laid the foundation for us to address this challenge more directly, and so we are about to initiate a larger scale international internship programme for PhD level education on innovation. Through this programme, students will gain experience of industry-targeted research questions and develop a deeper understanding of how organizational cultures differ around the world.

The contribution of Going Global to this process

Going Global has been instrumental in helping us understand current industry needs from around the world. Throughout the process of developing these initiatives, discussions with a wider group of industries and universities at Going Global over the course of several years have been an important catalyst. We have used the unique opportunity provided by the conference to share experiences and exchange opinions with many stakeholders, as initiatives like ours are difficult to discuss at specialist science and technology international conferences, which do not have an education focus. The outcome of sessions on human resource development, internationalization, PhD training and innovation at Going Global in 2013–15 has advanced our strategic thinking and helped to mobilize supporters from academia and industry from around the world. Ultimately, this has facilitated the design of an internationally relevant programme to train the next generation of innovation leaders.

The Deans Forum international internships: A way forward for PhD education

The members of the Deans Forum agreed in April 2015 to set up a new international internship scheme in order to develop PhD graduates who are equipped to work across the cultural divides between sectors and countries. The internship scheme will be implemented from the 2016 academic year. It is expected that between 30 and 50 PhD students per year will participate at this stage, with the intention of expanding the scheme.

The IBM Watson Research Center and Hitachi's Central Research Laboratory are the founding members on the industrial side. We are currently in discussion with several other potential partners, including

GSK and Rolls-Royce in the UK, and the members of the Kigyo Taiwa consortium in Japan. Industrial partners have shown a good understanding of the wider purpose of the scheme, with the majority seeking not only to recruit excellent PhD graduates, but also to strengthen the knowledge economy as a whole.

PhD students from member universities will select one of these international industrial partners, which offer them the opportunity to intern in different engineering sectors, and in different cultural and geographical settings. Research systems and management procedures vary widely from country to country, and students are strongly encouraged to choose an overseas placement in order to gain additional experiences and knowledge.

The benefits of PhD education offered through university–industry partnerships

We anticipate that the scheme will provide significant benefits for all involved, and indeed more widely. Participating PhD students will be given a valuable opportunity to work with a top-level industrial partner and to acquire knowledge and transferable skills that are impossible to attain within a higher education setting, making them more attractive to employers outside academia, not only in their home country but around the world. They will see the broad range of career options open to PhD holders within industry, that include not only research and development but also roles in management, production and marketing, informing their future career paths.

Development of and access to qualified human resources, meanwhile, are important motivations for industrial partners. Through the co-creation of new PhD initiatives such as this one, they will be able to shape the training of PhD students to ensure that they possess the skills and knowledge that will allow them to become effective researchers in the industrial context. Moreover, they will be given priority access to a group of intelligent young researchers, allowing them to benefit from their fresh ideas during the internship period, and to identify and cultivate relationships with those who show the potential to become valuable members of their teams after graduation. Conversely, working with international industry partners will not only enhance employment prospects, but more importantly help students gain a global outlook and deeper understanding of cultural and social differences.

For higher education institutions, there are potential advantages in multiple areas. Through such initiatives that provide both industrial and international experience to their PhD students, they will be better able to fulfil two of their key missions, the training of human resources equipped to work within a global knowledge-based economy, and the generation of innovation. These opportunities will attract the best minds to their PhD programmes, and these young researchers in turn will be enabled to develop to their full potential, creating a virtuous cycle. Furthermore, the strengthening of relationships with industrial partners has the potential to lead to other types of collaboration.

Initiatives such as this one are also in line with the priorities of national governments, for whom innovation creation and the development of highly skilled workforces are key policy objectives, thus helping universities to be accountable for their public sector funding. Finally, global society as a whole will benefit from the increased potential to develop new research ideas right through to actual products and services available in the real world, making people more aware of the contributions of PhD holders to industry and society.

Meeting the challenge of human resource development for innovation

Human resources are the most important national resource. Therefore, although the challenge of developing human resources for innovation is a substantial and difficult issue, it is one with which all stakeholders in a knowledge-based economy are deeply concerned. In particular, higher education and industry share a joint responsibility to ensure that the enormous human capital represented by the next generation of researchers currently studying on PhD courses is developed to its full potential in order to play a wide range of roles in a society with innovation at its core. The international internship scheme about to be launched by the leading representatives from both sectors who make up the Deans Forum is one innovative approach to tackling this challenge, and may serve as a useful reference.

As this scheme is still in its initial stages, it is intended that it will develop further. There is great potential to scale it up to incorporate new partners from industry and academia, allowing more students to participate and benefit. Through the process of collaboration, there will be opportunities to refine and improve the model, and also to identify ways to expand it into new areas. It may also be adapted for students at other levels of higher education, such as undergraduates, and in other disciplines besides engineering.

We hope, moreover, that this model will contribute to a broader change in PhD education, prompting a re-evaluation of how we train researchers and to what purpose. The model may serve as a starting point for senior management within universities or industry to take the initiative to develop similar broad, experience-based programmes at their own organizations. Going Global provides an unparalleled opportunity to interact with participants from both sectors, allowing us to disseminate information about our experiences to an international audience that may raise awareness of the issues and inspire others to approach this challenge in new ways, as well as to incorporate feedback and ideas from a wider group into our own programme and to network with prospective partners.

Going beyond individual organizations, this model has the potential to influence higher education associations and systems. Members of the European University Association's Council for Doctoral Education recently expressed interest in this internship scheme and other university–industry collaboration pioneered by the Deans Forum. Examples of good practice such as this one could also contribute significantly to broad higher education reform initiatives such as the Bologna Process by suggesting ways to bridge the cultural divide between higher education and industry.

The skills and knowledge obtained through PhD education have led to important economic contributions, but as the needs of the economy evolve, the gap between graduate skills and the industrial research context threatens to widen. Without teaching PhD students what innovation is and how to create it, rather than simply to produce new knowledge, we cannot prepare them to contribute fully to a knowledge-based economy. However, these skills cannot be taught solely within the traditional university context. Meeting this challenge will require a paradigm shift within the higher education sector as we reconsider what PhD education means and how to work together in new ways with our industrial partners to deliver it and create impact on an international scale. It is imperative that the higher education and industrial sectors jointly develop and implement various initiatives to train the next generation of PhD holders to become the bearers and creators of innovation.

Acknowledgements

I would like to express my deepest appreciation to Dr Lily Yu, Ms Emma Parker, Ms Azusa Tanaka and other British Council colleagues who have provided valuable discussions and support to complete this chapter.

Building knowledge transfer at Hong Kong Baptist University: A customer-oriented approach
Alfred K.T. Tan

Compared to the situation in many advanced economies, knowledge transfer is a relatively new notion for the higher education sector in Hong Kong. From the academic year of 2009/10 the Hong Kong Legislative Council has approved a new recurrent annual funding of HK$50 million for the eight public higher education institutions (HEIs) in Hong Kong to build up their capacity and broaden their endeavour in knowledge transfer. For the HEIs funding body in Hong Kong – the University Grants Committee (UGC), knowledge transfer is defined as 'The systems and processes by which knowledge, including technology, know-how, expertise and skills are transferred between higher education institutions and society, leading to innovative, profitable or economic or social improvements.' Specifically, UGC emphasized that knowledge transfer is a two-way process, where not only would the community enjoy realizable benefit from the knowledge transferred from the HEIs, but academics and researchers would also be enriched by having closer ties with the larger community. Thus, it is evident that the foundation of successes in knowledge transfer must be built upon good relationship building between the HEIs and the larger community.

In Hong Kong there are eight public HEIs comprising two large comprehensive universities – the Hong Kong University and the Chinese University of Hong Kong, an international research university – the Hong Kong University of Science and Technology, two universities with polytechnic roots – the Hong Kong Polytechnic University and the City University of Hong Kong, two liberal arts universities – Hong Kong Baptist University and Lingnan University, and one education institute – the Hong Kong Institute of Education. With such a diversity of HEIs, it is no wonder that knowledge transfer will have a very different focus and very different stage of maturity at each and every institution in Hong Kong.

Even with such diversity, there is bound to be a range of areas of common good practice wherein all the HEIs in Hong Kong, and other HEIs internationally, can learn from each other for the mutual good and the collective betterment of the knowledge transfer culture locally and internationally.

The Hong Kong Baptist University's experience

The Hong Kong Baptist University (HKBU) is a broad-based liberal arts university built upon the foundation of providing a Whole Person Education. Established in 1956, HKBU has more than 50 years of experience in providing broad-based and creativity-inspiring education while encouraging its staff and students to serve the community. With such a background, service to the community is not something new at HKBU but knowledge transfer in its other forms, such as technology transfer, commercialization, and entrepreneurship, and evidence-based knowledge transfer resulting from impact of academic research, are still at their infancy in the early days of 2009/10. At HKBU the knowledge transfer activities are promoted and administered via the Knowledge Transfer Office (KTO).

The following examples of knowledge transfer development at HKBU are highlighted to exemplify the importance of a customer-oriented approach in building good relationships between the staff of HKBU, the KTO, and the larger community, that in return produced tangible benefits towards building the knowledge transfer at the University.

Setting the right focus at KTO

When the KTO was established at HKBU, one of its fundamental tasks was to set the right focus on the support and services provided by this office both to the University and to the larger community. At HKBU knowledge transfer is not a compulsory activity for the faculty, so setting the right focus enables the KTO to best use its resources to bring about the highest return for HKBU in knowledge transfer.

The focus of the KTO at HKBU is 'to provide professional customer oriented knowledge transfer services'. This focus was developed after much analysis of the goals, strengths, and best return on investment for knowledge transfer at HKBU. With this focus, all activities at the KTO are planned and implemented to provide the best possible professional customer oriented knowledge transfer service to the staff and students of the University and to the larger community. With this as a constant practice, this focus has become the culture of the KTO at HKBU.

The culture of providing professional customer oriented knowledge transfer services has three distinctive elements in its focus. First and foremost, the knowledge transfer services provided must be of the highest professional standards possible. Only when the KTO provides such a professional service, are the interests of HKBU, the staff and students of the University, and the larger community best served. For every professional service that the KTO provides, it is very important that the delivery of that service is focused on the needs and wants of the customer – in other words, a fully customer oriented approach. This is very important, as the primary stakeholder of any knowledge transfer activity is the staff or student at the University. If their needs and wants are not met or aligned to the knowledge transfer activity, then the activity will not happen, or if it does, it will not be completed satisfactorily. Finally, the focus of the KTO is solely on the delivery of knowledge transfer services and nothing else. This focus entails not only doing what are the core activities of the KTO but also the discipline to forgo all opportunities falling outside of these core activities.

Focusing on the relationship between the different stakeholders is not new in many institutions globally. For example, PraxisUnico has long advocated the importance of customer relationship management as an essential element in successful knowledge exchange and commercialization among many higher education institutions in the United Kingdom. In private conversations with a number of Vice Chancellors in the UK, many also have identified faculty buy-in as a key factor in ensuring the successful implementation of the research impact agenda at their respective institutions.

In the following, the implementation and benefits of this sort of customer oriented approach are exemplified in the development of knowledge transfer at HKBU.

Customer oriented support for technology transfer

It is often cited that patent data is in itself an indicator of innovation and a key precursor to successful technology transfer. Hence, this example will illustrate how a customer oriented approach can successfully support and pave the way to successful technology transfer.

Before 2010/11, the number of patent filings and patent grants at HKBU were in the low twenties. Between the periods of 2011/12 to 2014/15 the total number of patent filings and patent grants at HKBU has grown exponentially with the number of patents filed now close to 200. Since its establishment, HKBU has always been a research and teaching university where innovative research outcomes have always been at the forefront. Give that there have always been good research outputs one might wonder what has contributed to the growth in patent applications alongside the ongoing research output. To better understand this, one must compare the patent support service provided at HKBU for the period pre-2010/11 and post-2011/12.

In the period pre-2010/11, all patent filings at HKBU were outsourced to law firms specializing in intellectual property laws and patent litigations. This is often the practice of many HEIs in Hong Kong and internationally. It is an effective way of managing the service without having to provide the equivalent level of professional expertise at the institutions. Some of the obvious drawbacks of this approach are time, costs and often, customer's satisfaction. As external law firms have their own private clients, and, in addition, they are stationed outside the campus, any patent filing process between a university faculty and the external lawyer will often take a considerable amount of time that can be weeks if not months. For an academic inventor timeliness is a critical issue as they are often under time pressure to publish their research outcomes, and further to meet key deadlines. A further consideration can be costs, since external lawyers will need to bill for the time they spent on each case together with the length of time they need to work with the academic inventor to finalize a given patent application. As a result, all too often the final costs for such patent filings are rather considerable. These two factors, taken together, will often result in rather poor customer's satisfaction for the academic inventor. The frequent complaint is that either the patent filing is too costly and takes too long to complete and/or the end result, i.e. the eventual invention filed, is not what was originally desired by the academic inventor.

In the period post-2011/12, the KTO at HKBU took a professional customer oriented approach to all patent filings at the University. While the final patent applications are still filed via external law firms, the KTO took on the task of providing a comprehensive patent application service, where all patent applications at the University are pre-processed to ascertain their patentability and to prepare the application to an advanced stage ready to be filed. As all these professional services are provided in-house, the KTO is now able to reduce the time required for filing a patent at HKBU from at least two months down to just two weeks. Furthermore, as most of their preliminary professional services are done in-house, the KTO was successful in reducing the patent filing costs at HKBU by more than 80 per cent. Most importantly, as the KTO is focused on delivering a professional customer oriented service to the academic inventors of HKBU, the year-on-year performance satisfaction rating of the patenting service at HKBU has been rated at above 95 per cent since 2012/13. By adopting a customer oriented approach in providing patent protection support at HKBU, the KTO has found great savings for the University in terms of time and costs for patent applications at HKBU. Ultimately, this has led to very positive customer satisfaction among the academic inventors, which also translated to better patents being filed and much more ownership in the commercialization process by the academic inventor.

Despite the exponential growth in patent applications at HKBU in the past four years, the KTO only filed approximately 60–65 per cent of all invention disclosures received from academic inventors at the University. Even more surprisingly, most of the applications that were rejected were done so with the support and agreement of the applicants. This is a good indicator of the strong ownership exhibited by the academic inventors at HKBU. Such enhanced ownership is attributed to the success of the customer oriented approach adopted by the KTO at HKBU.

Customer oriented commercialization and entrepreneurship support

On 14 March 2014 the very first commercialization company – the HKBU R&D Licensing Limited, was set up at HKBU to commercialize all intellectual property rights developed at and owned by the University. With a past track record of minimal patent licensing at HKBU, this commercialization company was able to license 13 of its patent rights to five technology spin-off companies from the University. These five technology spin-off companies were led by the respective academic inventors of the licensed patent rights. From testimonies of the academic inventors who led the commercialization of their own inventions, one of the key factor that led them to do so is the enhanced ownership they have on the patents they have filed at HKBU. Ironically, all 13 licensed patents and pending patents were developed in the post-2011/12 period.

Even in supporting entrepreneurship at HKBU, KTO has adopted the same customer oriented approach in providing the best possible professional entrepreneurship support services. For all the start-up companies from HKBU, the KTO provides a multitude of entrepreneurship support services for both funding and training. The KTO also provides entrepreneurship services for business incubation and enables match making with potential investors and potential customers. In all these entrepreneurship support and services, by focusing on providing professional customer oriented services, the KTO was able to incubate four student start-ups and five faculty-led technology companies, one of which was valued at HK$50 million within six months of its incorporation. Feedback received from the industry and venture capital investors indicated that the focus in delivering a customer oriented win-win strategy for both the University and the wider community is a key driver of the early successes found at HKBU.

Similarly, at world leading technology transfer universities such as Massachusetts Institute of Technology (MIT), Stanford University, and Harvard University, faculty-led start-up companies have proven to be the more successful model of technology transfer. Examples of such inventor-led start-ups from these universities are Akamai from MIT, Google from Stanford University, and Facebook from Harvard University. Moreover, in private conversation with the Director of Technology Licensing Office at MIT, it is well noted that at MIT one of the key factors behind their success is in the relationship they have built with their faculty and the industry.

Supporting the impact of academic research from the perspective of the customer

The Hong Kong UGC strongly believes that the transfer of knowledge between the HEIs and wider society helps bring about socio-economic impact and improvements to the community and businesses. This in turn also helps enrich the HEIs' research mission, thereby enhancing the international competitiveness of the local higher education sector. Hence, another major goal of the KTO at HKBU is to facilitate and support the development of research impact and influence from research at the University to the larger community.

Towards this goal, the KTO has developed funding programmes for support knowledge transfer activities that will build on the impact of good research at HKBU. Programmes such as the Knowledge Transfer Partnership Seed Fund and the Matching Proof of Concept Fund have been developed to provide not only funding support for faculty to make significant impacts in the larger community, but also, because of the way these programmes are structured, to ensure that their outcome will further enrich the research and inform the teaching of the faculty taking part. This is again focusing on the needs and wants of the faculty while providing support and services for their knowledge transfer activities.

Early success from these knowledge transfer programmes has already been achieved with faculty gaining further funding from competitive research funds based on the knowledge transfer work done under these KTO funding schemes. Moreover, due to the clear alignment between research, teaching and knowledge transfer, faculty at HKBU have shown a growing interest in doing more knowledge transfer. This is evident from the responses the KTO receives annually in its annual performance survey. Again, by aligning the interest of the faculty to the goals of knowledge transfer, the KTO at HKBU has been successful in building a strong foundation for a successful knowledge transfer agenda at the University. On the internationalization front, the successes of HKBU's KTO have attracted interest in knowledge transfer from regional and overseas organizations such as the universities in Macau SAR and China PRC, and the KT communities in Malaysia and Taiwan.

Conclusions

In conclusion, for a liberal arts university with no previous significant track record in technology transfer, commercialization and entrepreneurship, nor evidence-based knowledge transfer resulting from research impact, the KTO at HKBU, by adopting a customer oriented focus to knowledge transfer, has experienced successes in changing the academic culture of the institution. While recognizing that such a customer oriented approach may not have a similar effect at other HEIs, it is safe to say nonetheless that the success of the very personal approach of the KT at HKBU demonstrates that, in matters of knowledge transfer development, the building of interpersonal relationships is core to all successes in knowledge transfer.

3.6

Connecting international higher education and industry partners, forging future global music industry careers

Mark Thorley

Introduction

In 1997, Pierre Levy noted how emerging technology could offer the opportunity for a community to collaborate virtually, and by disregarding the traditional barriers of geography, organization and culture, give rise to 'collective intelligence'. Since that time, technology has continued to develop and writers such as Tapscott and Williams (2006) have shown how professionals in a variety of professional industries and contexts can 'peer-produce' for the sake of quality, speed and cost.

These concepts centre on catalysing creativity and innovation by utilizing emergent technology to bring together different cultures. Relevant to the work of higher education, this can take place at a variety of cross-sections – at the point where high technology meets creative fields such as music, where higher education interfaces with the world of business, and at the cross-section of different national or regional cultures. Although there is considerable potential, higher education institutions commonly fail to engage with these concepts. This is despite evidence that students themselves often connect with global peers outside of the formal curriculum, that business can be effectively involved in assessing student work (Thorley, 2015), and that there is general need for industry and education to increase their networks for the purpose of collaboration (Ashton, 2010).

This chapter outlines the approach and experience of a project funded by the UK's Higher Education Academy (HEA), which brought together Coventry University, industry organization Joint Audio Media Education Support (JAMES) and several international partners, including New York University, Stellenbosch University and the University of Michigan. The project's aim was to make the best use of the potential to marshal creativity and innovation through technology by facilitating peer working, peer assessment and employer-orientated assessment. This chapter explores in turn the potential to catalyse creativity and innovation, the project approach, the innovative approach and outcomes, issues of implementation, and the impact of such an approach on the academic and the institution.

The potential to catalyse creativity and innovation

The potential to catalyse creativity and innovation is in this chapter centred on the production of music. It is, however, grounded in a number of other concepts – collaborative learning, collaboration in music production, the global music production process and emerging social media use in music.

The fundamental approach to, and benefits of, collaborative learning have been explored extensively in the literature – these range from examples of texts focusing on instruction, such as Barkley *et al.*'s *Collaborative Learning Techniques: A handbook for college faculty* (2005) through to Bruffree's *Collaborative Learning* (1999). Whipple (1987) usefully sums up collaborative learning as a 'pedagogical style that emphasizes cooperative efforts amongst students, faculty and administrators'. The concept of breaking down the traditional role of educator and learner is therefore central, but furthermore (and shown here), technology can connect learners with collaborators outside of the institution (international collaborators or industry practitioners), thus widening the effect. As Whipple explains further, learners and educators are active participants in the educational process, the gap between educators and learners is bridged by collaboration, a sense of community is created, knowledge is created not transferred, the boundary between teaching and research becomes less distinct and collaboration creates knowledge in the community rather than in the individual.

The concept of collaboration is also explored in much of the literature on music production. As Negus (1992) explains, 'The work of recording industry personnel has often been characterized as a "collaborative" or "collective" activity coordinated according to various conventions, shared goals, consensual values or commercial formulas.' Furthermore, Kealey (1979) describes three 'modes of collaboration' in music production: the 'craft mode' (predominant in the postwar period), the 'entrepreneurial mode' (predominant in the 1950s) and the 'art mode', which followed. Interestingly, these take a chronological path, largely driven by developments in recording studio technology, and the amount of collaboration present in the role as outlined by Kealey increases with time. So while the recording engineer working in the 'craft-union mode' would have a formal and impersonal relationship with musicians, the 'entrepreneurial-mode' practitioner would be more open and fluid in his or her relationships, culminating in the 'art-mode' practitioner who would be seen by musicians as an essential collaborator in the production process. The concept of collaboration has therefore become more important with continued technological development and this is likely to continue.

Since the work of Negus and Kealey, the music business, like many others, has become more globalized, as multinational companies seek to maximize profit by best leveraging expertise irrespective of location. Even the seemingly isolated world of the recording studio forms part of an interconnected global network (Watson, 2014). To illustrate this, Figure 1 shows the global music production process made up of a series of stages, often managed by particular actors whose expertise allows them to specialize in that particular area. The person responsible for each stage needs to work with those in the previous and following stages – it is highly iterative, involves a variety of forms of communication and reflects the reliance of each actor on the quality of the work of the other actors. The overall process is therefore highly collaborative and now, using digital technology, highly globalized.

Figure 1: The global music production process

The broad field of emergent digital technology (including social media, streaming and compressed file formats) is also having a powerful impact upon individuals and organizations in terms of the manner in which they can connect and share music content. The world of music consumption has been touched by this in the sense that traditional ways of hearing about and sharing music have been swept away (O'Hara and Brown, 2006). For music producers, as Gaunt and Westerlund (2013) note, these technologies also present new opportunities for collaboration that are particularly relevant given the changing face of the commercial recording industry and the waning interest in traditional concert hall attendance.

The project

In response to these complex factors, the project funded by the HEA brought together Coventry University, industry organization JAMES and a number of international partners including the universities of New York, Stellenbosch and Michigan. Various activities took place that aimed to best utilize the opportunities with emergent technology, the potential already outlined, and the expertise and needs of the partners. For the purposes of this chapter, just three of the activities are outlined by way of demonstration, namely: two-way critical listening, three-way critical listening, and recording and mixing.

In the two-way critical listening activity, students from the host institution provided recorded material with supporting video evidence online, which the international partners listened to as part of a video-conference. A discussion followed about the recordings and technology and the techniques used. The same process then took place reciprocally, from the international partner to the host institution.

In the three-way industry critical listening activity, the host institution and international partner provided recorded material, which was listened to with a group of students from the host institution and a high-profile music producer from JAMES. Discussion took place, and the observations were shared with the international partner via social media.

In the recording and mixing activity, international HE and industry partners provided multitrack recordings. Students at the host institution then mixed or remixed that material. The resulting recordings were then assessed by the originating international HE or industry partner, the assessment feedback shared with learners at the host institution, and further critical discussion facilitated around the process.

Innovative approaches and outcomes

The innovative approach taken with the project produced a number of outcomes, the key instances of which are explained here. First, it became evident that there are now a proliferation of 'participation' tools, which, when combined with professional audio production technologies, produce a powerful catalyst. For example, audio and video files have been shared using FTP, Dropbox and other compression technologies. Similarly, ubiquitous streaming services such as YouTube and SoundCloud have been used effectively to facilitate not only asynchronous but also synchronous learning experiences – for example, a class in the UK can watch a class in the USA listen to material that has been produced in the UK. Video-conferencing technologies such as Skype and Google Hangout have similarly been used to foster real-time communication and collaboration. In this way, bringing together learners, higher education institutions and industry has, in accordance with Levy's point, broken down traditional barriers and created a 'collective learning' community experience existing in a technological space.

Secondly, where collaboration has been facilitated, in accordance with Tapscott and Williams's work, the end 'peer-produced' result has been of a higher technical and creative standard. For example, where students at the host institution used material from, and were assessed by industry professionals, their recordings were of a higher technical standard. This is because the source material was of a higher technical and aesthetic standard and the perspective of the industrial professional was different from that of an academic. Additionally, however, even material used from international academic partners produced a higher standard of response – partly because the providers of the material tend to want to provide impressive source material, partly due to the novel nature of the interaction, and partly because of the slight cultural differences evident in the material. An example of such an instance was where students who grew up in urban areas of the UK were able to remix a cappella choir recordings from South Africa – this produced creative results unique to the interaction.

Thirdly, completely new forms of feedback have emerged at the intersection of the partners and technology. For example, host institution students were able to watch the physical response of their international learning partners to their recordings in real time. This offers a very different experience from the tradition of written (or even verbal) feedback in that it is immediate and meaningful and reflects the cultural background of the learners involved in producing the response. Were it not for the combination of technologies and the provision of the learning partners' own creative content, this type of feedback would be unlikely to emerge.

Lastly, in order to make the best use of the contributing partners' expertise (right down to the level of individual learners), many possibilities arose from the interactions and relationships themselves. This means that the academic sometimes needs to take a back seat, facilitating new ideas and innovations that will come organically from the community.

Issues of implementation

Although the technology proved a powerful catalyst, challenges remain specifically around pedagogical, cultural and structural issues. The first is the central theme of how these kinds of collaborative activities fit into the curriculum. Given the attractiveness of the concepts, it would be easy to try such collaboration on a 'value-added' basis. However, this downplays its importance, risks a lack of engagement on the part of learners, and misses the point somewhat. In the case of this project, then, more successful activities were always mapped across to learning outcomes – typically, ones that referred to collaborative working (though not perhaps originally referring to industry or international collaboration) suited well.

Secondly, despite the attraction, where courses try to engage in large-scale interactions, there is considerable work, and risk, which can easily outweigh the advantages. If problems emerge (either with the technology, or with partner relationships), credibility is lost with the learners. This can be a common issue, particularly where universities are looking to engage in large-scale 'top-down' approaches that look exciting and attractive to potential learners. It is usually more appropriate to engage in small-scale, well-designed and rigorous collaborations that take advantage of, and offer benefits to, all of the partners.

Thirdly, when collaboration takes place across cultural boundaries (and these are particularly evident when engaging with industry), new levels of risk emerge. For this reason, careful thought needs to be given to provide fallback options should issues arise either with the technology or the relationships with project partners.

Impact on the academic and the institution

Working with partners in other international institutions and industry partners presents a significant challenge to the traditional role of academic and institution. In bringing together partners using emergent technology, much of the work takes place virtually and is based within structures and cultures that are external.

For the academic, as much of the strength in collaborative learning lies in bridging the gap between learner and educator, much is to be said for standing back from the process to allow learners to work with their international learning and industry partners. By doing so, genuinely innovative ways of working together arise from the colaborators themselves, as active parcipants in the relationship and the process. With this project, the most creative and innovative results came from interaction rather than dictating. That said, as has been outlined, the structural issues within the host institution mean that the academic needs to 'scaffold' the process in such a way that academic rigour is maintained. The academic also needs to have credibility and expertise with a variety of outside partners before undertaking such work. The reputation of the institution is not sufficient as it is the academic who is making the project work, managing the learning experience and mitigating against risk.

For the institution, as a global community develops between the learners and industry partners, it takes on a life and culture of its own. As it develops and expands, with such a diversity of contributors and users, it can become a resource with more depth and credibility than individual institutions. This has the potential to undermine or even contradict the culture and workings of the institutions involved in it. Participants may start to align their thought to that of the community rather than the institution in which they are based, as they see it to have more authority in their subject area globally. Additionally, the institution comes under pressure in its traditional role of holder of knowledge. In contributing to the community, much of the expertise and knowledge within an institution will either 'leak' due to porosity or have to be fed into the collaborations to make them work. Furthermore, the community will develop its own knowledge that exists within it, rather than in the institution. As such, the institution has to be quite comfortable with this shift and formulate ways of dovetailing its work with that of the community.

Summary

As the project has shown, the signicant potential in catalysing creativity and innovation through the application of technology can be realized. Fundamentally, the collaborative nature of music production lends itself to such an approach, and as technology increasingly brings global practitioners together (thus taking Kealey's 1979 concept further), it reflects the real world. Other disciplines that have similar production 'processes' (such as, for example, film) could follow the same approach. Though technology is the catalyst, it is the use of what may be called 'participatory' technologies (rather than merely production) that offers the greatest impact. Notwithstanding the strategies and cultural structures within institutions, it seems that small-scale activities can offer significant impact in terms of developing intercultural and international competences, whereas aiming for large-scale projects can be disproportionately difficult. Only when the activities are underpinned with appropriate academic rigour (with, for example, interactions tied into learning outcomes at course or university level), will they be meaningful. In accordance with Whipple (1987), though, the community will develop its own knowledge and expertise, which is difficult for the individual institution to capture and manage. The institution may then have to accept this as a challenge that is bearable given the impact of innovations such as new forms of feedback outlined. Lastly, as many of these activities involve students sharing their work openly with others, either to work with, or feedback on, trust plays a crucial part. This takes time, and highlights the importance of the technical integrity of systems used, and the academic integrity of all participants.

References

Ashton, D. (2010) 'You just end up feeling more professional: Media production and industry-ready personhood'. *Networks*, 10, 14–19.

Barkley, E.F., Cross, P.K. and Major, C.H. (2005) *Collaborative Learning Techniques: A handbook for college faculty.* San Francisco: Wiley.

Bruffree, K.A. (1999) *Collaborative Learning.* Baltimore: John Hopkins University Press.

Gaunt, H. and Westerlund, H. (2013) *Collaborative Learning in Higher Music Education.* Farnham: Ashgate.

Kealey, E. (1979) 'From craft to art: The case of sound mixers and popular music'. *Sociology of Work and Occupations*, 6 (1), 3–29.

Levy, P. (1997) *Collective Intelligence: Mankind's emerging world in cyberspace.* New York: Perseus.

Negus, K. (1992) *Producing Pop.* London: Arnold.

O'Hara, K. and Brown, B. (2006) *Consuming Music Together: Social and collaborative aspects of music consumption technologies.* Dordrecht: Springer.

Tapscott, D. and Williams, A. (2006) *Wikinomics.* London: Atlantic Books.

Thorley, M. (2015) 'Graduate meets employer – a model for embedding industry professional involvement in the development and assessment of student portfolios'. *Journal of Music, Technology and Education*, 7 (3), 325–9.

Watson, A. (2014) *Cultural Production beyond the Recording Studio.* New York: Taylor and Francis.

Whipple, W.R. (1987) 'Collaborative learning: Recognizing it when we see it'. *American Association for Higher Education and Accreditation Bulletin,* October 1987, 4–6.

Creative industries and global education
Christina Slade

The creative industries are the fastest-growing area of the United Kingdom economy and a catalyst for global development. This paper explores how one UK university connects cultures of creative education across national boundaries, ensuring our students are internationally networked and prepared for the new landscape of work.

The creative industries

'At the centre of the UK's digital transformation lie the creative industries. These span music, film, TV, books and the arts, but also include software, newspaper and magazine publishing, and advertising' (Bain and Co., 2014).

The creative industries as defined by the Department for Culture, Media and Sport (DCMS) in 2001 'have their origin in individual creativity skill and talent and ... have the potential for wealth creation through intellectual property'. The exemplars listed were:

- Functional content: architecture, cultural heritage (including museums, galleries and libraries), crafts, art and antiques, design, fashion and computer software.
- Expressive content: film and video, television and radio, advertising, computer and video games, performing arts (including theatre), music and publishing.

(DCMS, 2001)

These definitions have since served as the basis of statistics published for the UK government. In 2014, the UK's creative industries were worth a record £84.1 billion to the economy and showed an increase of 8.9 per cent (DCMS, January 2016). This growth is twice that of the wider UK economy.

Creative industries have always been global. Art, styles of architecture, music, plays, films and games do not respect borders. Each new technology, from print through television to the internet, has accelerated the pace of diffusion of cultural and creative forms, with social media giving rise to the phenomenon of cultural artefacts going viral and being viewed or used within hours by millions.

Estimates put the value of the creative industries for the global economy at $4.1 trillion US dollars (Montgomery, 2010: 36). The creative industries are decoupled from the rest of the economy. As in the UK, creative industries grow when other sectors do not. Moreover, they are of particular importance to emerging economies. There they have grown at an average of 12.1 per cent over the decade to 2011, while the global average was 8.8 per cent (UNESCO/UNDP, 2013.) The accelerating growth of creative industries in emerging economies can be correlated with the growth of internet and disposable income in these economies. The digital revolution also allows creative products to be reproduced at low (or even zero) marginal cost, meaning that creative industries will be important in reducing global inequality (Hajkowicz, 2015).

Creativity is at the heart of what universities do. Universities have long served as a prime conduit for creative and cultural innovation. Scholarly publication internationalizes innovation. Higher studies reinforce the globalization of ideas. A lecturer returning from graduate studies brings novel forms of practice, interpretations and innovation. Digital technologies underpin the newer types of creative industries – apps and digital marketing, but also new textiles, design and all those dependent on big data.

Creative industries are themselves creating new industries, new ways of conceptualizing the field. Since the 2001 definition, there have been modifications and glosses. Potts (2011) defines creative industries very broadly as activities embedded in social networks. Perhaps most interesting is the attempt to include the wider sphere of the creative economy in statistical measures (DCMS, June 2015: Ch. 3 and annexes).

Creative industries both employ graduates and rely on university education:

> More than half (58.8%) of jobs in the Creative Economy in 2014 were filled by people with at least a degree or equivalent, compared to 31.8 per cent of all jobs in the UK. One in every six jobs in the UK held by graduates in 2014 was in the Creative Economy. Between 2013 and 2014, there was an increase of 110,000 (7.3%) in the number of jobs in the Creative Economy held by individuals with at least a degree or equivalent.
>
> (DCMS, June 2015: 5.1)

The creative economy underpins a new world of work. Many traditional occupations are being digitized away, including roles in banking, administration and industry that were the traditional middle-class occupations of university graduates. Some new roles will be based on digital skills. Andrew Hugill, head of creative computing at Bath Spa University, listed ten jobs that did not yet exist for which we need to train our students for the world service in 2013. These include: 'collective intelligence officer; data ecologist; gamification consultant; pervasive mediatrician (mobiles)'. In the past two years, each of these then unheard of posts has been advertised.

The traditional job market is being 'hollowed out', a partner from McKinsey's, Jonathan Dimson, explained to UK vice-chancellors and senior educationalists (4 February 2015). While professional jobs in the financial and professional areas will continue, and low-paid jobs will survive, the middle tier is increasingly automated. Routine tasks will disappear. Dimson identified the creative digital sector as the major growth area.

Training for the creative economy is a particular focus of specialist institutions such as art colleges and the so-called 'modern universities', which have responded rapidly to new and emerging markets by developing multidisciplinary courses. Some 70 per cent of students of creative subjects study in such universities (Million+, 2015). While traditional universities also train those who join the creative industries, established pathways from university to work are changing. The change is made vivid in a 2012 Gazelle Global report. A simple 2 by 2 matrix divides the world of work along two axes – one the corporate vs the personal employer, the other axis business drivers – whether proprietary products or 'open solutions'.

In earlier years, graduates expected to leave university to work with a corporation, whether public or private. Those producing products in industry would fall into the proprietary corporate quadrant, while services such as education, banking, law, management consulting or medicine are 'open' corporates. Corporations tend to be hierarchical. Technical expertise is valued. They are places where careers can be planned. Universities were a prime route into success in the corporate world, whether in industry or in the services sector.

The new world of work is 'personal' rather than corporate. The proprietary quadrant in this case is where individuals work alone or in small teams to produce products such as novels, pots, apps or computer programs. This is the 'artisanal world' of the matrix. Value is typically shared across a team rather than distributed hierarchically through a bureaucratic structure. In the personal sphere of work, those who produce are very often 'entrepreneurs' as well as artisans. The 'entrepreneurial world' is the fourth quadrant of the matrix, open and personal. The focus is on open solutions and is customer based, globally relevant and project oriented.

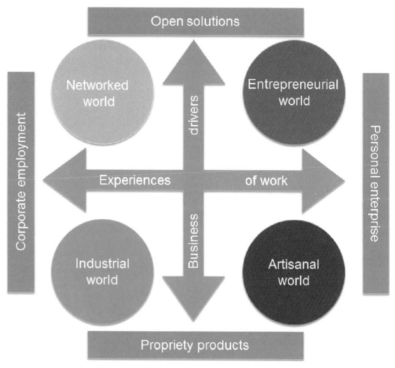

Figure 1: The future worlds of work

Source: 'The future worlds of work'. Gazelle Enterprising Futures.

Consider just one example of an entrepreneur producing an app, an artefact created in the 'personal' fashion of the new world. Naomi Alderman is a well-known novelist and a part-time professor at Bath Spa University. She researches interactive storytelling and game writing. She developed an iPhone fitness game and audio adventure called 'Zombies, Run!', working with a games studio, Six to Start, and funding the commercialization through Kickstarter. The app received almost five times the funding requested and has regularly topped the rankings in iPhone health and fitness apps. It has been featured in *The New York Times* and on Channel 4 News, and has been shortlisted for five Develop awards.

A 'personal' artefact has become globally successful. This is the new global landscape of creative training that has been the focus of Bath Spa University.

Bath Spa University

Bath Spa University began 155 years ago as the Bath School of Art. Bombed in the Second World War, the school moved to Corsham Court in Wiltshire. In the immediate postwar era it was acknowledged as a leading British art school, involved in the flowering of the English Modernist movement, attracting students from across the Commonwealth and an international group of teachers including Jim Dine. Following the war there was an acute shortage of teachers and a college for primary teachers was set up at Newton Park, a Georgian house and grounds near Bath that had been bought by the Duchy of Cornwall in 1942. The first principal, Miss Dawson, led a successful all-female college. Men were not admitted until the 1960s.

During the 1980s there was a flurry of amalgamations in the tertiary sector in Britain. The School of Art and the Teachers College in Bath were combined in 1983. The title, Bath Spa University, was granted in 2005, to be followed by 'higher degree research awarding powers' in 2008. Bath Spa University, a title conferred by the Privy Council and referring to the name of the town, offers a range of degrees from undergraduate to doctorates.

When I took up the role of vice-chancellor in 2012, Bath Spa was a perfectly formed and successful institution. Based in a world heritage city and in several historic buildings, it had developed a good reputation for student experience. The creative writing, music and art programmes were regarded as among the best in Britain. However, some areas were clearly challenging. As an arts-based university it had low graduate employability scores. Eighty-five per cent of students were from the west of England. Both the student body and the staff reflected the region, and were ethnically homogeneous. While individual academics had international networks, there were few active partnerships and the International Student Office had been closed down in 2010.

The greatest challenge at Bath Spa University was to attract international students. In 2011, there were 1.4 per cent international (non-EU) students and around 3 per cent EU and international students. This was the smallest proportion among all universities in the UK at that time. Very few students studied abroad. Their horizons were local: one graduate from 2011 remarked that the university had extended her horizons so much that she had considered taking a job in Swindon, 20 minutes away (Dossett and Devadasan, 2014). Yet higher education is and should be global. We owe it to our students to help them become globally aware, confident, cross-culturally adroit – global citizens. But we also owe it to them to prepare them for the new world of work. Bath is a 'creative hotspot', in a region where employment in the creative and digital sector is forecast to increase by 20 per cent by 2020 (West of England LEP, 2015). The creative industries, education, business and science are globalized. Our students need to have global networks and competencies.

In 2012 we developed a vision for the university:

> To be a leading university in creativity, culture and enterprise. Through inspirational teaching and research, we transform student lives. Based in a world heritage city and connected to a network of international partners, Bath Spa University will ensure that its graduates are socially engaged global citizens.

'Creativity' is a core value of the university, in terms of research, innovation and digital technology. We have developed our connection to the creative industries, a wide group of activities involving film, media, art and language, as well as education, design and creative computing. We focus on connectivity, and collaborative offerings, to emphasize not just the digital connectivity, but also the international, national and regional partnerships we encourage.

We have rapidly increased conventional internationalization through recruitment of international students. Over 950 of a student body of 7,000 are now international (including students from the European Union). There is a striking mix of student origins, with a very wide distribution, including the Faroe Islands, Colombia, Ukraine, Albania, Latvia, Gibraltar, Zambia and many others. Just 28 per cent of the international cohort is from China, or around 4 per cent of the student body, a much lower percentage than in the sector in general.

The vision for the university calls for our students to become socially engaged global citizens. I introduced a Certificate in Global Citizenship, based on a model used at Macquarie University in Australia (itself borrowed loosely from the USA). A small cohort of around 30 students is chosen in a competitive process from each intake year. Of this group we aim to have around 15 per cent non-UK-based students. As part of their courses, students must have at least two modules from a list that identifies material already taught across the university with a global focus. They attend a series of lectures by leading figures that touch on a wide interdisciplinary mix of global topics. They are asked to debate issues with the lecturers, then work together in teams to develop their understanding of the content of the special lectures. We have been able to attract scholarships and fund all UK-based students to assist them to study or work abroad.

I also led the establishment of the Global Academy of Liberal Arts (GALA), a network of international liberal arts institutions. Launched in 2014 by Professor Liz Coleman, a former president of Bennington and a TED speaker, GALA uses its networks and partnerships to internationalize students and staff experience. Students can learn virtually across campuses and are able to take courses and get credit across the network. Partners include the Tec de Monterrey in Mexico, the top-ranked university in Latin America, Claremont College in California, the J.M. Coetzee Centre at the University of Adelaide, the Communications University of China and the Foreign Languages Institute of Beijing, Queensland University of Technology, the University of Stockholm and the University of Utrecht. The network is formed on the basis of a convergence of highly reputable undergraduate and master's-level programmes, of research interest and of excellence. Our students travel within the network to study – this year to Mexico and Beijing as well as Los Angeles, Adelaide and Stockholm.

As leaders of the GALA network, Bath Spa proposed and developed a research project in the area of environmental humanities entitled 'Lost Waters'. This project brought together researchers, students and industry from Canada, Australia, the UK and Mexico. Artists from Montreal charted the lost canals of Montreal Island, a BSU student traced the tributaries of the Fleet in London, and we opened discussions between ecologists, artists and economists that then led to joint teaching. In another network, heritage management courses are shared between Claremont Graduate College in California and Bath Spa. Claremont College has strong links with the Getty Museum, while Bath Spa works not only with the Roman Baths and the many other local museums but also with the Victoria and Albert Museum in London. These networks enable students and staff to publish, work and move easily in the globalized world of the creative industries.

A final example of global integration is the 'three continents' degree with Santa Monica Community College in the USA and a variety of Asian partners. This degree gives ambitious students the chance to study in Asia, the USA and the UK. Students in Asia complete a foundation year with a partner in Hong Kong, Singapore or Malaysia. They then move for two years to Santa Monica College, where they complete a second (associate degree level) year and a third year, which is the penultimate year of the Bath Spa honours degree curriculum. Students then move to Bath for two years to complete their honours degree and go on to do a one-year master's. The focus is on a range of skills from the creative through to entrepreneurship. The students will have developed a unique range of contacts and cross-cultural skills when they graduate.

International students are important for universities not just as an income stream. All students need global networks, and experience with those from outside their own country or region. For a university such as Bath Spa, which focuses on the creative industries and on preparing our students for a global workplace, globalization is essential. We seek to open the minds of our students, to encourage innovation and entrepreneurship. We would like to be able to shape a student body to mix groups of different origins together. That is not easy and cannot be done by fiat: as university professors and professionals our role is to make interaction possible, and to create the conditions for understanding and friendship. Just as we aspire to foster interdisciplinary understanding and cross-disciplinary creativity, we hope to develop communities of difference where original and creative students have the confidence to move in a global world.

References

Bain and Co. (2014) 'Creative UK: Overview of the digital transformation of the UK creative economy'. Online. www.bain.com/publications/articles/creative-uk. aspx (accessed 17 November 2015).

Department for Culture, Media and Sport (2001) 'Creative industries mapping document'. London: HMSO.

Department for Culture, Media and Sport (2010) 'Measuring the value of culture: A report to the Department for Culture Media and Sport'. Online. http://tinyurl. com/jy97o4l (accessed 17 November 2015).

Department for Culture, Media and Sport (January 2016) 'Creative industries worth almost £10 million an hour to economy'. Online. http://tinyurl.com/ jcuvkdo (accessed 2 March 2016).

Department for Culture, Media and Sport (2015) 'Creative industries focus on employment June 2015'. Online. http://tinyurl.com/naj328t (accessed 17 November 2015).

Dimson, J. and Karim, D. (2015) 'Global challenges for higher education'. Speech presented to HEFCE Annual Conference (4 February).

Dossett, G. and Devadasan, R. (2014) 'Globalisation, work and the graduate experience: Moving beyond Swindon'. Research presentation at Bath Spa University, Bath, UK, July.

Gazelle Global (2012) 'Enterprising futures: The changing landscape and new possibilities of further education'. Online. www.stow.ac.uk/media/ gazelleenterprisingfutures.pdf (accessed 17 November 2015).

Hajkowicz, S. (2015) 'The potential of the creative economy'. CSIRO Australia. Online. https://agenda.weforum.org/2015/01/why-is-the-creative-economy-growing-so-strongly/ (accessed 17 November 2015).

Million+ (2015) *Creative Futures: Ten steps to support the creative economy*. London: Million+.

Montgomery, L. (2010) *China's Creative Industries: Copyright, social network markets and the business of culture in a digital age*. Cheltenham: Edward Elgar.

Potts, J. (2011) *Creative Industries and Economic Evolution*. Cheltenham: Edward Elgar.

UNESCO/UNDP (2013) 'Creative Economy Report: Widening local development pathways'. Online. www.unesco.org/culture/pdf/creative-economy-report-2013. pdf (accessed 17 November 2015).

West of England Local Enterprise Partnership (2015) 'Employment in the West of England 2015: Creative and digital'. Online. http://tinyurl.com/jgdj3fx (accessed 17 November 2015).

3.8

Global innovation networks: The anatomy of change

John Hearn, Joyce Achampong, Hilligje Van't Land and Paul Manners

A sustainable environment

Higher education and research are no longer privileged pursuits pursued by high priests in isolated ivory towers. That history and stereotype, itself only partly true, has given way to the increasing catalysis of change. The change is fuelled by rapid development and competition, and by a concert of factors and global dynamics affecting the international research universities that are the subject of this discussion.

The role of networks, formed by groups of universities in order to strengthen their capacity to compete, change, challenge and innovate, is to be experimental laboratories at the frontiers of change, where concepts and instruments may be developed, tested and assessed. If successful and viable, the proofs of concept may be adopted and implemented by their communities. In this paper, we take just three examples of international university networks, each different in scope, ambition and delivery. We ask how these networks adapt, evolve and introduce successful innovations to themselves but also serve as role models to their wider constituents and stakeholders.

In taking a look at the activities of the **Association of Commonwealth Universities** (ACU – founded 1913), the **International Association of Universities** (IAU – founded 1950) and the **Worldwide Universities Network** (WUN – founded 2000), along with the catalytic role of the **National Coordinating Centre for Public Engagement** (NCCPE – founded 2008), we are not promoting these as ideal models. We are testing their performance as examples of a new global teamwork in higher education and research, itself changing rapidly under drivers and change agents that can both encourage and threaten the future. We arrive at a short list of selected factors and features that will be influential now, and as far into that unpredictable future as we can see.

Teamwork time

There are now over 50 continuing international university networks of varying focus and levels of activity. Most have been formed in the past 10–20 years, and they are usually based on the premise that a team will achieve more than can the individual. They can provide capacities and opportunities that transcend and lift individual visions and missions. They can assist in the formation and competitiveness of prepared international citizens and leaders from established and emerging researchers and teachers. In addition, this teamwork allows for rapid group sharing and learning from successful experiments and interventions, while based on the historic strengths and qualities of universities in scholarship, teaching, community and international engagement.

The huge advances in the internet, the international fora for communication and meetings, such as the British Council Going Global conference, and the opportunities for easy and continuing teamwork through Skype and other platforms mean that the pace of change can only increase. That will require the retention of essential **core values and trust**, sometimes forgotten in the scramble for fame and fortune by individuals and institutions.

There are two further important points to make in defining our discussion. The first is that a focus on the three examples of networks represented here includes the many associates, stakeholders, NGOs and international agencies with which they work in flexible team formation to be fit for purpose. The second is that there are very many networks that are regional, national and even provincial and which have essential roles in the overall future of higher education and research, the development of talent, and the discovery and communication of knowledge.

As the world of higher education changes, new capacities and opportunities for **teamwork and service** are constantly emerging. Among these now are the **new overall framework** and transition from the Millennium Development Goals to the **Sustainable Development Goals**, with the vital requirement that knowledge gaps between developed and less developed economies do not expand; the engagement of universities as partners in support of major geopolitical initiatives such as the **Chinese 'Belt and Road'** and the **Trans Pacific Partnership**; and other regional or national programmes where new knowledge and innovation strengthen economies and improve lives. In the future, international university networks can engage actively, bringing new knowledge, evidence-based policy, open-minded experts and thought leaders to the table, and developing solutions and the best practical practice.

Future history

Networks can take time to build teams, and can review and reform them when opportunities arise that meet their vision and advance their impact. In 1913 the vision of the **Association of Commonwealth Universities** was to bring together the universities of the Commonwealth, whose diversity and distance are overcome by bonds of common language, aligned education systems and a desire to build better societies through higher education. Now there are over 500 member universities from developed and less developed countries across the Commonwealth. The unique mix of countries and institutions, as well as the global nature of the organization, provides fertile ground for **international collaboration and shared knowledge**.

The positive benefits of the association, and its dynamic community of stakeholders, have survived and strengthened through the turbulent histories, conflicts and transitions of the twentieth century from this experienced and tested network. The focus is now on membership, projects and scholarship administration and the ways in which these can impact on and advance wider society. Examples of innovation should include the **mobility of international staff and students** as key to preparing future citizens and leaders. These programmes are enablers to innovation and contribute towards prosperity, employability, human capacity development and international diplomacy.

Opportunities for university leaders, staff and students to benchmark and share knowledge and experience can provide the stimulus and impetus for creative thought and adaptive best practice. The resulting transformations are apparent across socio-economic and cultural barriers, and can be further developed as the **millennium goals** transition to **the sustainable development goals**. One innovation has been broad consultations across all of the members in considering the role and active engagement of Commonwealth universities in developing effective models and tools to influence the formation and implementation of the sustainability goals.

A further initiative is the role of universities as co-creators with the **Research Data Alliance** – a project that builds the social and technical bridges that enable open sharing of data across technologies, disciplines and countries. Further work in supporting **university research management** has led to the formation of associations across Africa to build a better appreciation of management infrastructure. The support of **early career researchers** is a pressing priority, with allied skills in the administration, assessment of effectiveness and impact of scholarships. There are numerous examples of individuals who have **progressed to leadership** across disciplines and society, including business, politics, academia and the professions. These leaders in turn contribute to growth, development and innovation of their own countries and beyond.

Defenders of the faith?

Since the early days of history, it has been recognized that knowledge is power, whether at individual, institutional, national or international levels. In terms of international higher education and university development, the influence and effects of the various **university rankings systems have had mixed impact.** This is not the place to debate the pros and cons of the rankings, other than to note two relevant points.

First, the rankings have produced positive contributions, in **aligning university performance against a set of criteria and indicators,** resulting in enormous interest and some prospects for improvement and transparency. Among the upper 2–3 per cent of universities who compete to be in the top 500, the indicators developed by the rankings systems are becoming more sophisticated, accountable and accepted, albeit with a wide degree of scepticism about their precision and accuracy.

Second, the negative effects of rankings systems are to **drive uniformity and lose diversity** – the very antithesis of intellectual thought and development. Universities, based in very different countries and cultures, with very different capacities and strengths, talents and resources, should not be slavish followers of fashion. In climbing the rungs of a linear ladder that forces one model, there is risk to diversity, identity, culture and soul. Playing to the imposed rules of others (and even paying to do so) is not always smart.

University networks can provide some datasets that celebrate diversity, and develop communities who learn from the pooled experience of members. The **International Association of Universities** (IAU), the UNESCO-based higher education organisation, includes over 630 members from around the world. The network is a global forum for leaders of institutions and associations to discuss, reflect and take action on issues of mutual interest. A strong theme of the network is to uphold the values of academic freedom and institutional autonomy, while promoting greater accountability.

The IAU promotes institutional effectiveness and the ideal of knowledge made available to all through collaboration and access to higher education. At the same time, it aims to give expression to the obligation of universities, as social institutions, to promote through teaching and research the principles of freedom and justice, human dignity and solidarity. These goals are achieved by strengthening international cooperation between universities and through partnerships between key organizations and stakeholders.

The IAU promotes healthy **cooperation and competition**, academic solidarity and the principles for which every university should stand: (i) the right to pursue knowledge for its own sake, and (ii) to promote and uphold the tolerance of divergent opinion and freedom from political interference. It advances equitable access, success and equal opportunities for students, researchers, faculty and staff, and inspires the pursuit of diversity and quality while respecting cultural differences.

Perhaps the emerging power and capacity of the rankings systems could encourage and achieve the ranking of national university systems against the fundamental principles and criteria promoted by the IAU. Governments look at rankings. Convincing data, where the political, social and economic climate and environment fall well below expectations, might convey to governments and agencies the sterility and drag imposed on national intellectual and economic development when talent is wasted or chained.

Evidence-based policies

Although there can be broad recognition of the major global challenges facing the future of human development, including a sustainable planet, the solutions to these challenges may not be uniform and may require a nuanced interpretation of instruments and solutions that can be applied in varied environments and countries. The argument for such international cooperation and comparisons encourage the contributions of research networks that can develop, evaluate and apply evidence-based technical and policy solutions.

Too often, the parallel streams of government, business, academia, international agencies and foundations, NGOs and specialist community groups proceed along their own paths without timely and adequate cross-talk that might conserve resources and build focus. The tools are becoming available to enable better integration of what must now be a multilayered approach to most global challenges. The **Worldwide Universities Network** (WUN) is a player in the search for relevant knowledge, opportunities for established and emerging researchers, communication with communities and policymakers, and the attraction of resources in the form of grants, scholarships and talent. The network has proved that **international teamwork can deliver more than individual institutions.**

The needs list for knowledge is endless. In considering priorities and the probabilities of successful engagement, WUN has focused on the four pillars of its global challenges: climate and **food security** and safety; **public health** in obesity, heart disease and diabetes throughout the life course; reform in global **higher education** and research; and **understanding cultures**. In some ways, this latter challenge is turning out to be the most catalytic.

WUN is now developing cross-cutting themes across the above pillars. These are in **migration, economics, web futures** and **big data**; as well as regional networks, with a **Global China Group** and a **Global Africa Group**. In addition, WUN is establishing global platforms in critical zones, farm platforms for intensification of sustainable production in plants and animals, and the development and balance of urbanization and green cities.

The network has restricted itself to a maximum core membership of 25 university partners, as effective research collaboration is complex. However, collaborative links and alliances are built, with over 200 'WUN-Plus Institutions'. Overall, WUN engages with the four global challenges and presently has 18 partner universities, 90 international and interdisciplinary research teams and over 2,000 researchers and students. An important current initiative is to build greater opportunity for **mobility for researchers, graduate and undergraduate students.**

WUN has pioneered innovations and instruments as a laboratory and test-bed for international engagement and the internationalization of peer research universities. The successful tools include the **Research Development Fund,** which provides seed funding for competitive proposals; the Sustainability Fund that catalyses major funding bids; 90 global teams addressing urgent challenges; policy engagement with international governments and agencies on key issues (including the Sustainable Development Goals); opportunities for established and emerging researchers to become **global citizens and leaders**; and focused workshops (not talk shops) that deliver research strategies and funding strategies to support the global teams. The WUN Interdisciplinary Research Groups (IRGs) represent global Rapid Research Response Teams, formed with the specific capacities needed to address present or emerging global challenges.

Public engagement

The UK's National Coordinating Centre for Public Engagement (NCCPE) was established in 2008 to address **university–society engagement.** Leading universities are moving from being relatively peripheral ivory towers to central societal powers. Sometimes they still retain distinct tribal cultures and practices that can appear arcane. There needs to be a greater establishment of mutual understanding and trust, and a joint approach to mutually desired rather than imposed solutions. In a dynamic democracy, where higher education and research may be undervalued or assumed, the consequences of lack of trust, avoidable misunderstanding, and the distraction and loss of talent is a national threat. The NCCPE brief is to coordinate initiatives and innovations that could trigger greater understanding and facilitate behavioural change – the last bastion of entrenched cultures!

In its approach, the NCCPE has worked extensively through networks. The UK Cabinet Office developed a paper 'Achieving cultural change: A policy framework', which identified four key activities in catalysing behavioural change: enable, engage, exemplify and encourage.

- *ENABLE:* remove barriers, give information, provide viable alternatives, educate and provide skills, build capacity, broker and support.
- *ENGAGE:* use networks, personal contacts, enthusiasts, co-producer teams, media and opinion formers.
- *EXEMPLIFY:* visible figures leading by example, achieving consistency in policies, establishing compelling and consistent messages.
- *ENCOURAGE:* financial incentives, reward schemes, regulations to promote desirable and sanction undesirable behaviours, contracts and codifications to frame expectations about behaviour, recognition and social pressures.

In addition, it is becoming clear that engagement is needed with networks outside of higher education to build common purpose and critical mass. A framework for such activity was developed by the Stanford Centre for Social Innovation, under a banner of 'collective impact', for which there are five conditions. The result is a model for bringing networks together to realize shared goals. This set of criteria can be fundamental to the effective working and success of any international university network, although the specifics will adjust to the vision, objectives and action plan of the network.

The five conditions of collective impact:

1. **Common agenda.** All participants have a shared vision for change, including a common understanding of the problem and a joint approach to solving it through agreed upon actions
2. **Shared measurement.** Collecting data and measuring results consistently across all participants ensures efforts remain aligned and participants hold each other accountable
3. **Mutually reinforcing activities.** Participant activities must be differentiated while still being coordinated through a mutually reinforcing action plan

4. **Continuous communication.** Consistent and open communication is needed across the many players to build trust, assure mutual objectives and create common motivation

5. **Backbone support.** Creating and managing collective impact requires a separate organization(s) with staff and a specific set of skills to serve as a backbone for the entire initiative and coordinate participating organizations and agencies.

Truths and trust

In this discussion so far, we have shown only three examples through very different international university networks. The platforms and capacities exist, and have done for a long time, to impact on discovery, transfer, policy and practice. The British Council Going Global 2015 provoked and facilitated some of the renewed debate. Competition has been core since cave days, but perhaps we are becoming more enthusiastic about cooperation when meeting common challenges. New technologies can assist with the tyrannies of time and distance, but they cannot impose teamwork: that takes intelligence, commitment and a shared vision, mutual respect and friendship.

Higher education and research are so obviously good, especially to us internal stakeholders, that we can risk some serious self-deception and complacency. There are urgent and compelling challenges, which should make us step back and consider that all is not perfect in our educational Garden of Eden. Numerous studies exist on trust in society, which rank politics, banking and other sectors – these often show a gap in the societal levels of understanding and appreciation of these sectors.

Higher education, which thankfully remains in relatively high regard in comparison to banks and politics, cannot revert to ivory tower thinking. While this is not the place for detailed examination, we can finish this contribution on a provocative note, which engages universities and networks in finding reforms and solutions — above all, achieving balance – to the following challenges and questions in higher education and research reform.

1. **The use and abuse of talent.** There is a long way to go before we can reach acceptable levels of equity and access so that bright and qualified individuals can develop and contribute. There is a long way to go to empower and engage women and minorities in higher education and research leadership.

2. **Standards.** Fifty years ago, 8 per cent of the population progressed to higher education in universities. This figure is now rising to 40 per cent

in many countries, at great cost to national investment and the taxpayer. There are benefits to society when managed well; and losses to diversity of career and to practical skills when balance is lost. Fifty years ago, less than 1 per cent of those starting BSc and BA degrees achieved first class honours. Now in many systems the figure rises to 30 per cent. Is the currency being devalued?

3. **Degree cost inflation.** The costs of higher education and degrees are unsustainable and unnecessary. They induce debt, which can blight early career and development of family and society. We must return to core values of scholarship and service.

4. **Glittering palaces.** Do we need to emulate the big end of town in chrome and steel, putting the costs of this bling before real academic talent, and consequently being unable to afford and support established or emerging leaders? A balance of buildings versus brains needs clear strategy and implementation.

5. **Curriculum reform.** Everyone talks about it, but few do it well. The inertia of the same old lectures without the excitement of fundamentals, frontiers and future relevance to each of our lives. New technology can make lectures into tutorials, with basic background available as MOOCs or equivalents.

6. **Interdisciplinary research.** What percentage of teachers and researchers grasp (maybe most students do) the entrancing challenges of working at six levels of interaction? The research grants system and university departmental silos need a balance between depth and breadth.

7. **Managerialism.** The rise of the university bureaucrat, often without experience of, or respect for, research or teaching, threatens and undermines the esteem and capacity of academic thought and impact. This culture results in disengagement of the academic discovery, learning and teaching enterprise from the 'corporate' university executive.

8. **'Strategic' plans.** If you download and read the strategic plans of the 20 universities above and below your peer ranking, they are all much the same: glossy, long, boring and soon forgotten. Save the money and build your own framework, with cut-through strategies to resource and achieve specific goals that have distinct advantages.

9. **International Higher Education.** This is the fastest-expanding part of the higher education universe. At best, it is a wonderful mix of cultures, values and practices that teaches understanding, tolerance and best practice standards to all. At worst, it degenerates into a money game to close budget deficits; injects the distractions of cheating (including easily available internet assignments), and subsidies to support non-competitive

research. A percentage of international student revenues should be invested in student support, language top-up, residences and further international business innovation and development.

10. **Leadership.** Some university executives are masters of establishing lofty and rightly inspiring objectives – and then not providing the resources to implement them. This 'set up to fail' delusion wastes time and talent, and can infect whole executives. Of course, we can always wait for the next strategic plan …

11. **Role models.** Fortunately the above provocations and practices are not universal. There are universities with great leadership, well-engaged researchers, teachers and students who show it can be done – and who address the above challenges and others! These role models and case histories should be the subject of serious intellectual analysis and trail-blazing study, well beyond the vagaries, gambling and gaming of the rankings roulette.

Conclusion

The case for international university networks as experimental laboratories and meeting places that can contribute ideas, new knowledge, comparative approaches and solutions to selected global challenges is real and should be supported. The catalysis and excitement of meeting colleagues in international engagement and environments expands minds and capacities. The development of new technologies and practices that can build and deliver collective impact from disparate networks and groups provides innovation and confidence in future progress. The acceleration of international engagement and internationalization can benefit individuals, institutions and nations and is the way of the future.

Further reading

Association of Commonwealth Universities, 'Progress and potential: Higher education playing its part in the Sustainable Development Goals', September 2015.

Boléat, M. (2003) 'Managing trade associations'. Online. www.boleat. com/materials/managing_trade_associations_2003_1.pdf (accessed 30 November 2015).

Hanleybrown, F., Kania, John and Kramer, Mark (2012) 'Channelling change: Making collective impact work'. Stanford Social Innovation Review. Online. http://connect.ala.org/files/2016.16%20Collective%20Impact%20Channeling_Change_SSIR.pdf (accessed 30 November 2015).

Hearn, J. (2014) 'Global research networks: Experiments in internationalization'. *IIE Networker*, Spring, 39–45. Online. www.nxtbook.com/naylor/IIEB/IIEB0114/index.php?startid=39

Hearn, J., Fenwick, B., Halevi, G., Lawton, W. and Chicherina, N. (2015) 'Teamwork time: experiments in international co-operation'. In M. Stiasny and T. Gore (eds), *Going Global: Inclusion, innovation, impact*. London: British Council and Institute of Education Press.

Knott, D., with Muers, S. and Aldridge, S. (2008) 'Achieving culture change: A policy framework'. Cabinet Office. Online. https://crawford.anu.edu.au/sparc/pdf/2010/achieving_culture_change.pdf (accessed 30 November 2015).

Section 4

Reflections

Editors' introduction to Section 4

Reflections

In this section the sole paper, by Jo Beall, Director Education and Society at the British Council, reflects on the role that universities play in the nation-building enterprise. She returns to the age-old discussion about higher education as a public or a private good, and in doing so moves our retrospective reflections on the 2015 Going Global conference in London towards a look forward to the 2016 event. Cape Town, South Africa, will play host to Going Global 2016, and it will provide a context in which to revisit debates about the internationalization of higher education and reflections on what she calls the 'processes of global economic integration, research collaboration, and competition for the brightest and best students and scholars' (Beall). The inter-relationship between internationalization and nation-states is one of crucial importance and significance. Going Global 2016 will give us the opportunity to explore this relationship further.

Universities and their importance to nations and cities
Jo Beall

Introduction

Higher education systems have a key role to play in positive social and economic change. Economically, they give rise to skilled workforces, while research universities are at the heart of innovation and knowledge economies. Socially, they foster wide public benefit through creating more informed citizens, more tolerant societies, more participative communities, and better living conditions. I have argued elsewhere that international development policy, particularly under the auspices of the Millennium Development Goals (MDGs), erroneously ignored the contribution of higher education to development and ultimately poverty reduction. It is also telling therefore that many national governments continued to recognize the importance of tertiary education to economic and social development, and have continued to invest in their universities and in research (Beall, 2015).

Here I look at universities and other higher education institutions within their spatial and locational contexts, namely the nation-states and city regions of which they are a part. I make the case that at national level, universities can be important not only to national economic development but also to the nation-building project. I also argue that universities and research institutions can play a key role in innovation systems and capital formation at local level, exemplified by their growing importance to the establishment and development of city-regional economies.

The synergies and disconnects between national higher education institutions and systems on the one hand and international higher education trends on the other, is a central theme of the Going Global 2016 conference in Cape Town. Going forward we need to pay similar attention to the relationship between universities and research and their city and regional economies and polities (Goddard and Puukka, 2008) and how international dynamics impact on this relationship. I suggest that there is much to be learned from the complex and interdependent relationship between town and gown from an international perspective and from understanding why it is that many city governments are paying closer attention to the contribution of higher education both to city-regional economies and to urban life more broadly.

Higher education: a public and private good

Nineteenth-century visions for universities were rooted in the religious foundations of education with a strong emphasis on teaching and learning, best exemplified perhaps in the contributions of Cardinal John Henry Newman in England. Alternatively they were concerned with the development of professional knowledge and research as advocated by his near contemporary in Germany, Wilhelm von Humboldt. In both cases universities were seen as contributing to the public good. In twentieth-century Europe higher education remained largely defined in relation to the public good and more particularly, to a country's national economic productivity. This constituted a key incentive for publicly funding the production and transmission of knowledge in the UK and across the continent.

Nevertheless, the notion of higher education as a public good has always been contested because of the private benefits that individual scholars and teachers accrue. Individualized notions of career advancement, educational attainment, and social mobility reinforced the idea of education as a private investment that delivers personal rather than public benefit. Twentieth-century debates as to whether higher education constitutes a public or private good have pivoted around the issue of public funding for universities. In Europe, the public good argument saw its heyday in the post-war dispensation, characterized as the region was by relative political stability, economic growth and a strong social contract. Since then, more and more national governments have shifted from a commitment to state funding to considering higher education as a private good, the cost of which should be born or shared by individuals through the payment of fees.

Moreover, during times of economic stress the private good elements of higher education tend to receive elevated attention as parents and students focus more intently on achieving educational outcomes that bring job opportunities and career prospects. In the UK this was most clearly articulated by the Dearing Report, which suggested that government and universities should 'encourage the student to see him/herself as an investor in receipt of a service and to seek, as an investor, value for money and a good return from the investment' (Dearing, 1997). More recently UK policy attention has re-emphasized not only private economic gains but also private provision and the contribution of higher education to national economic advancement. In relation to international higher education this has firmly focused on higher education as an export (Able and White, 2011).

Internationally, there is broad consensus that, however funded, higher education is both a public and a private good. There is acknowledgement of the role universities play in growing knowledge economies, the development of skills, the conduct and dissemination of research, and the contribution to commercial innovation. From the time of the economic downturn of the early 1970s and firmly reinforced by the 2008 economic crisis and its aftermath, efforts to diversify economies and increase global competitiveness have reinforced competition for the brightest research brains in order to enhance professional expertise and feed competing knowledge economies.

These drivers have tended to obscure the measurable public benefits higher education brings to social well-being beyond economic dimensions. For instance, it contributes to education itself as an end-to-end system from the primary to tertiary level, to health and nutrition, and to infrastructure and engineering. It demonstrably supports democracy through the strengthening of institutions, governance and the delivery of public services (Oketch *et al.*, 2014: 39–40). There is also a tradition of universities playing a constructive role in the arts, culture and the governance of cities, through civil society engagement, thus contributing to social reproduction as well as economic production in the cities and regions of which they are a part (Moulaert *et al.*, 2007). These benefits are as important as economic contributions in reinforcing the notion that public and private good benefits operate at both national and city regional levels.

Universities and nation-building

Historically there has been strong acknowledgement that universities can and do play an important part in the process of nation-building: in other words, the expectation that universities, as custodians and generators of national culture (particularly but not only through the humanities such as languages, history and the arts) can actively contribute to the establishment of national cultures, engage communities and promote political stability through the formation and strengthening of nation-states and through their contribution towards building and re-building national identities. Open to the flow of new ideas and providing as they do the intellectual spaces to contest existing and emerging social, political and economic structures, universities played a particularly important role in the post-colonial era, as newly independent countries sought to establish systems and institutions associated with nationhood (Enders, 2004). This trajectory is exemplified in the opening address to the Interim Council of the University of Ghana when it became independent from the University of London in 1961. Delivered by the President of the Republic of Ghana, Dr Kwame Nkrumah, he said the following:

> A very heavy responsibility is being entrusted to you. The whole future of Ghana depends to a very considerable extent on the success of our programme for higher education and research ... which is to produce a University which will serve the needs of African unity, will make practical and concrete contributions to the development of Ghana and the well-being of this country, and, indeed, all of Africa, and yet which will have a world-wide reputation

> (cited in Enders, 2004: 367)

Nkrumah's address reflects the belief held by African leaders at the time that higher education would be critical to the development and growth of their countries as well as the region and Africa as a whole and, in addition, being an active member of an international scholarly community was critical to the success of any nation and higher education system.

Universities naturally work across national and territorial boundaries, providing the institutional and operational frameworks for wider international knowledge exchange. Academic endeavour actively encourages scholars to be worldly, to seek out answers and collaborations, to look for others doing similar work and to present and test ideas. Historical images of medieval scholars moving between Bologna, Paris and Oxford suggest that from their earliest origins, universities could step across political borders and source learning and expertise from anywhere in the world (Bender, 1988). Indeed, it is the cosmopolitan values of international recognition, reputation and cooperation associated with scholarly endeavour that has tended to place universities at the centre of nation-building.

Jochen Hippler (2002) suggests that the term nation-building is 'both old and new'. Describing it as a highly complex concept that over time has had many political interpretations, he sees nation-building as the act of integration around a common ideology that leads to the establishment of a national identity and infrastructure. Importantly, it is recognition from other nations across the international community that cements and strengthens this identity. As Nkrumah clearly articulated, international recognition and engagement is critical to the success of any nation and paves the way for national unity.

Today, the expansion of international partnerships in higher education and research is increasingly being seen by national governments across the world as a means to deliver on national growth priorities (British Council, 2012). Universities as interactive institutions that work together with industry, commerce, government and community are increasingly seen as integral to national innovation systems (Mowery and Sampat, 2005). As such national policy makers and international economic actors are placing growing emphasis on capturing and providing incentives for a stronger relationship between higher education and research networks, and commerce and industry. In many emerging markets, national and local governments are explicitly linking this approach to economic development to the internationalization of higher education and research (Altbach *et al.*, 2009: xvii).

Internationalization and nation states

In unpacking international engagement it is useful to draw on Peter Scott's (1998) distinction between the more historically applicable and broadly positive concept of 'internationalization', being greater cooperation between states and across state borders, and 'globalization', referring to the more recent phenomenon of ever-increasing interdependence and convergence of economies globally and the associated liberalization of trade and markets. This distinction is of particular significance for countries where global economic integration has increased rather than reduced global inequalities but where an isolationist response means missing out on international encounters and partnerships that hold the potential for unlocking national and regional opportunity.

States are defined by sovereignty exercised over their territories and territorial boundaries in which their citizens share a single national identity, language(s) and cultural heritage. Late twentieth-century globalization scholars asserted that all that came under threat as a result of technology and communication changes, cultural fusion and economic integration (Castells, 1997) as well as global power dynamics undermining national and local authority (Mann, 1997). Even those that did not go so far as to see the state as existentially threatened, argued that nations were no longer as insulated from global processes as they once were and that the intensification of social relations that linked and shaped distant but globally connected localities had implications for governance (Giddens, 1999). When combined with late twentieth-century trends towards marketization and privatization of the public goods and services conventionally provided by the state in the post-war period, particularly in Europe and its colonial and post-colonial spheres of influence, many have argued that the state has been hollowed out and its functions usurped by other sectors, notably private but also the not-for-profit or voluntary sectors (Batley and Larbi, 2004).

Without wishing to deviate into these debates I would posit that states are not in decline although in many cases their functions have undoubtedly altered. In support of this argument, in developed and emerging market countries across the world it is rare to find the share of GDP going to public spending ever falling sharply and, despite withdrawal of the state from welfare provision in many countries, governments continue to regularly intervene through legislation, regulation, distribution and above all taxation. Martin Wolf has argued, for example, that it has been electoral resistance rather than globalization processes that have most significantly limited the ability of states to tax their citizens (Wolf, 2001). The relevant point here is that despite international economic integration and market liberalization it is unlikely that the nation-state and state intervention will disappear any time soon, particularly given the absence of legitimate and effective institutions of global governance, and this pertains to the sphere of higher education as much as any other area of policy.

Cities and universities

The contribution of universities to local and regional development is not a new phenomenon: 'For centuries, universities have had a deep and dynamic relationship with the economic, social and cultural life of the cities in which they are based' (Williams, Turner, and Jones, 2008: 4). Recently, however, the OECD, the World Bank, and other international agencies have recognized and promoted the idea that universities serve a broad range of functions at local and regional level, through education, research and through culturally related activities, with a particular emphasis on their contribution to economic development (OECD, 2007; Puukka, 2008). Today national and city governments increasingly see universities as pivotal to their economic innovation systems. Teaching and learning develops human capital and highly skilled graduates are recognized as key inputs for successful industrial development in a given locality (Puukka and Marmolejo, 2008). In some cases, such as India and China, growing large numbers of inexpensively trained graduates, particularly in science and engineering, has been crucial to meeting growing industrial demand in these emerging economies (Athreye, 2005). Research also contributes to innovation and innovation itself 'clusters around regions with vibrant communities, skilled people and universities' (Asheim and Gertler, 2005).

The late Jane Jacobs, the eminent economist, argued vigorously that cities rather than nations are the salient unit of analysis for understanding economic processes. She saw nations as political and military entities, noting that 'most nations are composed of collections or grab bags of very different economies, rich regions and poor ones within the same nation'. By contrast she suggested that cities 'are unique in their abilities to shape and reshape the economies of other settlements, including those far removed from them geographically' (Jacobs, 1984: 32). Why is this so? The first reason is agglomeration or the clustering of people and economic activity in space and the second is diversity, being the vast array of different people and multiple talents that congregate in cities. This in turn stimulates efficiencies, productivity and, above all, innovation (Beall and Fox, 2010; Beall, Guha-Khasnobis, and Kanbur, 2010).

Universities, industry, and government often work together and create innovative partnerships. In recent years, however, there has been much greater conscious effort to promote what has sometimes been dubbed the 'triple helix'. At the metropolitan or municipal level, this points to the need for collaborative efforts between local governments, firms, universities and individuals to strengthen the unique urban character of their city-regions. The so-called 'triple helix' has a strong international dimension that can perhaps best be exemplified by the role the Government of California and Stanford University played in the development of Silicon Valley. Here the aim and the outcome was to attract the most talented academics and world leading researchers, resulting in 52 per cent of all Silicon Valley firm start-ups and a quarter of all American patents being filed by or with the contribution of people of non-US origin.

From the vantage point of universities, as institutions primarily based in cities they make a significant contribution to the skills, ideas, creativity, and general environment and attractiveness of urban centres. Goddard and Vallance (2011: 2) ask whether universities are simply in the city or are fundamentally part of the city. Increasingly, universities work hard to play their part in setting the social, cultural and intellectual tone of a locality. Some universities also take very seriously their responsibility for community development as part of its strategic mission engaging in a wide array of community initiatives ranging from economic development plans in collaboration with local communities, extensive support to local schools and a variety of services to the local community (Goddard and Vallance, 2011).

In sum, creativity has replaced commodities as the foundation of economic development. Geography and institutions matter in developing agglomerations of talented and creative people to generate creativity and innovation. Talented people are not spread equally across nations but tend to concentrate within particular city-regions. Internationally the most successful city-regions are the ones that have a social environment that is open to creativity and diversity and therefore attracts the brightest and best from across different countries of the world. To attract creative people, whether in arts and culture or science and technology, requires openness to diverse people from different ethnic, racial and lifestyle groups. As Jane Jacobs so cogently argues, cities are such sites of attraction and provide distinct advantages when seeking to grow and attract knowledge-based economies and the diverse people involved in their creation.

Internationalization and city-regions

A striking feature of the late twentieth- and early twenty-first-century world is the rise of cities and their surrounding regions as important spaces in national and indeed global and local economic development. As a result, national and local governments have had to refocus their political and policy responses in order to deal with the spatial restructuring of global and local economic trends. Efforts to diversify economic activities away from extractive and commodity based industries towards manufacturing, service sectors and knowledge-based economies, have been accompanied by a propensity towards economic concentration in dense locational clusters. This has been reinforced by the fact that international investment and production are globally mobile and are attracted to localities that emerge or grow around economic clusters of similar firms or activities. These city-regions function as 'territorial platforms from which concentrated groups or networks of firms' engage with global markets, a process that has been intensified by international economic integration (Scott, 2001: 14). A number of urban scholars in the late twentieth century observed that global cities and city-regions were increasingly integrated into global economic systems in their own right and outside the direct control of nation-states (Sassen, 1991), leading some to argue that cities were trumping the nation-state as sites of social, political, and economic development and that globally networked megacities were outgrowing the physical and institutional infrastructure of the countries in which they were located (Ohmae, 2001).

To the extent that a network of semi-autonomous world cities exists within and across the global economy, they are few in number and it is important to recognize that urban and regional economic development is highly diverse within and among countries and across cities. While much scholarship on 'world cities' and 'global city-regions' focuses on cities of the global North, many of the largest global city-regions are in the global South, for example, Bangkok, Buenos Aires, Cairo, Jakarta, Lagos, Rio de Janeiro and Shanghai. Here the accompanying need for infrastructure provision, social development, and political reform is challenging and 'the effects of economic change are powerfully mediated by culture, by institutions, and by politics' (Keating, 2001: 375).

Let us take the example of Cape Town, the city-region hosting the 2016 Going Global conference. Although the Johannesburg-Gauteng city-region still dominates South Africa's overall national economy, with around a third of the national population and with responsibility for around a third of South Africa's national GDP, the Cape Town city region has seen a tenfold growth in its population over the last 50 years and has increased its share of national output in the context of South Africa's democratic transition. This transition has been accompanied by significant reorganization of local government, notably devolving considerable responsibility to local government for social services and some fiscal responsibility. In Cape Town a highly fragmented system with no fewer than 61 public authorities, divided by both geography and race, was brought together under a single Metropolitan Municipality, a significant part of the Province of the Western Cape. The latter has provided a regional vehicle for the delivery of education and other social services and for the co-ordination of the provinces' various municipalities.

In addition to changes at the national and city-regional level following the first democratic elections in 1994, there were changes in the international context as South Africa transformed itself from a pariah state to part of the global economy:

> Spurred by the development of finance, business services, logistics and tourism, Cape Town is becoming a service-based city-region economy, which today represents 69 per cent of the total regional GDP and employment. The integration of the region into the global economy has strengthened its position on a number of dynamic global value chains (agro-food, tourism and hospitality) and emerging clusters (financial and business services, logistics and creative and knowledge-intensive industries), while new demands for urban consumption (housing, retail and construction) driven by a positive business cycle and supported by public investments and social grants, have spurred internal dynamics

> (OECD, 2008: 14)

Even though the South African and Cape Town city-regional economies have seen considerable slowdown since 2008, each of these economic drivers holds considerable potential. Moreover, the city-regions universities and colleges play a critical role towards realizing this potential. Cape Town has strong specializations in biology, engineering and the life sciences and its reputation as the site of Professor Christiaan Barnard's successful performance of the world's first heart transplant in Cape Town has enhanced its reputation for medical sciences as well.

However, Cape Town city-region is not without its problems, notably unemployment among less skilled workers, the influx of people from other parts of South Africa and indeed the rest of the Africa compounding this problem. There is widespread poverty and the legacy of apartheid and economic and social inequality means that social cohesion is compromised. Health issues are considerable including the widespread prevalence of HIV/AIDS and large numbers of people in the city-region live in informal settlements or inadequate and overcrowded conditions: 'Although not as acute as in other African cities, income inequalities in the Cape Town city-region are extremely high by international standards' (OECD, 2008: 16) and this is in one of the most unequal countries in the world where the crime rates also top global league tables. In this context a key challenge for the city-region and for Cape Town's 'triple helix' between government at different levels, the private sector and the city-region's universities and colleges, is to foster more inclusive and sustainable social and economic development. Clearly economic growth will be insufficient to combat the high levels of unemployment and social exclusion that exist in the city-region. Much of the research at Western Cape universities is indeed spurred by the need to address the social problems that are evident in South Africa and the Cape Town city-region. However, there is more to be done, and tellingly, recent student protests and the 'fees must fall' campaign in South Africa suggest that affordability is an issue for students and that teaching and learning at South African universities must demonstrate increased sensitivity to the legacy of apartheid and continued social and economic disadvantage.

Conclusion

Across the world the concomitant social and political effects of economic clustering in city-regions have been considerable and are often beyond the wherewithal of local or city governments to resolve. In some cases city governments play a prominent role, in others it is state or federal structures that get involved, with the particular policy and institutional mix dependent on local circumstance. National governments may still be called upon to actively intervene in city and regional development. Significantly governments increasingly intervene through investment in human resources rather than physical infrastructure. Nowhere is this more evident than in the case of higher education and research. Here national governments play a critical role in supporting efforts to attract international students and inward investment in research, development, and technology transfer. However, local governments also play a role and are equally active, for example, in sourcing investment in science parks and promoting university-business linkages.

As the internationalization of higher education proceeds apace and as universities are affected by processes of global economic integration, research collaboration and competition for the brightest and best students and scholars, it is important to also view and understand higher education institutions within their spatial and locational contexts. I argue that universities have a key role to play in the formation and consolidation of nation-states through their social, political and cultural engagement and in national economic development strategies. Less widely recognized but equally important is the relationship between universities, colleges and research centres and the city regions of which they are a part. Cities and city-regions constitute key geographical or spatial sites for the contribution by higher education institutions to both private and public goods in a particular country and universities and colleges are critical components of local and regional social and economic development. However, higher education and research are important to national economic development and social policy, as well as to democratic processes and effective governance. As such, nation-states also remain central to debates and policy on the future of universities, colleges and research institutions, including the nature of engagement with international trends in higher education.

References

Able, G. and White, F. (2011) *Education: A Great British Export?*, London: Wild ReSearch.

Altbach, P.G., Reisberg, L. and Rumbley, L.E. (2009) 'Trends in global higher education: Tracking an academic revolution'. Report prepared for the UNESCO World Conference on Higher Education.

Asheim, B. and Gertler, M. (2005) 'The geography of innovation'. In Fagerberg, J., Mowery, D. and Nelson, R. (eds) *Oxford Handbook of Innovation*. Oxford: Oxford University Press.

Athreye, S.S. (2005) 'The Indian software industry'. In Arora, A. and Gambardella. A. (eds) *From Underdogs to Tigers: The rise and growth of the software industry in Brazil, China, India, Ireland, and Israel*. Oxford and New York: Oxford University Press. 7–40.

Batley, R. and Larbi, G. (2004) *The Changing Role of Government: The reform of public services in developing countries*. Basingstoke: Palgrave Macmillan.

Beall, J. (2015) 'Tertiary education: The unfinished business of the millennium development goals'. In Stiasny, M. and Gore, T. (eds) *Going Global: Inclusion, innovation, impact*. London: Institute of Education Press. 217–28.

Beall, J., Guha-Khasnobis, B. and Kanbur, R. (eds) (2011) *Urbanization and Development: Multidisciplinary perspectives*. Oxford: Oxford University Press.

Beall, J. and Fox, S. (2009) *Cities and Development*. London: Routledge.

Bender, T. (ed.) (1988) *The University and the City: From medieval origins to the present*. Oxford: Oxford University Press.

British Council (2012) *The Shape of Things to Come: Higher education global trends and emerging opportunities to 2020*. London: British Council.

Castells, M. (1997) *The Power of Identity, vol 2: The information age: economy, society and culture*. Oxford: Blackwell.

Dearing, R. (1997) *Report of the National Committee of Inquiry into Higher Education*. London: Her Majesty's Stationery Office.

Enders, J. (2004) 'Higher education, internationalisation, and the nation-state: Recent developments and challenges to governance theory'. *Higher Education*, 47, 367.

Giddens, A. (1999) *Runaway World: How globalisation is reshaping our lives*. London: Profile Books.

Goddard, J. and Puukka, J. (2008) 'The engagement of higher education institutions in regional development: An overview of the opportunities and challenges'. *Higher Education Management and Policy*, 20 (2), 11–41.

Goddard, J. and Vallance, P. (2010) 'Universities and regional development'. In Pike, A. Rodríguez-Pose A., and Tomaney, J. (eds) *Handbook of Local and Regional Development*. London: Routledge.

Hippler, J. (2002) 'Ethnicity, state, and nation-building – Experiences, policies, and conceptualization of nation-building in the globalisation process – A contribution to regional stability and global security?' *SEF-Symposium*, 11–12 December, Bonn: University Club.

Jacobs, J. (1984) *Cities and the Wealth of Nations*. New York: Vintage Books.

Keating, M. (2001) 'Governing Cities and Regions: Territorial restructuring in a global age'. In Scott, A.J. (ed.) *Global City Regions: Trends, theory, policy*. New York: Oxford University Press. 371–90.

Mann, M. (1997) 'Has globalization ended the rise and rise of the nation-state?' *Review of International Political Economy*, 4 (3), 472–96.

Moulaert, F., Martinelli, F. González, S. and Swyngedouw, E. (2007) 'Social innovation and governance in European cities: Urban development between path dependency and radical innovation'. *European Urban and Regional Studies*, 14, 195–209.

Mowery, D.C. and Sampat, B.N. (2005) 'Universities in national innovation systems'. In Fagerberg, J., Mowery, D. and Nelson, R. (eds) *The Oxford Handbook of Innovation*. Oxford: Oxford University Press. 209–39.

OECD (2008) *OECD Territorial Reviews: Cape Town, South Africa*. Paris: OECD.

Ohmae, K. (2001) 'How to invite prosperity from the global economy into a region'. In Scott, A.J. (ed.) *Global City Regions: Trends, theory, policy*. New York: Oxford University Press. 33–43.

Oketch, M., McCowan, T. and Schendel, R. (2014) 'The impact of tertiary education on development: A rigorous literature review'. DFID. Online. https://www.gov.uk/government/uploads/system/uploads/attachment_data/file/327901/Tertiary-education-2014-Oketch2.pdf.

Puukka, J. (2008) 'Mobilising higher education for sustainable development: Lessons learnt from the OECD study'. *Higher Education for Sustainable Development, vol 7*. Proceedings of the Fourth International Barcelona Conference on Higher Education, Global University Network for Innovation (GUNI), available at http://www.guni-rmies.net.

Puukka, J. and Marmolejo, F. (2008) Higher education institutions and regional mission: Lessons learnt from the OECD Review Project. *Higher Education Policy*, 21 (2), 217–44.

Sassen, S. (1991) *The Global City: New York, London, Tokyo*. New Jersey: Princeton University Press.

Scott, A.J. (ed.) (2001) *Global City Regions: Trends, theory, policy*. Oxford: Oxford University Press.

Scott, P. (ed.) (1998) *The Globalization of Higher Education*. Buckingham: Open University Press.

Williams, L., Turner, N. and Jones, A. (2008) *Embedding University in Knowledge Cities*. London: The Work Foundation.

Wolf, M. (2001) 'Will the nation-state survive globalization?' *Foreign Affairs*, January/February.

Conclusion

Going Global is a fresh and dynamic conference that allows the voices of post-secondary institutions across the world to be heard and to intermingle. These voices tell the stories of the issues, challenges and opportunities that all of us working in higher education are facing. They are of necessity works in progress as they offer windows on teaching, learning and research as it is happening now in Cambodia, China, Malaysia, Bahrain and a host of other locations around our diverse and complex world. The collective body of work represented in this volume results from these papers and is enriched by the authors' interactions with the audiences and their reflections since the conference itself.

The chapters tell stories of great diversity in the mix of influences from each geographical and cultural context and indeed celebrate this diversity. We are far from both Fukuyama's 'End of History' (1992) and Friedman's (2007) 'Flat World' as we have started out on a century that holds fresh and perplexing challenges and the inequalities of access and participation are as evident as they have ever been. Nevertheless, higher education is a crucial part of our evolving future and holds one of the most important tools humanity has access to which is disagreement and conflict. But, as Karl Popper (1959; see also Cook, 1979) told us it is conflict for a higher purpose – it is the cultivation of a sceptical and questioning approach so that we can work together as a human civilization to better understand the world we live in, to 'pop the hood' and see what are the mechanisms and forces at work that are driving such diverse phenomena as climate change and human creativity. The absolute freedom to disbelieve and question is fundamental to the advancement of knowledge. Higher education creates a space where this conflict is played out at a conceptual level – where criticizing is seen as positive and does not lead to imprisonment or persecution. Educators need to promote and defend this freedom at all costs.

Meanwhile, we are in a world where conflict is indeed resulting in human harm and eroding the quality and cohesion of human life. Higher education is a crucial element in redressing this balance and ensuring that the sum of human understanding continues to grow. Higher education has the power to produce better, more understanding humans as global citizens who have learned to question and interrogate ideas with the weapons of clear thinking and critical analysis. The mechanisms and concepts discussed in these papers are contributions to this over-riding and crucial agenda. To name but a few: mobility of students and staff ensure that conversations and debates cross frontiers; the development of inter-cultural values allows diversity to be valued and better understood, and clearly the creation of well-being is fundamental to humankind.

This book is about overcoming barriers and challenge. We often conceptualize internationalization as a pushing out process from a national base and globalization as something that happens to nation states from an undefined and all-encompassing world. The stories in this book testify to a middle ground, actors in our higher education world are reaching out beyond their own frontiers in new ways to new communities. These micro processes are at work in the Russian state education system; in Hong Kong's Baptist University; they are also at work in global initiatives in the music industry and in higher education management and are manifested in the very many concrete initiatives evidenced in the chapters. Together, these micro processes are knitting together the higher education community not from 'the West', 'the North'; from the 'Old World' or the 'New World' from Europe or Asia, but from everywhere. It is a truly global network of common interest.

There has never been a more important time for Going Global. We can argue that universities and institutions of higher learning have never been deterred by national barriers and over time have worked to eradicate as many other barriers such as those based on gender, faith and ethnicity as well. The purpose of Going Global is to continue this work by helping link up higher learning in this web of common interest across the planet in the service of a better world.

References

Cook, T.D. and Campbell, D.T. (1979) 'Popper and falsificationism. ' In Seale, C. (ed.) (2008) *Social Research Methods*. New York: Routledge. 43–7.

Friedman, T.L. (2007) *The World is Flat: The globalized world in the twenty-first century*. London: Penguin.

Fukuyama, F. (1992) *The End of History and the Last Man*. New York: Free Press.

Popper, K.R. (1959) *The Logic of Scientific Discovery*. London: Routledge.

Postscript

I am pleased to be able to contribute to this fifth volume of the Going Global series of books about global higher education. I am particularly pleased that this leading British Council conference is being co-hosted by the South African Department of Higher Education and Training in South Africa this year.

This comes at a very appropriate time for our university sector, as we strive to develop an implementation plan and process to give shape and form to the transformed, revitalized, expanded and integrated post-school system envisaged in our White Paper for Post-School Education and Training.

The White Paper, asserting as it does our South African constitutional values that contribute to all aspects of development here in our country and our continent, is connected in a close and mutually beneficial manner to a global network of higher education systems.

We welcome Going Global 2016 and look forward to seeing you all in Cape Town in May 2016.

Dr B.E. Nzimande, MP
Minister of Higher Education and
Training, Republic of South Africa

About the editors

Dr Mary Stiasny OBE

Mary Stiasny is Pro-Vice Chancellor (International) and CEO of the University of London International Programmes, almost certainly the world's first and oldest distance-learning provision, operating since 1858. With a fundamental commitment to provide access to study at university level to students wherever they are based, the University of London has always operated a policy of inclusion and openness to all students, at the same time maintaining its reputation for rigour and high standards. There are now more than 50,000 students around the world on under- and postgraduate programmes.

Mary started her career as a secondary school teacher and then moved to Goldsmiths College, University of London, as a teacher trainer. She was Deputy Head of the School of Education at Oxford Brookes University, then Head of the School of Education and Training at the University of Greenwich, before spending four years as the British Council's Director of Education and Training, followed by six years as Pro Director, Learning, Teaching and International at the Institute of Education (now the UCL IOE), until moving to her current role in 2013.

Mary has been a member of the UK UNESCO Education Committee and a Director of the UK UNESCO National Commission; she is currently a Trustee of the Council for Education in the Commonwealth, and is a Commonwealth Scholarships Commissioner. In 2013 she was awarded an OBE for services to higher education.

Tim Gore OBE

Tim Gore is CEO of the University of London Institute in Paris. This institute has played a part in Franco-British academic cooperation since the nineteenth century, becoming part of the University of London in 1969. Tim leads this unique Institute at a time of considerable change as it enlarges its teaching portfolio, enhances its research capacity and develops its strategic partnership with Queen Mary University of London. He was previously based in London as Director, Global Networks and Communities, for the University of London International Programmes, where he was responsible for their global engagement work. Prior to this Tim was the Director of the Centre for Indian Business, the University of Greenwich, where his role was to engage the University of Greenwich's intellectual capital with India. Tim previously held a number of senior leadership roles with the British Council working closely with educationalists, institutions, companies and governments to improve bilateral and multilateral educational links in Hong Kong, Singapore, United Arab Emirates, Jordan and India. He was awarded an OBE in 2008.

About the contributors

Joyce Achampong

Joyce Achampong is Director of Engagement at the Association of Commonwealth Universities and is responsible for member engagement, communications, and the delivery of the organisation's external relations strategy.

Originally from Canada, Joyce has worked in various aspects of educational management and development for almost ten years. Holding degrees in International Business, Political Economy, and European Policy and Management, she moved to the UK in 2003, subsequently working in the Campaigns and Communications team at the National Council for Voluntary Organisations. Prior to this, Joyce worked for the international development agency CUSO/VSO and as a consultant for the United Nations Association (Canada) on community engagement, fundraising and running high profile events. Before her role at the ACU, Joyce was Head of Events and Programmes with CASE Europe responsible for the design and implementation of their cross-cultural learning programmes such as Leadership in Development Management and the Vice Chancellor's Canadian Development Tour. She also managed, recruited and co-ordinated the first three cohorts of the very successful CASE/HEFCE Graduate Trainees Programme in Educational Fundraising.

Paul Kwadwo Addo

Paul Kwadwo Addo is an Assistant Registrar at the Vice-Chancellor's Office and Sectional Head for Quality Assurance and Accreditation at the Kwame Nkrumah University of Science and Technology, Kumasi, Ghana. Paul previously worked as Test Administration Secretary for the National Board for Professional and Technician Examinations (NABPTEX) where he was responsible for the effective conduct of HND Examinations and quality assurance in all the Polytechnics and other institutions in Ghana. Prior to this, he worked as a teacher at all levels with the Ghana Education Service.

He has several publications by way of peer-reviewed papers, book chapters, and technical reports to his credit and has attended and presented papers at several conferences around the world including British Council Going Global 2014 and 2015. His interest is in the areas of leadership and management in higher education culminating in ways that seek to continually raise standards of teaching and learning experience and total quality management.

Paul is a Fellow of the Ghana Institute of Management (GIM), a Member of the Ghana Association of University Administrators (GAUA), and the Institute of Public Relations, Ghana (IPR). He is currently conducting research for his doctorate degree in educational leadership in Florida, USA.

S. Kojo Mbra Assan

S. Kojo Mbra Assan works with Kwame Nkrumah University of Science & Technology (KNUST) in Ghana as an Assistant Registrar and a Member of the Ghana Association of University Administrators (GAUA).

Prior to his work at KNUST from 2004, Mr Assan obtained a Master's degree in Economics, and a Bachelor's degree in Economics and Sociology. Both credentials were earned at KNUST. He is currently in the second year of the Higher Education Administration PhD programme at University of Florida, Gainesville.

Mr Assan's research interests include institutional research, financial aid and student outcomes, higher education governance systems and how they impact institutional effectiveness.

Pavel G. Arefiev

Pavel Arefiev is a Principal Researcher at the National Training Foundation, Russian Federation. His area of responsibility covers analysis and evaluation of research output and also principles and methodology of developing academic careers in universities. Pavel Arefiev has been recognized as an expert in the areas of science policy and evaluation since he started work as principal researcher on the national project, Russian Index for Science Citation, in 2005. Now he is a peer in several nationwide university projects including the Russian Academic Excellence project '5 to 100'. He is a long-term reviewer and also author for leading Russian journals in Higher Education. His authorship comprises several dozens of journal and conference papers and two multi-authored monographs. He received the Best Journal Paper award at the annual National Competition 'PRO-Education' in 2013. He also has teaching experience as a visiting lecturer in several Russian universities.

Irina V. Arzhanova

Irina V. Arzhanova, MEd, PhD, DSc, Associate Professor, is an Executive Director at the National Training Foundation, Russian Federation. Irina Arzhanova has 20 years of experience working in the field of education and science, managing, developing and implementing key Russian and international projects. Supporting successful cooperation with federal and regional education authorities, institutions of professional education as well as national and international organizations, she managed large Russian projects in the field of education and science, including: implementation of the Bologna process in Russia; the national priority project on education; organizational and analytical support of development programmes in leading universities in Russia; designing and approving template methodology for national ranking of higher education institutions; developing information technology and ICT-testing tools for schools. She is author of numerous articles and publications dedicated to the development of higher education in Russia and international education.

Graeme Atherton

Dr Graeme Atherton has been working in the field of widening access to higher education (HE) since 1995. He founded and leads both AccessHE and the National Education Opportunities Network (NEON). AccessHE is a network of more than 200 schools, colleges and Higher Education Institutions (HEIs), working together in London to widen access to higher education. NEON is the national professional organisation for social mobility through widening access to higher education in England. He holds visiting professorships at London Metropolitan University and Amity Business School and is chair of the Global Access to Post-Secondary Education (GAPS) initiative. His latest book, *The Success Paradox: Why we need a new theory of social mobility*, is published in 2016 by Polity.

Marina Y. Baryshnikova

Marina Y. Baryshnikova, PhD in Pedagogy, is a Deputy Executive Director at the National Training Foundation, Russian Federation. Marina Baryshnikova has extensive experience in the field of education, with a special focus on ICT and E-Learning. She successfully managed the implementation of several significant projects, including monitoring R-and-D grants for the Russian Science Foundation and providing analytical support for the Federal Programme 'Scientific and Scientific-pedagogical Personnel of Innovative Russia'.

Jo Beall

Jo Beall is Director Education and Society and a member of the Executive Board at the British Council. A graduate of the London School of Economics, Jo's past roles include Professor of Development Studies at the LSE and

Deputy Vice Chancellor of University of Cape Town. She is a specialist in international education, international development, and cities in fragile and conflict situations, and a regular speaker at major conferences in these fields. Her work has taken her to Africa, Asia, and Latin America, with extensive periods of research in Afghanistan, India, Pakistan and South Africa. She has written numerous books and articles on a wide range of topics including governance and civil society, women and development, and cities and fragile states. She is a Fellow of the Academy of Social Sciences and was recently awarded an Honorary Doctorate by the Open University.

Nilton N. Cometti

Nilton Cometti obtained his Bachelor's in Agronomy from the Federal University of Espirito Santo (1985), Master's in Agronomy from Universidade Federal de Santa Maria (1989) and PhD in Agronomy (Soil Sciences) from the Federal Rural University of Rio de Janeiro, with study abroad at Utah State University (2003). He is currently a professor at the Federal Institute of Espirito Santo, and also professor and advisor at the Federal University of Espirito Santo in the Graduate Program in Vegetable Production, and the Professional Masters in Science and Mathematics Education at IFES. He served as Dean of Education at the Federal Institute of Brasilia from 2011 to 2013, and currently acts as General Co-ordinator of Planning and Management of the Federal Network of Vocational Education, Science and Technology, at Brazil's Ministry of Education.

Catriona Cunningham

Catriona Cunningham is an Academic Development Partner at the University of Stirling. She previously worked as a consultant in academic practice at the Higher Education Academy in the UK where she led the work in modern languages. She is also a former lecturer in French and in education at Queen's University, Belfast, as well as at Edinburgh, and the University of the West of Scotland, with a research background in francophone postcolonial literature. Her most recent research is in the area of internationalization and interculturalism in HE, particularly its impact on academic identities.

Dmitriy O. Derman

Dmitriy O. Derman, PhD in Economics, is a Head of the Department of Higher Education at the National Training Foundation, Russian Federation. Dmitriy Derman has been engaged in the various projects of transformation of the higher education system in Russia, including creating national research universities, federal universities and the project '5 to 100'.

Sir Ciarán Devane

The British Council was established over eighty years ago to create a basis of 'friendly knowledge and understanding' of Britain by making the most of the cultural resources of the country to create opportunities, to build connections and to engender trust. Sir Ciarán Devane took up the role of Chief Executive in January 2015. Ciarán has focused on ensuring that all stakeholders understand and value the contribution that soft power, cultural relations and the British Council makes to security, prosperity and influence, and that the organization and staff are aligned behind that vision.

Prior to this, Ciarán was Chief Executive of Macmillan Cancer Support from 2007 to 2014. He transformed the scale and impact of the charity, both on its own and in collaboration with other organizations, and raised its profile as an authoritative voice on cancer and on health matters, leading to Macmillan being the UK's 'Brand of the Year' in 2014.

Ciarán was educated at University College, Dublin where he gained first-class honours in biochemical engineering. He then started his career as an engineer and manager for Imperial Chemical Industries (ICI) before becoming a management consultant, mostly with Gemini Consulting. He specialized in complex change programmes with companies such as AstraZeneca and RollsRoyce. He holds a Masters degree in International Policy and Practice from George Washington University, and has also held non-executive roles on the board of organizations ranging from small local charities to NHS England. He is currently on the board of Social Finance Limited. Ciarán was awarded a knighthood in 2015 for his services to cancer patients.

Hans de Wit

Hans de Wit is Director of the Center for International Higher Education (CIHE) at Boston College. Previously he was Director of the Centre for Higher Education Internationalisation (CHEI) at the Università Cattolica del Sacro Cuore, Milan, in which capacity he was project leader of the European Parliament Study, Internationalisation of Higher Education, on which the chapter is built. He is the founding editor of the *Journal of Studies in International Education* and founding member and past president of the European Association for International Education (EAIE).

Philip Esterhuizen

Besides international work experience in South Africa and the Netherlands, Philip has worked as an educator and as an academic in the Netherlands and the United Kingdom. He has been involved in curriculum development with universities in the Republic of Ireland, the Netherlands and England. In teaching and facilitating healthcare professionals in a wide range of areas and settings, Philip uses confluent education as a theoretical framework. He is an Academic Representative in the Inclusion and Equality Committee in the School of Health at the University of Leeds.

Dawn Freshwater

Dawn Freshwater is Senior Deputy Vice Chancellor at the University of Western Australia and Professor of Mental Health at the University of Leeds. As an academic Dawn has a track record of research in the fields of offender health, psychological therapies, mixed methods research and leadership strategies. In her leadership capacity she has championed and led the successful implementation and award of the Athena Swan charter and led a British Council funded study to examine the impact of globalization on leadership. Dawn contributes widely to national and international research and education reform and policy both in an advisory capacity and as an expert in her field.

Anne Marie Graham

Anne Marie Graham is the Head of Programme, Outward Student Mobility at the UK Higher Education International Unit. She leads on the implementation of the UK Strategy for Outward Mobility, which aims to increase the proportion of UK domiciled students accessing international opportunities during their studies. Anne Marie has managed projects in UK and European higher education in the fields of languages, communication and intercultural skills. She is the author of several research reports, including labour market intelligence for the British Academy, the University Council of Modern Languages and Skills CfA and a review of public service interpreting and translation training in higher education for HEFCE's Routes into Languages. In addition to her work in the higher education sector, Anne Marie has more than ten years' commercial management experience in the language services industry.

Elizabeth Halford

Elizabeth Halford is Head of Research and Intelligence at QAA. She joined in 2012, having previously held senior academic and management positions in further and higher education, most recently as Head of Validation and Review at the University of West London. Elizabeth holds a doctorate in Education from UCL IOE, and is a Fellow of the Higher Education Academy, with research interests in higher education policy and widening participation.

Catriona Hanks

Catriona Hanks is the Outward Mobility Policy Researcher for the Go International Programme at the UK Higher Education International Unit. Previously she worked for the World Bank in Washington DC, administering their Joint Japan/World Bank Scholarship Program, and leading their Robert S. McNamara Fellowship Program. She graduated with a Master's degree in International Economics and European Studies from Johns Hopkins University in Bologna, Italy and Washington DC, in 2012, and an undergraduate degree in Music from the University of Oxford in 2007.

John Hearn

John Hearn is the Board Executive Director and Chief Executive of the Worldwide Universities Network, Chairman of the Australia Africa Universities Network and Professor of Physiology (Medical School) at the University of Sydney. He was awarded his PhD from the Australian National University (ANU) and served for 6–7 years each in leading research, teaching and administrative positions at the Universities of Edinburgh, London UCL, Wisconsin, ANU and Sydney. Most recently he was Vice-President (Research) at ANU 2000–4 and Vice-President (Academic and International) at Sydney 2004–13. He has published 210 research papers and edited six books in reproduction and fertility, stem cell biology and biotechnology. He has worked globally in research capacity development, especially in China, India, Thailand, Kenya and Brazil. He is a senior scientific adviser to the Australian Government, British Council, Swedish STINT, World Health Organisation and OECD in Higher Education and Research.

Laura Howard

Laura Howard is President (2014–16) of the European Association for International Education (EAIE). She currently holds a lecturing post at the University of Cadiz, Spain. Laura has more than 15 years' experience in international relations management. On a national level, she chaired the Commission for International Promotion, which was created within the International Relations Commission of the Spanish Rectors' Conference, from 2008 until 2010. She was Vice-President of the Compostela Group of Universities between 2007 and 2015. Laura has published articles and papers and presented at international conferences extensively on many issues related to international higher education, and is one of the authors of the recently published report, *Internationalisation of Higher Education*, prepared for the European Parliament.

Fiona Hunter

Fiona Hunter is Associate Director at the Centre for Higher Education Internationalisation (CHEI) at the Università Cattolica del Sacro Cuore in Milan and was co-leader for the European Parliament Study on Internationalisation of Higher Education. She is Co-Editor at the *Journal of Studies for International Education* (JSIE) and past President of the European Association for International Education (EAIE) where she is now a member of the newly formed Knowledge Development Taskforce. She is also is a consultant and trainer working with public, private and faith-based higher education institutions around the world on strategic change.

Wendy Jordan

Wendy Jordan has been Director of the British Universities Iraq Consortium since 2010, which works directly with the Higher Committee for Education Development Iraq to enable Iraqi students to study in the UK. It is a network for sharing information and facilitates contact between its members. She has a long association with the Middle East, having worked in Oman for three years and travelled extensively in the region as the Regional Education and Training Adviser while at the British Council. She worked in São Paulo, Brazil, for the British Council, running a major arts programme and managing the Chevening scholarships. Currently she is a member of the Associate Faculty at Henley Business School.

Susanne Kammüller

Susanne Kammüller is senior desk officer for TNE in the Transnational Education and Co-operation Programmes division of the German Academic Exchange Service (DAAD). Her remit includes questions of TNE policy, strategy and funding, quality assurance and TNE statistics. Susanne has ten years of professional experience in international higher education with the DAAD, including various roles in the DAAD's regional sections for south and south-east Asia. She studied English literature, Indology and political sciences and holds a Magistra Artium degree from Bonn University.

Tom Kennie

Tom Kennie is a founding director of Ranmore, a 'niche' provider of senior level leadership development to more than 120 higher education institutions globally. His work in HE leadership development is informed by 13 years as co-programme director (with Robin Middlehurst) of the UK Top Management Programme for Higher Education (TMP). He has also worked for ten years with King's College, London, and the Harvard School of Dental Medicine on a programme for senior dental leaders. He is joint programme director of a new 'Leading Globally Engaged Universities' (LGEU) programme with the International Association of Universities, and in collaboration with specialist occupational psychologists has developed a new personal insights profiling tool focused on Globally Engaged Leadership. His earlier career included more than ten years as a full time academic and work in the corporate world in human resource management. He is a graduate of the University of Glasgow, did his doctoral work at Imperial College, London and completed an MBA at the University of Sussex.

Takehiko Kitamori

Professor Kitamori is a Professor in the Department of Applied Chemistry, School of Engineering, the University of Tokyo (1998 – present). He was Dean of the Graduate School of Engineering (2010–11), Vice President (2012–13) and Special Assistant to the President (2014) of the University of Tokyo, responsible for Human Resource Development and Internationalization. Professor Kitamori's extensive professional career includes positions at leading Japanese industry and academic institutions including Hitachi and Kanagawa Academy of Science and Technology. He has received numerous honours for innovative research, including an Award from the Science and Technology Agency, the Ichimura Award for Science and The Chemical Society of Japan Award for Creative Work. He is the recipient of an Honorary Doctorate from Lund University.

Alexandr V. Klyagin

Alexandr Klyagin, PhD in Economics, is a Deputy Head of the Department of Higher Education at the National Training Foundation, Russian Federation. Alexandr Klyagin has strong experience in managing and supervising educational and youth development national projects, including youth volunteering and social project management. Previously he served as associate professor for the Russian State University for Economics. He received his professional education and PhD degree at Plekhanov Russian University of Economics.

Jane Knight

Dr Jane Knight, Ontario Institute for Studies in Education, University of Toronto, focuses her research on the international dimension of higher education at institutional, national, regional and international levels. Her work in more than 70 countries with universities, governments and UN agencies helps to bring a comparative, developmental and international perspective to her research, teaching and policy work. She is the author of numerous publications on internationalization concepts and strategies, quality assurance, institutional management, trade, education hubs and cross-border education. She is co-founder of the African Network for the Internationalization of Education and sits on the advisory boards of several international organizations, universities and journals. In 2010 the University of Exeter awarded her an Honorary LLD; in 2011 she was the recipient of the Outstanding Researcher Award from the European Association for Institutional Research, and in 2013 she was awarded the Gilbert Medal from Universitas 21 for her contribution to higher education internationalization.

Annamarie Lawrence

Annamarie Lawrence is a lecturer in the Business School at Bahrain Polytechnic, a government-owned higher education institution with a focus on industry integration and twenty-first-century skills. Annamarie works to identify industry-based project work for students and to mentor students acting as project consultants to industry. She has also been involved in a number of national initiatives for the development of innovation, research and university business collaboration in the Kingdom of Bahrain. Prior to Bahrain Polytechnic, Annamarie worked as a consultant on various multi-stakeholder economic development/education projects for the New Zealand government. Annamarie has also had management consulting experience in the private sector while working for PWC in Sweden and Bain and Co. in London. Her research interests are in the role of education policy within developing innovation systems.

Jonathan Ledger

Jonathan Ledger is Chief Executive Officer of the Proskills UK Group. Jonathan's industrial skills expertise includes more than 25 years' experience of training and assessment delivered in workplaces throughout the UK and across the globe in 22 countries. Jonathan is a renowned expert in policy development and strategic implementation working with governments and their agencies, NGOs, donors, employers and industries to develop sustainable business growth through high-impact skills. A postgraduate in Management and also Learning and Development Provision, Jonathan is a member of the Institute of Directors, Institute of Quarrying and Chartered Management Institute.

Proskills is twice a co-winner of the British Council's prestigious Skills Partnership of the Year award for its outstanding achievements in vocational education in Egypt for the printing sector (2014) and for creating high-impact systemic change in partnership with building materials manufacturer Viglacera, Vietnam (2015). Proskills is currently delivering vocational programmes in China and Vietnam ranging from NQF development to skills standards and curriculum development, train the trainer and certification services.

Paul Manners

Paul Manners is Associate Professor in Public Engagement at UWE and founding director of the UK's National Co-ordinating Centre for Public Engagement (NCCPE). The NCCPE was established in 2008 to support universities to embed innovative approaches to involving the public in their work. The NCCPE is widely recognized for its expertise in supporting organizational change, partnership working, impact assessment and innovation in engagement.

Paul's whole career has been education related. He trained as a secondary English teacher and after teaching for five years, joined the BBC where his credits include the long running BBC2 series, 'Rough Science'. He was an executive producer in BBC Learning, responsible for a number of broadcast-led public engagement campaigns, including the People's War project, gathering tens of thousands of personal reminiscences about World War 2 into an online archive. He is chair of the National Trust's advisory panel on Collections and Interpretation.

John McNamara

John is an economist and Director of Research at McNamara Economic Research (MCER), a consultancy based in Ireland with a data driven focus on the international higher education sector. John has particular expertise in research and analysis of transnational education. Prior to establishing MCER in 2011, John worked as an economist with Enterprise Ireland in Dublin, and more recently as a senior economist with the Economist

Intelligence Unit in London with responsibility for managing the custom research education portfolio. John has a BA in Economics from University College, Dublin and an MSc in Economics from the National University of Ireland, Galway.

Robin Middlehurst

Robin Middlehurst is Professor of Higher Education and External Policy Adviser in the Vice-Chancellor's Office, Kingston University, London. She also serves as a policy adviser to the Higher Education Academy, is a trustee of the British Accreditation Council and Advisory Board member of the Observatory on Borderless Higher Education. Robin's research includes borderless education and internationalization, governance and leadership, quality assurance and enhancement in higher education. Previous roles have included: Director, Strategy, Research and International at the Leadership Foundation; co-designing and co-directing the UK's Top Management Programme for Higher Education; Director of the Quality Enhancement Group of the Higher Education Quality Council (now QAA); academic posts at the University of Surrey and Institute of Education, London; and serving as a governor in two UK universities. Professor Middlehurst has published extensively on higher education policy and management and undertakes consultancy for governments and higher education agencies in the UK and overseas.

Cameron Mirza

Cameron Mirza is a highly skilled leader of change with vast international experience of leading public sector reform within the UK and Middle East including working within two UK prime ministers' delivery teams. He has 15 years' international reform experience across the public and private sector specializing in education and social impact reform at the highest level. In 2004 Cameron was part of the team that integrated work-based learning into schools with the launch of the young apprenticeship programme, and in 2008 was part of the team led by Sir Keith Ajegbo that reviewed citizenship and diversity in the school curriculum.

As director for projects and strategy for the kingdom of Bahrain since 2011 he has co-authored a national higher education strategy and the nation's first industry-led graduate skills guide. Cameron has led on several key reforms ranging from regulatory reform to a curriculum and teaching review, and capacity-building within the sector. He was responsible for Bahrain's improvement in seven out of eight indicators in one year for the innovation ranking in the global competitiveness report produced by the World Economic Forum in 2015.

Rajani Naidoo

Rajani Naidoo is Professor of Higher Education and Director of the International Centre for Higher Education Management at the University of Bath. Before this she was an inaugural faculty member at an institution that aimed to contribute to the development of an alternative model of higher education in post-apartheid South Africa. She is a graduate of the universities of Natal, London and Cambridge. She sits on the research and development steering group of the European Foundation of Management Development, is co-editor of a book series on global higher education (Palgrave/Macmillan) and an editorial board member of numerous journals including the *British Journal of Sociology of Education*. She has worked on executive development for university leaders, on a wide range of funded research programmes on international higher education and keynoted conferences in many parts of the world. She has published on topics including the global commodification of higher education, new forms of imperialism, and higher education and global wellbeing.

Ruth Najda

Ruth Najda holds an MA (Education) and MSc (African Studies) and has more than 30 years' experience as an educator in cultural awareness, global citizenship, collaborative intercultural partnership working and enabling pedagogies. She is a writer and editor of online and face-to-face training materials on these themes for professional practitioners and for school, undergraduate and postgraduate students. She is currently the adviser for the British Council's intercultural fluency initiative.

Patricia G. Owusu-Darko

Patricia G. Owusu-Darko is a Senior Lecturer in Food Science at Faculty of Applied Science in Kumasi Polytechnic and the Director for the Graduate School. She was formerly the Director for International Affairs and Institutional Linkages.

She has a PhD from the Strathclyde Institute of Pharmacy and Biomedical Sciences, University of Strathclyde, Glasgow, UK; an MPhil in Biochemistry and a BSc (Hons) in Biochemistry both from Kwame Nkrumah University of Science and Technology. She is a resource person for the Root and Tuber Improvement and Marketing Programme (RTIMP) of the Ministry of Food and Agriculture (MOFA), Centre for Biodiversity

Utilization and Development (CBUD) of Kwame Nkrumah University of Science and Technology (KNUST), Ministry of Social Welfare, Nestlé (Ghana) and the Ghana Tourism Authority.

She is a reviewer for the following journals: *International Journal of Technology and Management Research*, *Food Control*, *Journal of Food Chemistry*, and the Sunyani Polytechnic Lecture Series. She has attended several national and international conferences.

Sibilla Robutti

Sibilla Robutti conducted research on intercultural competence as Study Abroad Coordinator at St Mary's University Twickenham, London, a role to which she was appointed in 2013. She was previously the main researcher in the 'Developing Employability through the Study Abroad Experience: A structured and supported activity to enhance international experience' project, funded by the Higher Education Academy. The project developed online resources to support experiential learning in mobility. Former research focused on the impact of work placements on graduate employability. Sibilla also has experience working as Intercultural Mediator with refugees, and has studied and worked in four different EU countries and in India. She holds an MA Res in Anthropological Research Methods from SOAS, an MA in International Co-operation and Development from Sciences Po Bordeaux and an MA in International Relations and Human Rights Protection from the University of Turin.

Dorothea Rüland

Dorothea Rüland has been Secretary General of the German Academic Exchange Service (DAAD) since October 2010. Between 2008 and 2010, she was Director of the Center for International Co-operation at the Free University, Berlin. She first joined the DAAD in 1980 and until 2008 assumed various roles in several regions of the world. In 2004 she was appointed Deputy Secretary General of the DAAD. From 1999 until 2004 she was in charge of diverse DAAD activities in Asia, Africa and Latin America; from 1994 to 1999 she was head of the office in Indonesia. She is a member of several national and international associations and administrative boards. Dorothea Rüland studied German Literature, History and Musicology and holds a PhD from the University of Freiburg.

Elizabeth J. Sandell

Elizabeth Sandell is a professor in the College of Education at Minnesota State University, Mankato, MN, USA. She received her BA (Social Work),

MA (Educational Administration), and PhD (Education) from the University of Minnesota. She has travelled to all 50 states in the USA and to six continents. Her research agenda includes development and evaluation of approaches to multicultural and diverse education in the USA. During the past eight years, she has mentored more than 40 undergraduate students (including eight from Russia) who have presented oral and poster sessions at the Minnesota State University, Mankato Undergraduate Research Symposium, and at annual National Conferences on Undergraduate Research (NCUR).

Melissa Schuessler

Melissa Schuessler is the Faculty International Director at the Leeds University Business School. She is responsible for the international strategy including partner engagement and the internationalization of research and student education. As a Fellow of the UK Higher Education Academy, she is committed to preparing students for global careers by working closely with international employers and lecturing in intercultural competence and graduate employability. With a Master's in Intercultural Education and Internationalization from Durham University, her research includes measuring and assessing intercultural competence, creating institutional frameworks for internationalization initiatives and operationalizing new international programmes.

Neil Shaw

Neil Shaw has nearly 25 years' experience of working in international education. He currently manages the British Council's Global Employability Portfolio, which includes leading on the organization's Intercultural Fluency products. He has also worked as an Educational Adviser for the British Council, specializing in Skills and in ICT in Education. Prior to joining the British Council in 2003, Neil worked for the National Museums of Scotland on international research and development projects in the area of education and culture. He is an experienced teacher and lecturer and has worked at school, college and university level.

Christina Slade

Christina Slade is Vice-Chancellor of Bath Spa University. Former roles include Dean of the Schools of Arts and of Social Sciences at City University, London, Dean of Humanities at Macquarie University (2003–8) and Professor of Media Theory at the University of Utrecht. Trained as a philosopher of logic and language, her research has focused on issues of the media since 1990. Her monograph, *The Real Thing: Doing philosophy with media* (2002) examines the role of reason in the media, while *From Migrant to Citizen: Testing language, testing culture*, (2010) jointly edited with Martina Möllering, looks at linguistic, legal and philosophical aspects of citizenship testing. Her most recent monograph, *Watching Arabic Television in Europe: From diaspora to hybrid citizens* was also published in 2014 by Palgrave Macmillan.

Alfred Tan

Dr Tan is an entrepreneur, IP attorney, engineer, research scientist, inventor and a university senior administrator. He started his career in academia before successfully leading his own technology start-up, and he has a number of patents to his name. He then returned to academia to further his career as a published professor in engineering and technology in Hong Kong and Australia. Dr Tan is a Senior Member of IEEE and a Member of Engineers Australia. He is also a registered Australian Trade Marks attorney and a patent consultant. He is a Certified Patent Valuation Analyst and consults for venture capital firms. He is currently head of the Knowledge Transfer Office, Hong Kong Baptist University.

Mark Thorley

Mark Thorley's work combines research, consultancy and academic leadership and draws upon his background as a classically trained musician, technologist and entrepreneur. He presents at conferences throughout the world, and his research appears in a variety of publications ranging from Oxford University Press and the Audio Engineering Society, through to the *Journal of Popular Music and Society*. He has also acted as Principal Investigator on funded projects including a number for the UK's Higher Education Academy. He has authored and been director of a number of academic programmes in the UK, and collaborated extensively with other institutions in the United States, Australia and South Africa. He was a Director of the Music Producers' Guild, and a Senior Fellow of the Higher Education Academy, before becoming Head of Music and Creative Technologies at Coventry University.

Hilligje Van't Land

Hilligje Van't Land is director of Membership and Program Development at the International Association of Universities (IAU). She was educated in France, the Netherlands and Canada and obtained her PhD in contemporary literature from Groningen University. She commenced her academic career working in the humanities and taught comparative francophone literature at universities in the Netherlands, Canada and France. She has worked with the IAU for 14 years where she is in charge of membership development and of thematic priorities in sustainable development and intercultural dialogue. She recently co-edited the book *The Promotion of Intercultural Learning and Dialogue through Higher Education*. She is Editor in Chief of *IAU Horizons*, the association magazine. She works with the IAU Secretary General on the Association's annual and general conferences, and runs the project on the changing nature of doctoral programmes in sub-Saharan Africa.